Divagations

The Belknap Press of Harvard University Press • Cambridge, Massachusetts, and London, England • 2007

The Author's 1897 Arrangement

Together with

"Autobiography"

and

"Music and Letters"

Divagations

STÉPHANE MALLARMÉ

TRANSLATED BY BARBARA JOHNSON

The translation of Mallarmé's "Mimique" (Mimesis) previously appeared
in Jacques Derrida, *Dissemination*, trans. Barbara Johnson, copyright
© 1981 by the University of Chicago Press. Reprinted by permission.

Design by Annamarie McMahon Why

Library of Congress Cataloging-in-Publication Data
Mallarmé, Stéphane, 1842–1898.
    [Divagations. English]
    Divagations : the author's 1897 arrangement ; together with
  "Music and letters" / Stéphane Mallarmé ; translated by Barbara
  Johnson.
      p.   cm.
    ISBN-13: 978-0-674-02438-0 (alk. paper)
    ISBN-10: 0-674-02438-9 (alk. paper)
    I. Johnson, Barbara, 1947–   II. Mallarmé, Stéphane, 1842–1898.
  Musique et les lettres. English.   III. Title.
  PQ2344.D5E5   2007
  848'.807—d22
                                     2006043745

For B.D.L., who made me want to live.

—B.J.

Contents

Autobiography

Paris, Monday, November 15, 1885

My dear Verlaine,

I am late for you, because I was trying to find the unpublished works of Villiers de l'Isle-Adam, which I lent hither and yon.† Enclosed please find the almost-nothing I located.

But precise information about that dear old fugitive I don't have: even his address. Our two hands simply find each other, as if they had last clasped each other the night before, at the bend in a road, every year, because God exists. Besides that, though, he's always right on time at meetings, so if you want him for your *Poètes Maudits* [Poets of the Damned] or *Hommes d'Aujourd'hui* [Contemporary Men], look for him at Vanier's, where he's sure to have a lot to do, with the publication of *Axel*. He'll be there at the appointed hour, I guarantee. Literarily, no one is more punctual than he is; it's up to Vanier to get his address, or Darzens, who has recently represented him with that gracious publisher.

If all else fails, you'll walk with me some Wednesday at dusk, and suddenly he'll join us, and all those details about his civil status, which I've forgotten, will be available, since they concern the man himself.

Now I'll turn to me.

---

†Mallarmé was responding to Verlaine's request for information for his latest series of sketches of contemporary poets. Villiers was the bourgeois Mallarmé's favorite outsider. [—*Trans.*]

Yes, I was born in Paris on March 18, 1842, on the street that is today called the Passage Laferrière. My paternal and maternal families present, ever since the Revolution, an uninterrupted series of functionaries in the Administration and the Registry; and even though they were almost always at the top of their profession, I escaped a career that was planned for me from birth. In several of my ancestors, I find traces of a taste for holding a pen for something other than recording Acts: one, no doubt before the creation of the Registry, was in charge of bookstores under Louis XVI—I saw his name at the bottom of the King's Privilege in the original French edition of Beckford's *Vathek*, which I had republished. Another wrote mocking verses for women's Confirmations and Almanacs of Muses. As a child, I knew, deep in the interior of a family Parisian bourgeoisie, Monsieur Magnien, a second cousin several times removed, who had published a rabid Romantic volume called *Ange* [Angel] or *Démon* or something, which I occasionally come across now, listed at a very high price, in the catalogues booksellers send me.

I call my family "Parisian" because we've always lived in Paris, but our origins go back to Bourguignon, Lorraine, and even Holland.

I lost, while still a small child of seven, my mother; then was adored and cared for by my grandmother; then I went through numerous boarding schools and high schools, a Lamartinian soul with the secret ambition of one day replacing Béranger, whom I had met at a friend's house. It seems that this plan was too complicated to be put into execution, but I kept trying to fill hundreds of notebooks with verse, which were always confiscated from me, if I remember correctly.

When I entered into life, it was impossible, as you very well know, for a poet to live from his art, even by lowering it several degrees, and I have never regretted it. Having learned English simply to be a better reader of Poe, I left for England at the age of twenty, mainly to get away; but also to speak the language and teach it, to settle down in a quiet spot and need no other living: I was married and it was urgent.

Today, more than twenty years later, and despite all the wasted hours, I believe, with sadness, that I made the right decision. It's that, besides the verse and prose pieces I wrote in my youth and those that followed and echoed them, pieces which have been published all over the place every time a new Literary Review started up, I have always dreamed and attempted something else, with the patience of an alchemist, ready to sacrifice all vanity and all satisfaction, the way they used to burn their furniture and the beams from their ceilings, to stoke the fires of the Great Work. What would it be? It's hard to say: a book, quite simply, in several volumes, a book that would be a real book, architectural and premeditated, and not a collection of chance inspirations, however wonderful . . . I would even go further and say *the* Book, convinced as I am that in the final analysis there's only one, unwittingly attempted by anyone who writes, even Geniuses. The orphic explanation of the Earth, which is the poet's only duty and the literary mechanism par excellence: for the rhythm of the book, then impersonal and alive, right down to its pagination, would line up with the equations of that dream, or Ode.

There, now, is the admission of my vice, laid bare, dear friend, which I have many times rejected, my spirit bruised and tired; but I am possessed by it and I will succeed, perhaps—not in drafting the whole of it (one would have to be I don't know who for that!) but in showing a fully executed fragment, making its glorious authenticity glow from the corner, and indicating the rest, for which a single lifetime would not suffice. To prove, by means of these finished pieces, that this book exists, that I knew what it was I couldn't accomplish.

Nothing, however, is so simple, and I made haste to collect the known pieces, which have, from time to time, attracted the attention of charming and excellent minds—you first and foremost! All this had no immediate value for me other than keeping my hand in: however successful these pieces may be, as a whole [word missing], they barely make an album, not a book. The publisher Vanier may well rip those shreds away from me, but I'll merely stick them on pages as one collects pieces of cloth to commemorate an occasion, immemorial and precious only to oneself. With that damning epithet "album" in the title, the *Album de vers et de prose* could go on indefinitely (next to my personal work, which, I think, will be anonymous—the Text there speaking on its own, without the voice of an author).

Those verse and prose poems can be found, or not, besides in the opening volumes of certain Literary Reviews, in out-of-print Luxury Editions of Vathek, the Raven, the Faun.

I've had to grab whatever offered itself as a lifeboat in hard-up moments, but apart from those potboilers (*Les Dieux Antiques; Les Mots Anglais* [Antique Gods; English Words]) about which the less said the better, concessions to needs or even to pleasures have not been frequent. Nevertheless, despairing of the recalcitrant book of myself, and having unsuccessfully dragged proposals and sample chapters all over, I undertook to write—covering dress designs, jewelry, furniture, theater programs, even dinner menus—my own fashion magazine, *La Dernière Mode* [The Latest Fashion], whose eight or ten published issues, when I divest them of their dust, suffice to plunge me into a reverie for a long time.

In the final analysis, I consider the contemporary era to be a kind of interregnum for the poet, who has nothing to do with it: it is too fallen or too full of preparatory effervescence for him to do anything but keep working, with mystery, so that later, or never, and from time to time sending the living his calling card—some stanza or sonnet—so as not to be stoned by them, if they knew he suspected that they didn't exist.

Loneliness necessarily accompanies that type of attitude: and beyond my path from home (now No. 89, rue de Rome) to the various establishments to which I have owed an account of my time—the lycées Condorcet, Janson de Sailly, and Rollin Collège—I travel little; preferring above all, in an apartment defended by the family, a stay with a few old cherished pieces of furniture and a page that is often blank. My great friendships have been with Villiers and Mendès, and for ten years I saw dear Manet every day—his absence now seems to me unbelievable! Your *Poètes Maudits* [Poets of Damnation], dear Verlaine, and Huysmans' *A Rebours* [Against Nature] interested young poets in my Tuesdays, which had long been empty—poets who adore us old folks (besides the Mallarméans), and people even speak of my influence, where in fact there were only coincidences. Very much attuned, I went ten years ago where similar talented young minds go today.

Well, there you have my whole life—lacking in anecdote, in contrast to those that fill the newspapers, where I've always been seen as very strange: I've looked hard and found nothing, except for private troubles, joys, or losses. I've put in an appearance wherever they perform a ballet or play the organ—my two almost contradictory artistic passions, whose meaning will nevertheless burst out—and that's all. I forgot to mention my wanderings, which I pursue whenever my mind gets dead tired, on the edge of the Seine and the forest of Fontainebleau, where I've gone for ten years. There, I seem to myself quite different, thinking only of riverboating. I honor the river, which swallows up in its waters whole days—yet days that don't seem wasted or lost, or surrounded by any aura of guilt. I'm a simple passer-by in my little mahogany boat; I'm a furious sailor, proud of his fleet.

Good-bye, dear friend. You will read this over, written in pencil to try to approximate a good chat between friends, in the shadows and without raised voices; you will glance at this and see the couple of biographical details you know to be true. I am very upset to hear that you're ill, and with rheumatism! I know all about that. Use salicylate only rarely, and under the care of a good doctor, since the dosage is very important. Once I suffered from fatigue or even a mental absence after using that drug, and I blame it for my insomnia. But I'll visit you and tell you all this in person and bring along a sonnet and a page of prose, which I'll compose for the occasion and which will go wherever you put them. But you can begin without those two baubles. Good-bye, dear Verlaine. Give me your hand.

DIVAGATIONS

Preface

This is a book just the way I don't like them: scattered and with no architecture. Decidedly, no one consciously escapes journalism, or, if one tries to, one produces some anyway for oneself and let's hope for certain others and can't help throwing toward the light, over the heads of the multitudes, some truths.

One always has the excuse, through all this chance, that any coherence found in the book was aided by its assembly, and perhaps, too, by always saying the same thing.

In addition to the poems or anecdotes at the beginning, which the reading public has given an exaggeratedly positive fate to, and obliges me (toward the public) not to omit, the Divagations that appear here treat a single subject of thought—if I look at them with the eye of a stranger, they resemble an abbey that, even though ruined, would breathe out its doctrine to the passer-by.

Anecdotes

or

Poems

Over the world as it ends in decrepitude is a pale sky that may perhaps dissipate with the clouds—streaks of used sunsets that bleed into the dormant waters of a river, submerged beneath rays and drops. The trees are bored, and, beneath their whitened foliage (whitened by the dust of time, not by the dust of roads), rises the tent of the Revealer of Things Past: many a lamppost waits for dusk and revives the faces of an unhappy crowd, crushed by immortal sickness and the sin of centuries, the men next to their puny companions, pregnant with the miserable fruits with which the earth will perish. In the anxious silence when all eyes gaze pleadingly at the sun that, under the water, plunges deeper with the despair of a cry, here is the simple come-on: "No sign tells you about the spectacle inside, for there isn't one painter today capable of rendering even its sorrowful shadow. I bring, alive (and preserved through the ages thanks to all-powerful science), a Woman of yesteryear. A certain original and naïve madness, an ecstasy of gold, I don't know!—what she calls her hair—curves with the grace of cloth around her face illuminated by the naked gash of her lips. Instead of useless clothing, she wears a body; and her eyes, like precious stones, cannot equal the look that emerges from the whole of her happy flesh: her breasts lifted as though eternally filled with milk, their tips pointed toward the sky, her legs, smooth and glistening, preserving the salt of the primordial sea." As they remember their poor spouses—bald, morbid, and tremulous—the husbands press forward; their melancholy wives, too, out of curiosity, want to see.

When everyone has contemplated their fill of the noble creature, the last vestige of an age already accursed, some indifferent, for they won't have had the strength to understand, but others, upset, their eyelids wet but resigned, just look at each other; while the poets of that time, feeling their extinguished eyes reignite, will make their way toward their lamps, their brains spinning with a vague glory, haunted by Rhythm and in utter forgetfulness of living in a time that has outlived beauty.

EVER since Maria left me to go to another star—Which one? Orion? Altair? Or you, green planet, O Venus?—I've always cherished solitude. How many long days I have spent alone with my cat! When I say "alone," I mean without another material being—my cat is, rather, a mystical companion, a spirit. I can thus say I've spent long days alone with my cat, and alone with one of the last authors of Latin decadence: for ever since the white creature went away, strangely and singularly I've been attracted to anything that could be summed up in the word "fall." Thus, my favorite time of year is those last, lazy days of summer which immediately precede autumn, and my favorite time of day for walks is when the sun perches for a moment on the horizon before setting, casting yellow copper rays on the gray walls and red copper rays on the window panes. Similarly, the literature my spirit turns to for pleasure is the dying poetry of Rome's last moments, so long as the verse gives no whiff of the revivifying Barbarian invasion to come, and there is no hint of the faltering beginnings of the childish Latin of the first Christian prose pieces.

I was reading, then, one of those beloved poems (whose layers of makeup have more power to charm me than the healthy flesh of youth), and was burying one hand in the fur of that pure animal, when a barrel organ began to sing languidly and melancholically under my window. It was playing in the avenue of tall poplars, where the leaves, even in the spring, seem to me mournful, ever since Maria went along it with her candles, one last time. Yes, truly, instruments of sadness: the piano shimmers, the violin lights up the rent heartstrings, but the barrel organ, in the twilight of memory, made me desperately dream. Now that it was murmuring a joyously vulgar song that could scatter gaiety into the suburbs—an old-fashioned and banal tune—how is it that that ditty went straight to my heart and made me weep, like a romantic ballad? I savored it slowly and did not throw a coin out the window, both in order not to move, and for fear of finding out that the instrument was not playing alone.

To whom did this Saxony clock belong, with its slowing down of time and its thirteen strokes, its flowers and its gods? Imagine it traveling from Saxony by way of one of those old-fashioned diligences.

(Strange and unique shadows hang from the worn glass panes.)

And who looked into your Venetian mirror, deep as a cold fountain, surrounded with tarnished gold serpents? Ah! I'm sure that more than one woman bathed the sin of her beauty in it; and perhaps I can catch a glimpse of a naked ghost if I look hard.

—You meanie, you often say naughty things.

(I can see cobwebs at the tops of the windows.)

Our sideboard, too, is very old; look how the fire casts a red glow upon it; the deep, muffling purple curtains are the same age, and so are the chairs whose colors have disappeared, and the old prints on the walls, and all our old things. Doesn't it seem to you as if the songbirds and the blue bird have also faded with time?

(Don't think about the spider webs that tremble above the grand casement windows.)

You have affection for all that, and that's why I can live with you. Didn't you once, O sister of the yesteryear look, want one of my poems to contain the words "the grace of wilted things"? You, too, dislike new things; they are frightening, with their noisy healthiness; you'd feel obligated to wear them down with use, and that's very difficult for those who shun activity.

Come here, close the old German almanac you are reading with such attention even though it came out more than a hundred years ago and the kings it announces are all dead, and, lying on the antique carpet, my head resting on your charitable knees and pillowed on your faded dress, O tranquil child, I'll talk to you for hours; the fields are gone and the streets are empty; I'll talk to you about our furniture. . . . Are your thoughts wandering?

(Those spider webs are shivering at the tops of the tall casement windows.)

Have unknown words ever played about your lips, the haunting and accursed fragments of an absurd sentence?

I went out of my apartment with the distinct sensation of a wing sliding along the strings of some instrument, languid and light, which was replaced by a voice that, with a downward intonation, pronounced the words: "The Penultimate is dead," in such a way that

The Penultimate

ended one line and

Is dead

floated free within the fateful pause, the signifying void, more uselessly in the absence of all signification. I took a few steps down the street and recognized in the "nul" sound the tight string of a forgotten musical instrument, which glorious Memory had just revisited with its wing or its palm, and, putting my finger on the secret behind the mystery's artifice, I smiled and pleaded, with all my intellectual wishes, for a different speculation. But the sentence came back, a virtual reality, detached from any previous stroke of plumes or palms, heard henceforth only through the voice, until finally it articulated itself all alone, animated by its own personality. I walked along (no longer contenting myself with mere perception), reading it at the end of a line, and once, like a test, trying to make it fit my speech; then I said it with a silence after "Penultimate," in which I felt a painful pleasure: "The Penultimate," then the taut forgotten string, stretched over the *nul* sound, which broke, no doubt, and I added, in the manner of a funeral oration, "Is dead." I hadn't discontinued the attempt to return to my ordinary thoughts, alleging, in order to calm myself down, that of course "penultimate" is a lexical term signifying the next-to-last syllable of a word, and its appearance merely the unwanted residue of the linguistic labor through which my noble poetic faculty daily sobs to see itself interrupted; nevertheless, I was tormented by the sound and by the impression of untruth created by the haste and facility of the affirmation. Harassed, I resolved to let the sad words just wander on my lips, and I walked on, murmuring comfortingly, as if offering condolences, "The Penultimate is dead, she is dead, really dead, the poor desperate Penultimate," thinking that in this way I might allay my anxiety, and not without a secret hope that, by expanding the speech, I might bury her once and for all, when, horrors!—brought into existence by some easily deducible nervous magic—I felt that I had, my hand reflected in a shop window stroking something, the very voice (the original, which undoubtedly had been the only one).

But the irrefutable supernatural force intervened and the anguish under which groans my theretofore controlling spirit began when I raised my eyes, in the street of antiquities I had followed instinctively, and saw that I was standing before the shop of a lute seller who had antique musical instruments for sale hanging on his wall, and, underfoot, yellowed palm fronds and ancient birds' wings, half in shadow. Then I fled, strange person, probably condemned forever to wear mourning for the inexplicable Penultimate.

Poor pale child, why are you singing as loudly as you can
your grating and insolent song, which loses itself among the
cats, lords of the rooftops? It won't penetrate the shutters of
even the first floor, because unbeknownst to you there are
heavy silk curtains behind them.

But you are fated to go on singing, with the self-assurance
of a little man alone in the world, who, counting on no one,
works for himself alone. Have you ever had a father? It seems
you don't even have an old woman who makes you forget
hunger by beating you when you come home without a dime.

But you are working for yourself: standing tall in the streets,
covered with faded overalls made like those of adults, your
premature thinness too great for your age, you are singing to
eat, intently, without bringing your nasty eyes down to the
other kids playing on the pavement.

And you sing so loud, so loud, that your bare head, rising
in the air as your voice gets higher, seems to want to take leave
of your puny shoulders.

Little man, your head may very well leave your shoulders
for real, when, having sung all day in the city, you go on to
commit a crime. A crime is not hard to fall into, my lad; all
one needs is the courage to act on a wish, and, among the lamentable . . . Your little face looks energetic.

Not a nickel is thrown into the wicker basket your long, emaciated hand is holding as it droops against your pants leg without hope: you'll fall in with a bad crowd, and one day you'll commit a crime.

Your head is still rising and trying to leave you, as if in advance it knew, while you go on singing a tune that is becoming threatening.

It will bid you farewell the day you pay the price for me, and for those who are worth even less than me. You probably came into the world toward that, and already you are starving; we'll see your name in the papers.

Oh! Poor little head!

The Pipe

YESTERDAY, I came across my pipe as I was preparing for a long evening of work, the cozy kind of work one does in winter. Gone were the cigarettes with all the childish joys of summer, thrown into a past lit with sun-blue leaves and the rustle of muslins, and taken up again was my serious pipe, the pipe of a scholarly man who likes to smoke for a long time without getting up, so he can work more diligently. But I wasn't prepared for the surprise that the abandoned pipe had in store for me; as soon as I took the first pull, I forgot all about the important books I had to write, and, amazed, moved, I felt the whole of last winter coming back to me. I had not touched my faithful friend since coming back to France, and all London, London as I lived it entirely by myself a year ago, appeared: first, those dear fogs that muffle our brains and that have, over there, their own particular smell when they seep through the casements. My tobacco smelled like a dark room whose leather furniture was covered with a dusting of coal ash and on which lounged the scrawny black cat; those hot fires! And the maid with her red arms pouring the coal, and the sound of that same coal banging from the tin bucket to the iron storage bin in the mornings—while the mailman gave his solemn double knock, which kept me alive! I could see again through the windows the sickly trees of the deserted square—I could see the Channel, so often crossed that winter, as I shivered on the bridge of a steamer wet with mist and black with smoke—with my poor beloved wandering on the deck in traveling clothes: a long dust-colored dress, a coat that clung damply to her icy shoulders, and one of those straw hats without feathers and almost without ribbons which wealthy ladies throw away on arrival because they have been so battered by sea and wind, and which poor beloveds refurbish and wear for many more seasons. Around her neck my beloved was wearing the terrible handkerchief that one waves when saying goodbye forever.

Hᴏᴡ ꜰᴀʀ from procuring its much-touted pleasures the civilized state really is! One should, for example, be astonished that in every big city there doesn't exist an association of dreamers who happen to be there, an association supporting a journal that recounts current events from the particular perspective of dreams. *Reality* is just an artifice, good for anchoring the average intellect among the mirages of a fact; but it therefore rests on some universal agreement: let us see, then, whether there isn't, in the ideal, a necessary, obvious, and simple aspect that can serve as a type. I want, for my own sake, to write down the way this Anecdote struck my poetic eye, before the mass of reporters have chewed it over into the pabulum required to give everything its common character.

The little theater called Prodigalities had just added the exhibition of a living cousin of Atta Troll or Martin to its classic performance of *The Beast and the Genius;* in order to show that I had the double-ticket invitation kicking around somewhere in my house, I put my hat on the vacant seat next to me, the absent friend indicating a general tendency to stay away from the naïve spectacle. What was happening in front of me? Nothing, except: out of the gauzy muslin surrounding twenty pedestals right out of Baghdad came a smile and arms open to the mournful heaviness of the bear: the hero, one of those evocative sylphides, and their handler, a clown, in his haughty silver nakedness, were tormenting the animal with our superiority. To enjoy, as the crowd does, the myth enclosed in all banalities—what a comfort! And in the absence of neighbors to

tell my thoughts to, I just had to pursue, in the ordinary splendid effect of the stage, my dreamily imaginative search for
symbols and images. Though I had no memories of habitual
evenings here, the unexpected and unprecedented accident
nevertheless riveted my attention: one of numerous waves of
applause, offered according to the enthusiasm of the spectators for the theatrical illustration of Man's authentic privilege, just when it was reaching its crest, stopped short, for unknown reasons, and was unable to spread itself around. The
crowd was all ears when it was necessary to be all eyes. The
hero's gesture—his hand clenched in air opening its five fingers—had attracted the crowd's sympathy by, I saw now, its
ingenious suggestion that he had caught something in mid-
flight, a figure (nothing more) of the ease with which anyone
at all can get an idea. Moved by the slight breeze in the wake
of the gesture, the bear rhythmically and gently interrogated
that exploit, putting one taloned paw on the beribboned human shoulder. The spectators all held their breath, the consequences were potentially so damaging for the honor of the
race: What was going to happen? The other paw hung down
calmly beside the arm along the body suit; and one could see,
in this couple united in a secret bond, something like an inferior man, thickset and good-natured, standing upright on his
two widely planted furry legs, hugging the other fellow, in order to absorb the practices of genius, his black-nosed muzzle
reaching only halfway up the chest of his brilliant and supernatural brother; the latter, in turn, his mouth twisted with im-
precision, tried to signal something to a horrible head propel-
ling a golden paper fly by means of a visible wire that, in the
midst of this panic, expressed the real denials. An obvious
spectacle, larger than the stage, with the gift, proper to art, of
lasting a long time; to complete it, I welcomed into myself the
speech denied to the denizen of arctic wastes, not letting myself get distracted by the probably fatal stance of the mime,
depository of human pride: "Be kind" (that was the sense),
"and rather than lacking charity, explain to me what's good
about this world of splendor, dust, and voices, in which you

have had me live. My urgent request is just, and you can't simply answer, overcome by a merely feigned anguish, that you don't know, subtle elder brother, already launched deep in the realms of wisdom; while I, to make you free, am still garbed in the nebulous atmosphere of caves where I'll reconfine, during the night of these humble eras, my latent force. Let us authenticate, through this close embrace, in front of the multitudes gathered here for that purpose, the pact of our reconciliation." The absence of a single breath united with space to make me wonder what absolute place I was living in, where one of the dramas of astral history could elect to take place in this modest theater. The crowd disappeared in this emblem of its spiritual situation, and magnified the stage: the gaslights, modern dispensers of ecstasy, all alone, with the impartiality of an elemental thing, prolonged, to the farthest reaches of the house, their luminous sound of anticipation.

The charm broke: it was when a piece of meat, unadorned and brutal, crossed my vision, coming from a gap in the curtains, a few seconds ahead of the moment the bear usually got his reward. A substitute bloody shred presented to the bear who, refinding his instincts anterior to discovering a higher curiosity through the magic of theatricality, fell back on his four legs and shuffled off with the food amid Silence, sniffing, preparatory to sinking his teeth into his prey. The crowd breathed an incomprehensible sigh of relief with almost nothing fake about it: rows of glistening lorgnettes looked for the splendid imbecile sizzling in his fear; but saw an abject meal preferred, perhaps, to what the animal would have had to do to *our image* to reduce it to something equally palatable. The curtain, after hesitating to do anything to increase the danger or the emotion, dropped all of a sudden with its advertised prices and banalities. I got up like everyone else to go and breathe outside, astonished that I had not, however, felt the same impressions, this time again, that my fellows had, but serene: for my way of seeing was, after all, superior to theirs, and was maybe even the genuine one.

As an orphan, I wandered around in black with my eyes vacant of family; in the square, the tents of a fair were being put up, and I could see my future living that way: I liked the smell of travelers, and could forget my comrades among them. I could hear no chorus coming through a crack in the scenery, no soliloquy intoned in the distance, since dramas required the holy hour of lamplighting; I was hoping to talk to a boy too wavering to represent his people, his nightcap fitting his head like Dante's; who was taking in, in the form of toast with soft cheese, already the snows of summits, lilies, or other white things constitutive of wings inside: I almost begged him to share his superior repast with me when he gave some quickly to a famous older brother who had surged up against a neighboring canvas doing somersaults and other well-known gymnastic feats that go along with daytime. Unfettered, the lithe one pirouetted up to me in his body-suit lightness, surprising in my opinion, and started in: "Your parents?" "I haven't any." "Go on, a father's a riot, don't you know. . . . Even last week, when the soup didn't come, he made the funniest faces when the master lashed out with kicks and punches. . . . My dear boy!" and triumphed by lifting his glorious leg easily up to my face, "He astonishes us, Papa," then he bit off a piece of the chaste tidbit that the younger brother held out. "Your Mommy—perhaps you don't have one? Since you're alone? Mine swallows rope to the crowd's applause. You don't know, parents are funny folks that make you laugh." The parade heated up, he left me; and as for me, I sighed, suddenly upset at not having parents.

Silence! It is certain that beside me, as in a dream, stretched out to the rocking of the coach under whose wheels dies an interjection of flowers, any woman, and I know one who can see though this, would exempt me from the effort of proffering a single vocable: to compliment her aloud on her inquiring outfit, almost an offer of self to the man in whose favor the afternoon draws to a close, would only imply, compared to all this fortuitous closeness, a certain distance from her features ending in a dimple that turns into a witty smile. But thus does reality not consent to our plans: for pitilessly, outside the last rays one sensed luxuriously fading from the polished surface of the carriage, there was something like a shouting voice, in the midst of too much tacit felicity for a nightfall in the suburbs, stormy, in all directions at once and senselessly, recalling the strident ordinary laughter of things and their triumphal fanfare: in fact, if the cacophony heard by anyone suddenly ceases, it is not the start of a new silence more attuned to one's idea, but rather an echo of the noise that was there, remaining raw before the haunting of existence.

"The X Festival! . . ." I'm not sure what suburban meeting point the child transported in my idleness named, her voice free of any boredom; I obeyed and ordered the carriage to stop.

Without some compensation for this departure, some figurative explanation plausible for my spirits, I threw myself into the symmetrical opposite of what I had expected, as festive glass lanterns align themselves little by little into garlands and other attributes; I decided, since solitude was impossible, to immerse myself totally in the hungry and hateful kind of outburst I had always avoided in gracious company: ready and without surprise at the change in our program, my companion's candid arm resting on mine, we wandered down the alley, keeping one eye on the crowd, now divided into two echoing lines of revelers, so that it could enclose the whole universe in there for a time. Subsequent to the waves of would-be spectators willing to see anything that would dissipate our stagnation, entertained by the sunset—which was, in fact, strange and purple—we were brought up short by a poignant human spectacle as much as by the fiery clouds: garnished with no painted car nor sign in capital letters stood a stall, apparently empty.

To whomever this torn mattress, capable of improvising here—like the veils in all times and temples—the hidden secret! belonged, its frequentation during the fast had not stirred up in its owner before he unrolled it the banners of common hopes or the hallucination of some marvel to reveal (except the banality of his hunger-filled nightmares); and yet, moved by the holiday quality of exception to daily misery that a meadow takes on when the mysterious word "festival" redefines it, trampled by many shoes (for the same reasons a hardened coin can weigh down the pockets of clothing, and work its way down with the sole purpose of being spent), him too! Anyone denuded of everything except the notion that he should be among the elect, or else to sell, to exhibit, but what, had given in to the feeling of confidence inspired by the gathering. Or, more prosaically, maybe the trained rat, unless he himself, this beggar counted on the athletic prowess of his muscles, to mobilize the crowd's attention, might be lacking at that very moment, as often happens whenever a man is on the spot under the widest general circumstances.

"Beat the drum!" proposed like a great lady Madame . . . you alone know Who, pointing to an old-fashioned snare drum out of which rose, unfolding his arms as if to signal the pointlessness of approaching his little theater without prestige, an old man seduced, perhaps, by the camaraderie of living so close to an instrument of sound and summons, and ready to be conscripted into her vacant design; and then, among all the most beautiful things imaginable, the throat of the woman of the world tightly closed by a jewel, as if the absence of answer to the riddle shone brightly! there she was, totally involved, to the great surprise of my silent clown persona, faced with the crowd's approach, attracted by the deafening sound of *ra*'s and *fla*'s which drowned out my invariable and (at first, even to me) obscure come-on: "Step this way, everyone, it hardly costs anything, and we will give a refund to anyone dissatisfied with the show." The old man's belongings glowed around him as he joined his previously emptied palms together in thanks, and I waved the banner to signal the start of the performance, put on my hat, and stood ready to strangle the desirous standing masses, but curious to see the secret of her preference for this dreamless spot over my company, to see what my evening companion would think up.

Down to about knee level, she emerged, on a table, above the crowd of heads.

In a flash, it came to me, electrically, like a fountain springing up where it wasn't expected, this thought: that, lacking everything, she, as fashion or the sunset circumstanced her beauty, without any supplement of dance or song, for the crowd amply repaid the donation required at the door; and in that same instant I knew my duty in the perils of the subtle exhibition, that the only thing to do, when attention flagged, was to have recourse to some absolute power, like a Metaphor. Quick! Keep talking until certainty replaces doubt on the faces of the crowd; keep explaining, until they're ready to bow to the evidence implied in speech itself, and until they're willing to part with their coin for one of those poetic, superior, and exact presumptions: in short, the certainty that they have not been duped.

Casting a last glance at her hair that seemed to wreathe in smoke and then light up gardens and fairgrounds with the increasing paleness of its crepe hat, of a color that matched her statuesque dress, advancing one leg toward the audience, all in hydrangea.

So:

> The hair, the theft of fire at the far
> West of desires ends its course
> And comes to rest (I would call it a diadem dying)
> On the forehead crowned with a braid of its former
>   source
>
> But without gold to sigh
> That this smoldering cloud
> Igniting the always interior fire
> Originally the only one allowed
>
> Extends to the jewel of the spectator's true or mocking
>   eye
> To offer the hero's nakedness maligns
> Her who without moving either star or fire on her
>   finger
> Stands simply and gloriously for woman, signs
>
> That her hair alone casts rubies on doubt's dark night
> Like a joyous and tutelary torch's light

With my help around the waist of the living allegory who was already finished, perhaps because I had nothing more to say, I eased her down gently to earth: "Let me point out to you," I said, now down to the crowd's level, cutting short their aston-

ishment at this dismissal through an apparent return to authenticity, "Ladies and Gentlemen, that the person who had
the honor of submitting herself to your judgment needs, in
order to communicate to you the sense of her charm, no costume or other theatrical prop. Her natural being, which already alludes, through the history of women's outfits in general, to one of the primordial motifs of Woman, is enough,
as your sympathetic approbation convinces me." There was
an absence of assenting agreement except for a confused
"Of course!" or "That's true," or "Yes!" arising from several
throats and a few generous pairs of hands applauding. We
quickly made our way to the exit, and out into a vacancy of
trees, night, and crowds, among whom we expected to mill
around. We found only a waiting circus child with white
gloves who dreamed of stretching his hands out toward some
haughty garter.

"Thank you!" murmured the lady, breathing in the air of a
constellation or of leaves, drinking in, not to calm herself
down—she had never doubted her success—but rather at
least to restore her habitual frigid voice: I have in my head
memories of things that can't be forgotten.

"Oh!" I said modestly, "it was just an aesthetic commonplace . . ."

"Which you might never have introduced, who knows? my
dear, the pretext of formulating thus before me in the joint
isolation of our carriage—where did it go?—let's go back to
it; but this is forced out by the punch in the stomach caused by
the impatience of people to whom willy-nilly you have to proclaim something quickly, even if it's a reverie . . ."

"Which doesn't know itself and hurls itself naked with fear
through the crowd; that's true. Just as you, my dear, would

not have heard so irrefutably, despite its doubling by the final lines, my come-on made after an old mode of sonnet,† I bet, if each word hadn't bounced off various eardrums before coming to you, made to charm a mind open to multiple meanings."

"Perhaps!" agreed the same, accepting my thought with good humor, in the same breath with the cool night breeze.

---

†Used in the English Renaissance. [—*Author*]

I HAD been rowing for a long time, with grand, lazy gestures, my eyes focused inside me in utter forgetfulness of
moving, the laughter of daylight swirling all around, when so
much immobility seemed to have been grazed by an inert
sound and the little boat kept going by half. I knew I had
stopped only from the initials now visible on the oars, recalling me to my identity in the world.

What was happening? Where was I?

To see my way clear in this adventure, it was necessary to
recall my early departure in this hot, bright July, toward the
bright spaces between the dormant vegetation of an always
narrow and meandering rivulet, in search of water plants and
with the aim of reconnoitering the placement of the property
of the friend of a friend to whom I was to say hello. Without
being stopped by the ribbon of any plant here rather than
there, the reflection of the landscape any more likely here than
there to dissipate in the impartial rhythm of the oars, I had
been beached on a tuft of reeds, the mysterious end of my
quest, in the middle of the river: where, immediately expanding into a fluvial thicket, it lay with the nonchalance of a
swamp, and rippled with the hesitant movements of a spring.

A detailed inspection taught me that the tuft of herbage
that came to a point in the current was masking the single arch
of a bridge, extended on each side by a hedge around a lawn.

It was then that I realized: Ah! Madame X's park! The un-known woman I was supposed to greet.

What a pretty neighborhood during the summer! The na-ture of someone who would choose a retreat so humidly im-penetrable could only be right up my alley. One could be sure that she made this spot her inner mirror, far from the hubbub of July afternoons; she spent time here, and soon the silvering mist that coats the willows became the transparency of her gaze, which knew every leaf.

I imagined her entire lustral self.

Bent in two in the sportive attitude maintained by my curi-osity, and in the spacious silence where everything evoked the stranger, I caught myself smiling at the incipient enslavement that a feminine possibility suggested, which wasn't badly sig-nified by the ties attaching the rower's shoes to the hull; how often we become one with the instrument that transports us!

"She could be anyone . . . ," I was going to conclude.

When an imperceptible rustle made me wonder whether the inhabitant was haunting my leisure, or even—I hardly dared hope—the pool.

The steps ceased. Why?

The subtle secret of the feet coming and going conduct the spirit wherever the shadow that inhabits the lace and the petti-coats wants, the skirt brushing the ground as if circumscribing the heel and the toe with a gentle wake, concealing the way the first steps open, pushing all the rest to fall back into a kind of train, but something escapes, and moves along with its savvy double arrow.

Does the pedestrian even know herself why she stopped; and isn't it just to raise my head too high to look out from those reeds belying all that mental somnolence that masks my lucidity, and examine the mystery too closely?

"Whatever you look like, Madame, I feel the precision of your face destroys something installed here through the rustling of an approach. Yes! It can be most authentically tied or buckled or closed with a diamond: the belt won't be able to withstand the fingers of the explorer. So vague a concept suffices, and nothing will transgress the pleasure of a generality that permits—nay, demands—that all faces be excluded, to the point that if one is unveiled (don't go and lean it over the furtive threshold where I reign), it would dispel my desire, with which it has nothing to do."

I could try to introduce myself, wearing this getup of an aquatic marauder and using chance as my excuse.

Apart, we are together: I immerse myself in her vague intimacy, in the arrest above the water where my dream suspends the hesitant one, better than any visit, followed by others, can authorize. How much meaningless small talk would it take, compared to the discourse I proffered so as to not be heard, to rejoin the intuitive accord we have now, one ear to the ground or to the sand, to hear that everything has fallen silent!

The full stop is measured by the cadence of my determination.

Advise, O my dream: What should I do?

Give a last good look at the absence enclosed in this solitude, and, as one plucks, in memory of a site, one of those magical closed water lilies that spring up all of a sudden, enveloping with their hollow whiteness a taste, made of intact dreams, of the happiness that didn't take place and that your held breath feared would be destroyed by an apparition, and depart with it: silently, rowing gently but rapidly home, trying not to leave any splashes or waves at the feet of the unknown suggesting the theft of the ideal flower.

If, attracted by the feeling of something different, she appeared—the Meditative or Haughty one, the Shy or Forward one—too bad for the ineffable face I will always not know! For I accomplished the maneuver according to the rules: I extracted myself, turned around, and followed the curve of the river, carrying with me like a noble swan's egg, from which flight will never arise, my imaginary trophy, which will never fill with anything but the exquisite vacancy of itself, that every woman, in summertime, on the pathways of her park, likes to pursue, arrested perhaps for a long time by some water to cross or by some stagnant pool.

SPRINGTIME induces organisms to commit acts which, in any other season, would be foreign to them, and many natural history treatises are full of descriptions of this phenomenon in animals. How much more interesting it is, then, to gather materials about the climatic transformations observable in individuals made for spirituality! Barely out of the irony of winter, I myself remain in an equivocal state unless it is replaced by some absolute or naïve naturalism, able to find pleasure in the gap between two blades of grass. Since nothing in the present case could profit the crowd, I retire, in order to meditate on it, under one of those shade trees I noticed yesterday around the town. It is precisely at the heart of their quite ordinary shadowy mystery that I will show you a striking and graspable example of such springtime inspirations.

Great was my surprise when, earlier today, in a deserted spot in the Bois de Boulogne, walking soundlessly through the woods, I saw, through the thousand interstices of the screen of saplings good for concealing nothing, convulsed in regular beats, animated from his tricornered hat to his silver-buckled shoes, a cleric, who, in the absence of any witnesses, was giving himself to the inviting grass. Far be it from me (and far also, one hopes, from any providential plan) to make my presence felt: I felt guilty like someone falsely scandalized seizing a pebble in the pathway, I hoped that my smile, however complicitous, would not redden the face concealed behind the two hands of the poor man, any more than the redness already brought on by his solitary exercise! My foot quick, since it was necessary that my presence not cause any distraction, needed agility: and strength to resist the temptation of a backward glance; I had to content myself with imagining the almost diabolical continuation of his writhing, right, left, and front, that produced that chaste frenzy. Everything, whether rubbing himself or flinging out parts of his body, whether rolling or sliding, brought satisfaction: and stopping short, ignoring the tickling of some tall stems against his dark ankles, in that special robe worn to signify that one is all in all to oneself, even one's own wife, was impossible. O solitude and cold, silence dispersed in the underbrush, you heard, perceived by senses less subtle than anxious, the muffled pounding of cloth, as if the night hiding in its creases were shaken out, finally freed! And the muffled banging of the rejuvenated skeleton against the earth imparted new life; the disciples didn't even have to look at you. Intoxicated, it was enough to seek in oneself the cause of a pleasure or duty, not at all explained by the ecclesiastic's return, across a lawn, to the familiar seminar pranks. The warm verdant breath of spring eventually dilated the immutable texts inscribed in his flesh, and he, emboldened by the pleasant arousal of his sterile thinking, had come to recognize, through contact with Nature—unmediated, sharp, violent, positive, stripped of all intellectual curiosity—the general well-being. And, candidly, far from the obedience and constraint of his occupation—the canons, the prohibitions, and the censures—he rolled around, in the beatitude of his native simplicity, happier than a mule. The moment the goal of his walk was finished, he stood up abruptly like a waterspout, not without brushing off the pistils and juices that clung to his person, and in order to go back unnoticed into his congregation and the habits of his ministry; it was necessary for the hero of my thought—I'm trying not to deny anything here—I have the right not to think about it. Doesn't my discretion about enjoyment as it first appeared have as its recompense to fix forever that passer-by's fantasy, completing it as I wish? The image stamped with the mysterious seal of modernity, at once baroque and beautiful?

GLORY! I only got to know it yesterday, irrefutable, and nothing that anyone calls by that name can interest me.

Hundreds of posters catching the last uncomprehended golden rays of the day, a betrayal of the letter, have gone by, to all corners of the city, my eyes remaining at the level of the horizon, lingering there because of the start of a railway trip, before collecting themselves in the abstruse pride that the approach of a forest gives out in its moment of apotheosis.

Suddenly, a discordant cry inserted itself into the exaltation of the hour, announcing a familiar name, Fontainebleau, and I wanted, the glass of the compartment having been violated, to strangle the loudspeaker: Shut up! Don't shed light, through your indifferent barking, on the shadow that has here gotten into my spirit, despite the wagon doors banging in the egalitarian wind, and the omnipresent tourists disgorged. A misleading calm of deep forests spreads an extraordinary state of illusion—what do you say?—that made these travelers leave the capital, and get off at your station, good employee, shouting out of duty, from whom I can't expect, not partaking of the intoxication distributed to everyone by the conjoined liberality of Nature and the State, a bit of silence long enough for me to isolate myself from this urban delegation toward the ecstatic torpor of foliage too still not to be scattered in the air by the least commotion; here, without violating your integrity, take this coin.

Beckoned by some inattentive uniform, I approach a barrier and, without saying a word, give him, instead of that corrupting coin, my ticket.

Obedient, nevertheless, agreeing to see only asphalt stretching along the track, I still can't imagine that in this pompous and exceptional October, among the millions of vacuous existences bringing here the enormous monotony of the capital city, to be effaced by the sound of a whistle blowing in the mist, that anyone other than me got away furtively, and sensed, this year, bitter and luminous sobs, many a hesitant floating idea that deserts random perches and branches, a shudder and something that calls to mind autumns beneath big skies.

No one! And, flying away from the arms of doubt like someone who has the key to some secret splendor, too inappreciable a trophy to make an appearance; but without thereby throwing myself toward that immortal daily guard of tree trunks or trains spewing passengers onto one of the superhuman prides of the world (but wouldn't it be necessary to verify the authenticity?) or crossing the threshold where torchlights stand guard and consume any dream that existed prior to their splendor, reflecting in royal colors the sunset clouds, awaiting the universal sacredness of a royal intruder who needs only to appear: I waited as ordinary movement took over the crowd and, dwindling down to the proportions of some childish illusion, carried it off somewhere, revealing the train that had left me off here alone.

F OR A long time, I thought that my ideas were exempt from any accident, even a real one; preferring over chance to plunge into their deepest principle to provoke an upsurge of the truth.

A taste for an abandoned house, which would seem favorable to such a disposition, makes me change my mind: every year the identical contentment, the outside stairway growing greener and greener, a winter shutter opened against the wall as if there had been no interruption, the eye wandering over a spectacle that had been immobilized in the past. It was a sign of faithful returns, but this time the worm-eaten shutter opened on a ruckus, refrains, arguments, below: I remembered reading about the invasion of workers expected in the unhappy domicile I haunt the corner of, proceeding to offend the place where solitude had reigned for so long, with the laying of a train track. I remember agonizing at first—should I go or shouldn't I?—but overcoming my hesitation, I said the hell with it, too bad! I'll go defend the property as mine. A certain tenderness, exclusive now, for houses that have failed to be listed among a town's historic sites; I become the one who presides over its decline; improbably, this spot appreciated for its decrepitude and uniqueness is turned, through the workings of progress, into a mess hall for railroad workers.

Road graders and diggers, by means of whom, a piece of worn velvet between their legs, the pile of earth seems to move; they stretch out, during breaks, in a ditch, the blue-and-white stripes of their shirts, little by little, resembling the surface of water (clothing that says Oh! Man is the very source he's searching for): my co-occupants are the same ones I meet on the roads, in my mind, embraced like workers par excellence: rumor has it that these intruders are indeed road workers. Lazy and strong, swarming wherever the earth needs modification, they find, in the absence of a factory, in the open air, a certain independence.

Their bosses, unbothered, their word absolute, are probably elsewhere.—I am the resident noisophobic, and I'm surprised that almost everyone notices bad smells, but not bad noises. This crowd goes in and out, shouldering shovels and picks: which invites one to think of things in the back of one's mind, and forces one to proceed directly from notions one tells oneself *are nothing but literature*. My devoted enemies begin their day going into the crypt or cellar we share and standing in front of the row of double utensils, the shovel and pickaxe, sexual—whose metal, summing up the worker's strength, fertilizes fields where nothing grows. I am overcome with religious feelings, in addition to annoyance, moved enough to kneel. No officer will come to dislodge the intruders—local customs, tacit agreements—slipped in behind our backs, and even with payments to the owners: I'm on my own to try to restrain them from trespassing. Whatever language I use will, of course, imply that I disapprove of them, since in general promiscuity displeases me: but I imagine myself holding forth more or less as follows:—Comrades—for example—you can't imagine the state of someone trying to find in a landscape, maybe this one, the coherence he lacks; even the crowd stops short before this landscape, where the deep woods reinforce the isolation I seek in both forest and pool. Given my case, when people swear, gasp, fight, or wound each other, the discord produces, in the luminous suspension of air, the most intolerable, and, if you must know, invisible of gashes.—It's not that I fear the inanity of my plight in the eyes of simple men, who would take my speech, surely, rather more seriously than the eleven citizens—neighbors—I tried it out on, who immediately laughed at it. These drinkers have a sense of the marvelous, and, after working very hard, they might imagine superior delicatenesses somewhere, and understand the need to break out; they wouldn't see it as a sign of privilege, would not take umbrage at a manifestation of something not social but personal. They would restrain themselves for a while but soon habit would take over again, unless someone responded right away, equal to equal.—When work stops for awhile, we feel the need to band together among ourselves: Who is it that shouted, me, him? the sound of his voice increases me, and, drawn out of my fatigue, it's already like starting drinking for free, to hear someone else shouting.—Their chorus, however incoherent, is thus to them necessary. I quickly abandon my defense, with the same sensitivity that heightened it; and I hold out my hand to the intruder. Ah! Property, with all its proper and express usages, is closed, as the People would say, to the dreamer, from the deep shade of forests to the spacious retreat it offers: I must have avoided it, obstinately, for years—to say nothing of having the means of acquisition—in order to satisfy some instinct of owning nothing and simply passing through; at the risk of having the residence, as now, open to any adventure, which is not quite a chance occurrence, for it brings me closer, depending on my attitude, to the proletariat.

I can see this season alternating between sympathy and uneasiness. . . .

—Or waiting, to end the suspense, for someone to confront me: in the meantime my only strategy is to close off the garden, planted and arranged by my hand, its terrace on the water, the room we live in facing the fields. . . . No stranger is allowed to cross this threshold, as some cabarets say; the workers can get to their workplace by renting and cutting a road in the fields.

"Piece of crap!" accompanied by the sound of feet kicking the grate, suddenly bursts out: I know whom the title names, and, even though it comes from a drunkard, a tall boy with his face against the bars, it disturbs me in spite of myself; is it class? not at all; I don't measure, between individuals, any difference, and at this moment simply don't succeed in considering that madman, staggering and bellowing, a man, or denying my resentment. Pulling himself erect, he examines me with animosity. It is impossible to wipe him out mentally: I want to complete the work of alcohol and lay him in advance in the dust so that he will cease to be this vulgar and mean colossus; without my having to lose to him first in a fistfight that would illustrate, on the lawn, the class struggle. In the meantime, he overflows with new insults. The ill that will ruin him, drunkenness, will provide, in my place, his downfall, to the extent that, conscious of it, I feel guilty about my muteness, seeming oblivious to his situation, which makes me complicit.

I am racked with contradictory states, pointless, distorted, and affected by the contagion, the shiver, of some imbecilic ebriety.

Even the calmness, obligatory in this place of echoes, I have, particularly on Sunday evenings, unto silence. I love the fragility of that hour, which takes on the transparency of the day, before flowing lucidly before the shadows into some sort of depth. I like to observe, in peace, that crisis; to have it undersigned by someone. My chums appreciate the instant in their own way, colluding, between supper and bedtime, over salaries, or having interminable disputes as they sprawl amid the furnishings. Excluded, I don't know whether to stay or leave the window, where I look at what you can see from the oldest part of the building; I gesture to the group, but without effect. That is always the case, I'm afraid; it is hard to be together; contact among men cannot, I fear, ever happen. "I say," a voice pipes up, "that we're all slaving here for the profit of others."—"More than that," I add under my breath, "you are doing it so as to be paid, and to be legally what you are." "Yes, the bourgeois," I hear, unconcerned, "want a railroad line."—"Not me, in any case," for a laugh, "I didn't call you to this luxuriant, echoing countryside, overturned as much as I am bothered." This frequent conversation, marked with mute restrictions on my side, doesn't reach up, like a jewel under a spell, to the fluid sky. All the ordinary mouths remain silent and close to the ground, as if to disgorge there the vanity of their speech. I am about to conclude: "Maybe I, too, work. . . ." "At what?" nobody would have objected, admitting, because of accountants, that work could be transferred from the arms to the head. "At what?" echoes silently, inside, my conscience alone; "Anything useful, at least, in the general process of exchange." Sadness that what I produce remains, to people like this, essentially, like the clouds at dusk or the stars in the sky, vain.

Then one day I hear a sudden silence. What is happening?

The labor squad has come to the meeting place, but lies defeated. One after the other, they have fallen on the grass, barely completing their first effort, scattered as if bombed by a projectile, the body as if asleep faced with the unfeeling clod.

And so I walk by them, freely admiring and dreaming.

No, my view can't, from the window I'm leaning out, go all the way toward the horizon, without part of me stepping over the window sill, awkward and lacking in social graces in my turn, to become part of the swath of workers: whose mystery and duty I should understand, unlike the majority, and a lot of those more fortunate. Bread hasn't sufficed for them!—

first, they have toiled most of the week to obtain it, and now, maybe tomorrow, they don't know, they crawl around in vagueness and dig without movement—which makes, in their fate, a hollow equal to the one they have been digging every day in the reality of the roadbed (but of course, it might be the foundation of a temple). Without saying what it is or elucidating this ceremony, they honorably reserve the dimension of the sacred in their existence by a work stoppage, an awaiting, a suicide. Out of the pride inherent in daily work, simply to resist and stand tall, comes knowledge, magnified by the pillars of a stand of tall trees; some instinct seeks it in a large number, soon to be thrown away, of little glasses; the workers are, with the absoluteness of a ritual gesture, less its officiants than its victims, if one takes into consideration the evening stupor of the tasks and if the ritual observance comes more from fate than from will.

Constellations begin to shine: I wish that, in the darkness that covers the blind herd, there could also be points of light, eternalizing a thought, despite the sealed eyes that never understood it—for the fact, for exactitude, for it to be said. I will thus think exclusively about them, about those whose abandon blocks my access to the vesperal distance more than their daily commotion ever did. Keeping watch over these artisans of elementary tasks, I have occasion, beside a limpid, continuous river, to meditate on these symbols of the People—some robust intelligence bends their spines every day in order to extract, without the intermediary of wheat, the miracle of life which grounds presence: others in the past have built aqueducts or cleared fields for some implement, wielded by the same Louis-Pierre, Martin, Poitou, or the Norman. When they are not asleep, they thus invoke one another according to their mothers or their provinces. But in fact their births fall into anonymity, and their mothers into the deep sleep that prostrates them, while the weight of centuries presses down on them, eternity reduced to social proportions.

Volumes

on

My Divan

Muse of impotence, who dries up the sources of rhythm and forces me to reread; opposed to inebriants, I give you the intoxication that comes from others.

A landscape haunts me like opium. Up above and at the horizon is a bright cloud, with a narrow blue burrow in it for Prayer. For vegetation, there are suffering trees whose pained flesh is wrapped around exposed nerves, their visible growth accompanied, despite the immobility of the air, by a violin's mournful sound, which, at the extremities, vibrates into leaves. Their shadows spread out like taciturn mirrors in the flower beds of an absent garden, setting forgetfulness and the future into its black granite edges. Bouquets of flowers are strewn on the ground all over, along with several fallen wingfeathers. One ray at a time, day casts off its boredom, bursts into flame, and spews incomprehensible splendor—Is it makeup? Blood? Strange sunset! Or is this torrent of tears lit up by the fireworks of that artificer Satan moving behind the scenes? Night only prolongs crime, remorse, and Death. Therefore you veil your face in sobs, less because of this nightmare than because of the fragments of attempts to go free implied in any exile; what, oh, what is the Sky?

THE STORY of Caliph Vathek begins at the summit of a tower from which one can read the firmament down to an enchanted underground cave; every serious or funny or prodigious scene holding the two extremes apart. What magisterial architecture inheres in the narrative and its no less beautiful idea! Something fated or perhaps merely predetermined by the law hastens the descent of the powerful to hell; the prince goes down there accompanied by his whole kingdom; but he stands alone on the edge of a cliff: he had wanted to deny the State Religion to which omnipotence was tired of being joined through a universal genuflection, and turned to the practice of magic, which is linked to insatiable desire. The whole ancient mystery of absolute power is contained in this drama, acted out by three characters: a perverse and chaste mother, prey to both ambitions and rites, a nubile young woman, and a languid, precocious husband, bound by joyous betrothals. Attended by delicious, devout dwarves, ghouls, and other figures that go with the mystic or earthly surroundings, something unexpected arises from the fiction: not knowing the modern arts of painting, these images, chosen to render the ugliness or uniqueness of each character, seem to present an almost lyrical clownishness, and the silhouettes convey a mounting outline of passions and ceremonials. The expansion of these details almost covers up the narrator's great dream. So much newness and *local color* grabbed in passing by the recent fad of Eastern imitations, the depiction of an orgy, would amount to nothing, compared to the grandeur of the visions opened up by the subject, in which hundreds of impressions, each more captivating than a mere procedure, are revealed in their turn. Is it necessary to isolate each effect through a brief, distinct formula? I'm afraid of saying nothing when I announce *the mournfulness of very vast, monumental perspectives* joined with *the curse of having a superior fate*. And finally *the fright*, caused by *the secrets and dizziness* brought on by *the oriental exaggeration of numbers: the remorse* that sets in *over vague and unknown crimes; the virginal languors of innocence and prayer; blasphemy, meanness, the crowd.*† Poetry (whose origin cannot be elsewhere and which hasn't become a habit among us), unforgettably linked to the book, appears in some odd juxtaposition of quasi-lyrical innocence with the enormous or vain solemnities of the practice of magic. At that moment is colored and heightened, like the black vibrations of a star, the freshness of natural scenes, until it hurts; but not without imparting to this approach to dreams something simpler and more extraordinary.

---

†Quotations. [—*Author*]

Capsule

Sketches and

Full-Length

Portraits

No one, that I recall, was more wrapped up in the visible folds of illusion, descending to us, with his open gesture that meant, "Here I am," with a drive more vehement or supernatural, than that adolescent; no one knew, at that point in youth, that flashing out in him was the whole destiny of Man—not his own, but possibly that of Man himself. Perhaps we didn't see that mental scintillation, eternal like a diamond solitaire, because, distracted by our consciences, we stopped looking. I don't know, but I think, going back over those early years now, that his arrival must have been extraordinary, or that we were all crazy. Both, maybe, and I'm happy to affirm it. He waved very ancient or future victory flags, the kind extinguished on forgotten pillars that let their doused but still burning embers fall: I swear we saw some.

What he really wanted, this suddenly appearing stranger, was in fact, I think very seriously: to reign. Didn't he go to inform himself, when the newspapers announced that a throne was vacant, the throne of Greece, that it would be incontinent of him to rush to validate his right to it due to his ancestral sovereignty, having something to do with the Tuileries: he chewed over the idea just a minute too long, for he made up his mind a minute after they had offered it to someone else. In any case, the rumor, plausible enough, was never denied by the person concerned. Thus, this candidate for any surviving throne took up residence among poets; this time, his mind made up, he said, and wiser, he wanted "to add to the illustriousness of my race the only truly noble badge of glory remaining in our time—that of being *a great writer.*" The epithet stuck.

What relation could there be between feet trained to walk beside the sea with a breeze from the ancient oak grove, or solitude brought back to oneself in the quiet of a deserted chateau, a noble and provincial calm belonging to ancient Saint-Brieuc, concentrating so that a booming silence would erupt from the pipe organs of the retreats into abandoned abbeys in pursuit of juvenile science, and a group, lost in deepest Paris, of high school graduates, banding together intuitively? Exactly in the midst of this group dropped the young Philippe Auguste Mathias of the prodigious name. Nothing will disturb, either for me or for all who saw him arrive, even though they are now widely scattered, that bolt of lightning etched indelibly into the memories of François Coppée, Léon Dierx, José de Hérédia, Paul Verlaine, and Catulle Mendès.

A genius! That's how we understood him.

In our gatherings, the beginnings of a generation, trying at least to catch a reflection of borrowed glory, we assembled, in case one of us would reveal himself to be the Elect one: whenever he was felt to be present, everyone suffered the same turmoil.

I can see him now.

His ancestors were present in the way he shook his ample, indecisive, graying mane, as if to say, "Let them stay there, I'll make do, even though it's harder now"; we had no doubt that his pale blue eyes, which came from skies other than the vulgar ones we knew, were contemplating their next philosophical exploit, undreamed of by us.

Certainly he surprised the group among which, not without reason, he had landed. He was a walking genealogical chart:

Rodolphe-le-Bel, lord of Villiers and of Dormans, 1067, the Founder; Raoul, lord of Villiers-le-Bel, 1146; Jean de Villiers, married, in 1324, to Marie de l'Isle, and their son, Pierre I, who, taking the name of an extinct family of lords of l'Isle-Adam, was the first Villiers de l'Isle-Adam; Jean de Villiers, his grandson, who was the Grand Marshall of France, and who let himself be heroically massacred, in 1437, in Bruges, for the Duke of Burgundy; and finally, one of the first Knights of Malta and one of the last Knights of Rhodes, a valorous fighter vanquished by Suleiman through the restoration of Charles V, we find Philippe de Villiers de l'Isle-Adam, one of the Knights of Saint John of Jerusalem (the sound of it making it seem more general); to so many echoes sleeping in genealogical treatises, the last descendant added other names that to us, artists united around a limited goal—I'll say in a minute what it was—echoed, perhaps, with equal distances, but belonged, at least, to our world: Saint Bernard, Kant, Thomas de la Somme, and mainly, designated by him, the Titan of the Human Spirit, Hegel, by whom that extraordinary reader seemed to be recommended, among other visiting cards or letters of introduction, having forced their dusty volumes, in those retreats, to go together with an understanding of modern life and multiplied, on the threshold of his days, in monasteries—Solemmes, la Trappe, and several imaginary ones—to make their solitude complete (because, once he had entered into the struggle of production, he had nothing but what would be to his detriment to learn from life). He had read a considerable amount, both once and for all and in the course of years to come, notably anything having to do with Man's eventual grandeur, whether in history or in himself, or in the doubt about any realization—or, on the other side, what is promised by religion: for he was prudent.

We, motivated by a different tendency, were grouped together: to play for real, before handing on, in excellent condition, tuned definitively and consciously, an old instrument that has sometimes been out of tune, French verse, and some members of the group turned out, while working, to be superb instrumentalists.

The somewhat rusted sign of *Le Parnasse Contemporain* has blown down now—where was the wind blowing from? Nobody knows; but it's a fact: the old French metrical system (I don't dare call it French poetry) is undergoing, as I write, a marvelous crisis, unknown in any epoch or to any nation, in which, among the most zealous reworkings of all genres, it is forbidden to tamper with prosody. But the Parnassian experiment was not meaningless: it provides the reference point between the daring leaps of Romanticism and true freedom; and marks (before it dissolves altogether into something identical to the original melody of each voice) the official rhythm and the challenge of fixed metrics.

A lesser concern, it seemed, for an intellectual prince who appeared from his lands or the mists of reflection, to win by any means and to get for his family, having waited outside time, a quasi-mystic, recent sovereignty, our obsession weighing little in the frail hand that was cooking up truths whose revelation was supposed to illuminate; one would expect it hardly to signify, except for the particularity we professed, that verse was nothing other than a perfect word—vast and native—and our adoration was directed at the virtue of words: which could not be foreign to him who was trying to conquer everything with a word, his name, around which he saw gathering, materially, to be perfectly honest, a huge chandelier,† which can today be discerned only by imagination. The cult of the word that the writer in verse would, more than

†Mallarmé's word here is *lustre,* with its ties to *illustration* and *illustrious*— a chandelier which, before the days of electric lights or even gaslights, was used to illuminate theaters. The image of a single artificial light source made up of sparkling fragments of glass and perfectly balanced, often stands, in his writing, as a figure for poetry. [—*Trans.*]

anyone else, solemnize (and which, beyond any doctrine, is nothing but the glorification of the very intimate life of the race, a celebration of its native, natural speech) bound up the ties between random others and him: not that Villiers disdained the deployment of words in verse—he kept in his suitcase, along with the plaque from Malta, among the means of capturing the modern world, a volume of poetry, already visionary, about which he judged it proper not to breathe a word, among enamelers and engravers on semiprecious stones, preferring to account for himself, unseen, as an author, elsewhere, which, in a beginner, denotes character. And he would even, after not having appeared for a while, make his enthusiasm lapidary, and treat the newcomers among us to *lieder* or to other short songs.

Thus he came,† that sufficed, for him; for us, it was surprise itself—and for years, so long as a shadow of his life was mobile, and during these last, recent years, when, in the home of one of us, could be heard a call at the door that attracted attention through its pure, obstinate, fateful sound, like the sound of an hour missing from clock faces, wanting to stay, invariably, repeating that sound, with friends themselves elderly, who, despite fatigue, beckoned him in, exhausted, discouraged, but driven by the old obsession with arrival.

Villiers de l'Isle-Adam appeared.

He always brought a festival atmosphere with him, and knew it; and now, perhaps, it became even more beautiful, more humbly beautiful, or poignant, this sudden intrusion of ancientness, incessantly repeated, than it had been the first time it erupted in reality; despite the fact that he had divested

---

†Mallarmé no doubt has in his head Boileau's famous sentence, differently meant but quite appropriate to the young poets' preoccupations, about the codifier of classical French verse: "Enfin Malherbe vint. . . ." [—*Trans.*]

himself of mystery right away, and its vague ruins, crumbling then between faith and soil, had settled; we nevertheless suspected him of harboring other mysteries no less dark and sinister; that assailed the desperate nobleman always barely escaping from torment. One was taken aback by his munificence in paying for his refuge, as soon as he had shed his crude overcoat still imbued with the outdoors' bad weather: one admired his haste to reappear as himself, very correct and almost elegant despite his difficulties, and his certainty that in this shelter, not preoccupied with dates—days, or even years—he was awaited. One has to have heard him talk for as much as six hours in a row! He felt rushed, and, in order to avoid long explanations, found an elegant kind of shorthand, leaps and summersaults of thought that worried the cordial shelterers. As his hand-to-hand struggle with adversity diminished him, one sometimes caught sight of some youthful trait, and since he never wanted to appear inferior to what he once was, he playfully mocked and multiplied it with painful intimations, and to those to whom not one inflexion of his voice, not even its silence, remained foreign, he signified that "I was right, back then, to produce myself thus, in the exaggeration caused perhaps by the enlargement of your ordinary eyes, in the guise of a spiritual king, or he who cannot be; if only to give you the idea. I was the real actor playing myself! playing a truth that no one reaches in himself, except in moments of lightning and then one expiates them for their duration, as I have; but you see that it exists (that of which you felt through me a dim impression, since here I am conscious, and using the same language that, for others, serves to deceive, to converse, to greet) and henceforth can perceive, behind each of my terms, the desired and silenced gold on the far side of all human loquacity, now dissolving, now radiating, in a veracity of trumpets inextinguishable for their superior fanfare."

He fell silent. Thank you, Fugitive, for having spoken, you are understood.

Midnights indifferently thrown aside for his wake, he who always stood beside himself, and annulled time as he talked: he waved it aside as one throws away used paper when it has served its function; and in the lack of ringing to sound a moment not marked on any clock, he appeared—all the uncommon lucidity of that supremely rigorous mind, even in deliberations that were out of the ordinary, focused on something mysterious, while the doorbell rang, late, and filled up space, and the host said: "It's Villiers" when, in weakened form, was repeated for the thousandth time his original arrival. One waited anxiously to discuss with him an enigmatic last point that was, nevertheless, clear to *him*. A timely question, indeed, strange and of great interest, but which few men here below have occasion to ask, he himself might not have asked his own, so great was the conflict. Yes he would! From the point of view of History, he had been punctual, as well as to the assignation of fate, not untimely or reprehensible: for it is not contemporary with any epoch, not at all, that those who exalt all signification should appear, those who are ordered by fate to be the naked expression; they are projected several centuries ahead, and appear, stupefied, testifying to something that, normal at that time, enlarges magnificently through their regret, and, one of them, he found in the exile of their nostalgia, his spirit turned toward the past, his pure vision.

THE TOMB loves silence right away.

Acclamations, reputation, speech aloud ceases, and sobs over abandoned poems will not follow all the way to this place of discretion the one who hid himself so as not to hide the sense of his poetry, with their presence, their fame.

Thus, for our part, in fraternal mourning for many, we will forgo any literary intervention: it unanimously occupies the newspapers anyway, as if the blank pages of the interrupted work, blown out of proportion, could go and announce his disappearance to the mists and to the public.

Nevertheless, Death laid this slab expressly for any foot to step on to give an explanation or dispel a misunderstanding. Saying goodbye to the dearly departed beckons, and, if it happens that the sovereign human face reappears one last time, thinking that he was misunderstood, he'll say: "Take a better look at who I was."

Let us teach, Sirs, in passing, to whoever stayed away, because of incompetence or misunderstanding about the external sense of our friend, whose outfit, like all of his outfits, is perfectly correct for the occasion.

Yes, didn't *Les Fêtes Galantes* [The Gay Entertainments], *La Bonne Chanson* [The Good Song], *Sagesse* [Wisdom], *Amour* [Love], *Jadis et Naguère* [Long Ago and Recently], and *Par-*

allèlement [In Parallel] pour out, from generation to generation, when juvenile lips are open for a few hours, a river of melody, which quenches their thirst with a sweet, eternal, and French torrent—the conditions, a bit, for his visible nobility: we would deeply mourn and venerate him, we who watched powerless to intervene even with sympathy into his absolute stand toward his fate.

Paul Verlaine, his genius taking refuge in the future, remains a hero.

Alone, all of you who found a luxurious or advantageous retreat in his accommodation—all alone, let us consider, though, as an example of something that seldom comes back to us though the centuries, that our contemporary braved, in all its horror, the state of being both a singer and a dreamer. Solitude, cold, inelegance, and want are injuries their victim would have the right to respond to through others inflicted voluntarily on himself—here poetry almost sufficed—which ordinarily constitute the fate of a child walking straight into existence with his guileless daring, directed by his inner divinity: granted, he may die a beautiful death, but the offenses will have been necessary, and they extend to the end, painfully and impudently.

Scandal? On whose side? Everyone's. By one person amplified, accepted, sought: his bravura, in not hiding from his destiny, harassing it, rather by defiance, cutting through its hesitations, became thus his terrible honesty. We witnessed that, my friends, and testify to it: out of that or some pious revolt, the man showed himself to his Mother, whoever she was, a lady veiled, the crowd, inspiration, life; in any case she stripped the poet bare, and he remained loyal, sensitive, and imbued with honor.

We salute with this homage, Verlaine, and with dignity, your remains.

Arthur Rimbaud

Letter to Mr. Harrison Rhodes†

I TRY to imagine that, on one of the rare Tuesday evenings when you came to my house to do me the honor of hearing my friends converse, suddenly the name of Arthur Rimbaud was balanced on the smoke of several cigarettes; installing, to satisfy your curiosity, a certain vagueness.

Maybe you want to know what the person was like: but at least we have the published works—*Une Saison en Enfer* [A Season in Hell], *Illuminations,* and the volume *Poèmes* published long ago, which ever since have exerted, on recent poetic events, an influence so particular that, once one has mentioned him, one can but keep an enigmatic silence, and reflect, as if a lot of silence and reverie imposed themselves, or as if one were struck by some unfinished admiration.

You can doubt, my dear host, whether the principal innovators at the present time, even one, exceptionally and mysteriously, the magnificent elder, *who raised the baton,* Verlaine, have really undergone, in any depth or directly, Arthur Rimbaud. Nor does the freedom now allowed to verse or, better, springing out of it, claim derivation from him who, except for his stuttering very last verses or his absolute cessation, strictly

---

†Harrison Rhodes was the editor of *The Chap Book,* a North American journal in which Mallarmé's text first appeared (May 15, 1896), doubtless written directly to Rhodes, who had solicited his contribution. [—*Trans.*]

observed the official forms. Consider his most magical effects produced by the opposition between a world before the Parnassians—even before the Romantics—or very classical, and the sumptuous disorder of a passion about which one could say nothing except that it was spiritually exotic. He burst on the poetic scene like a meteor, ignited by no motive other than its presence, streaking alone in the sky, and extinguished alone. Everything would have remained the same since then without this considerable passage, just as no literary circumstance prepared for it: but the personal case remains, indelible.

My memories: rather, my thoughts, often addressed to this Someone, here: I'll make them into a chat for your immediate benefit.

I did not know him, but I saw him, once, at one of those literary banquets, arranged in haste, at the end of the War— the *Dinner of Naughty Goodfellows*—named by an antithesis, and made famous by the painting and by Verlaine's description, in *Les Poètes Maudits*, of Rimbaud. "He was tall, well built, almost athletic, with the perfectly oval face of an exiled angel, with disorderly brown hair and pale blue eyes that were disturbing." With a mysterious something about him either proudly or meanly flaunted, that recalled a daughter of the people, and his laundrywoman appearance, because of his enormous hands, reddened with chilblains resulting from rapid changes of temperature, which might have indicated even more terrible jobs, since they belonged to a boy. I later learned that they had signed some beautiful poems, unpublished; in any case his sardonic mouth, with its pouting and mocking expression, had never recited one.

> As I descended the impassive Water,
> I felt I was no longer guided by the haulers' lines:
> Loud-mouthed redskins had used them for practicing
>   slaughter,
> And had nailed them to totem-pole-like pines.

And

Mellower than the flesh of sour apples to little tots,
The green water seeped into my hull,
Washing away the blue wine and vomit spots,
Scattering my rudder, and making my grabbing-hooks
dull.

And

I dreamed of greenish nights filled with blinding snows,
Of kisses coming slowly up to the eyes of the sea,
Of saps circulating that no one knows,
And the yellow awakenings of phosphorus singing in
harmony.

And

Sometimes, a martyr tired of those poles and those
zones,
The sea whose sobbing rocked me gently in the breeze,
Turned toward me its shadow-flowers with their suckers
in yellowish tones
And I stayed there like a woman on her knees.

And

I've seen cosmic archipelagos! And islands whose skies
In their delirium are open to the hardy traveler;
Is it in these bottomless nights that sleeps, hides, and
sighs
Your flock of golden birds, O future Vigor?

And everything—everything!—should be rolled out, as a
pathbreaker stretches awake before producing a brilliant general awakening, for this poem, "The Drunken Boat," was already done at the time: all poems remembered and repeated—
like "Les Assis" [The Establishment], "Les Chercheuses de
Poux" [The Lice-Hunters], or "Premières Communiantes"
[First Communions], which seemed to come from a puberty

both perverse and superb—held their tongues before this gan-
gling newcomer. Our curiosity, among friends, was spared the
public rumors, which said that this was his fourth escape, at
seventeen, from his native Charleville to Paris on foot; at first
sumptuously (the boy having sold all his class prizes in rhetoric); torn between his home (a mother of peasant origins and
an absent father, a military man who had long since departed)
and his friends: the Cros brothers, Forain, and of course
the always irresistible Verlaine: a tug-of-war resulted, which
ended up with Rimbaud sleeping on coal barges, or falling
into an outpost of fighters for the Commune. The big oaf
cleverly passed himself off as an independent sniper for the
Commune fallen on hard times, and his companions hastened
to take up a collection for his benefit. These are small, miscellaneous details, quite suited, in fact, to one who was violently
ravaged by literature; the worst of all perturbations after his
having spent many long, slow, studious hours on benches or in
libraries, now master of a style that was perhaps premature
but sure of itself, intense and exciting, spurring him to tackle
unprecedented subjects—in search of "new sensations," he
insisted, "not known," and he flattered himself that they could
be found in the bazaar of illusions vulgarly known as big cities; in which the demon adolescent did discover, one evening,
a grandiose vision, prolonged by drunkenness alone.

Cheap anecdotes are not lacking around someone who had
lost the thread of his existence; they fell naturally into the
newspapers. What purpose would it serve to recycle these stories and string them together like pieces of colored glass? Fit
to be worn around the neck of some Negro king, as caricatur-
ists would later laughingly represent him, a poet lost in an unknown tribe. But your ambition would be to see, in this mass
of details, the *broad outlines* of a significant destiny; which,
even in its apparent deviations, ought to maintain the rhythm
of a singer along with a strange simplicity. Nevertheless, while
thanking you for making me remember all together what I

know of the personality that seduces you, dear friend, I can't resist sharing with you the following anecdote that Théodore de Banville once deliciously told me. The goodness of that Master was palpable. We went to him right away. One of our own needed the conditions, we explained in some sort of jargon, to make *great art*. Banville asserted that, with this in mind, talent became secondary; first one needed a room to call home: he could rent one in the eaves of his own house, rue de Buci; then a table, ink, and pens, and some paper; and white bedsheets for moments when he wasn't dreaming on his feet or in his chair. The wandering young man was thus installed: but great was the stupefaction of the methodical donor when, at the hour when the inner courtyard united the smells of all the dinners, he heard, on each floor, shouting, and saw, naked, framed by the roof up above, someone waving wildly and throwing over the roof tiles, perhaps so they would go down with the last rays of the sun, his ragged clothes: while the host worried about that, er, mythological garment so close to God, Arthur Rimbaud explained to the author of *Les Exilés*, who had to agree with the logic of the position, and only castigated his own lack of foresight, "It's just that I can't occupy a bedroom so clean, virginal, with my old clothes infested with lice." The host didn't consider himself correct until he had sent a change of clothes to the newcomer, and invited him to the evening meal. For "clothing and lodging don't suffice when one wishes to produce remarkable poems, it is also essential to eat."

When the prestige of Paris was about used up, and Verlaine was beginning to have marital problems and vaguely feared pursuit as a low-grade functionary of the Commune, it didn't take much to convince Rimbaud to visit London. There the couple led a life of orgiastic poverty, breathing the free smoke of coal fires, drunk on reciprocity. A letter from France to one of the fugitives said that all would be forgiven so long as he abandoned his companion. The young wife, between mother and mother-in-law, expected a scene of reconciliation when she arrived at the appointed place. Here I refer to the story as delicately traced by M. Berrichon,† the most poignant scene in the world, given that its two heroes, one wounded and the other delirious, were two poets roaring in agony. Entreated by all three women together, Verlaine had renounced his friend, but saw him, by accident, at the hotel room door, flew into his arms to follow him, ignored the chilly requests by the latter to do nothing of the sort, "swearing that their affair was forever dissolved"—"even without a penny," although they had come to Belgium precisely in order to make money for the return trip, "he was leaving." That attitude repulsed Verlaine, who pulled the trigger of a pistol he happened to have on him, before he dissolved in tears at Rimbaud's feet. It was said that things couldn't remain, as it were, all in the family. Bandaged, Rimbaud, still determined to leave, came back from the clinic, and was shot again, in the street. The shooting, decidedly public now, earned the faithful friend two years in the prison of Mons. One can say that nothing enables us to decipher him—alone, after this tragic incident—in his ultimate crisis, which interests us because he ceased everything literary: friends and works. Facts? He is said to have gone back to England—goal unknown—before 1875; then went to Germany, where he held teaching posts, and used his gift for languages, which he collected, having sworn off any heightening of his own; went to Italy, first by train to Saint-Gothard, then on foot; he crossed the Alps, stayed a few months, then pushed on to the Cyclades, and, finally tired of isolation, allowed himself to be officially repatriated.

Not before he had been brushed by a breeze from the East.

Somewhere in there is the mysterious yet natural date on which it is generally agreed that he rejected dreams—through his fault or theirs—and amputated from himself, wide awake, all trace of poetry, finding, perhaps, far away, very far away, a new state of being. The oblivion that covers him includes the

†"Verlaine héroïque," *La Revue Blanche*, February 15, 1896. [—*Author*]

vast spaces of deserts and seas. His tropical escapades had perhaps less to do with the marvelous or sumptuous settings, since it's as a soldier hawking his wares that he shows up in 1876, among the Dutch military headed for Sumatra, where, after a few weeks, he deserts again and boards, at the cost of his travel bonus, an English ship, before becoming, audaciously, a slave trader in his turn, amassing a fortune he loses in Denmark or Sweden, from which he is again repatriated: he becomes Director of Marble Quarries in Cypress in 1879, after a stint in Egypt, in Alexandria, and elsewhere—and he spends the rest of his days "trafficking." His total renunciation of Europe, with its intolerable climate and practices, push him on to Harare, near Abyssinia (lately, the theater of military events), where, like the desert sands, a total silence covers all acts committed by the exile. He traffics, on both coasts of Aden—did anyone ever see him in this godforsaken spot? Surrounded magically by precious objects—ivory, gold dust, and incense—like someone whose hands once caressed pages, or perhaps oblivious to the special qualities of his wares, too imbued with Thousand-and-One-Nights–style orientalism or with local color: but as for landscapes drunk in with thirst for vastness and independence! And if, once the instinct of verse is renounced, everything diminishes as you pass through it— even living, unless life is virile and savage, civilization failing to outlast, in the individual, the call of a supreme sign.

An unexpected report, in 1891, circulated in the journals: that he who was for us and always will remain a poet had landed in Marseilles with a fortune, and, world traveler, arthritic, he let himself be operated on, and had just died. His coffin took the road to Charleville, where in the old days he had found refuge from all kinds of agitation, thanks to the piety of a sister.

I know, at least, the gratuitousness of putting oneself in the place of someone else's mind: this one, in any case, must have spoken a lot when he was alone. To organize the fragments of someone else's life into intelligible and probable parts, in order to translate the whole into a story: what impertinence! All I can do is push to the limit this kind of misdeed. But, at least, I inform myself. Once, during his travels, around 1875, his high school friend and confidant, M. Delahaye, who wrote a memoir from which this draws heavily, discreetly asked him about his former goals in some such terms as this—"Well then! and literature?" to which the other turned a deaf ear, finally replying with simplicity that "no, he no longer did that," stressing neither regret nor pride. "Verlaine"? about whom the chat became pressing: nothing, except that he avoided, as unpleasant, the memory of procedures that were, in his opinion, excessive.

The usual fantasies of abandoned or fabulous treasures, habitual on the part of the crowd, caught fire at the idea that there were among his effects unpublished poems, perhaps written down there. Their breadth of inspiration and their virginal accent! They were spoken and dreamed about as if they really existed; quite rightly, since one should never neglect, mentally, any of the possibilities that swarm around a figure; they belong to the original, even seemingly unlikely ones, putting in place a legendary foundation before it completely dissipates. I feel, however, that prolonging the hope of a mature work is harmful, here, toward the exact interpretation of a unique adventure in the history of art. That of a child too precociously and peremptorily touched by the wings of literature, who, barely having had time to live, used up its stormy and magisterial destiny, without recourse to any possible future.

Another speculation, this one much more plausible and intriguing, concerned a manuscript disavowed by the incisive eye of our vagabond, who, on his return, learned of the expanding fame of his youthful splendors, and their influence among the opulent fruits of a next generation, much more attuned to his glory than those, back there, around the oasis: Would he have denied those works or collected them? Fate, in a warning to the man about the role he was playing, no doubt so that he would stop vacillating, cut off the foot that descended on foreign home turf: or else, between the patient and the voices that called him, especially that of the great Verlaine, he took refuge in the muteness offered by a wall or a hospital curtain. It was forbidden that, to breathe in the surprise of his fame, and immediately set it aside, or, at the opposite extreme, deny it and cast an envious eye over this past that had grown during his absence, he would return, himself, to the new significance, and in his own language, utter the beautiful syllables ARTHUR RIMBAUD. The proof, alternatively, had the hardness and meaning that he had, if the name were removed. However, one must, squeezing the hypothesis until it yields up the eventual beauty of this glorious career, after all, without compromise—with anarchy or intellectually—presume that the person concerned would have greeted the news of his fame with icy disdain, as concerning someone who had indeed been him, certainly, but was in no way him now. Unless the impersonal phantom pushed his lack of literary interest as far as to demand, crossing Paris, to add to the wealth he had brought back with him, his royalties.

APRIL, 1896

To the sharply drawn portrait in pencil, joining here a portrait in words seems a superfluity: because the author, with his monklike or Saracenlike profile under a pile of medical compresses, as the collection explains, is perfectly comfortable, faced with white pages, with their silence.

There was so much noise before. . . .

It was the newspapers that almost disfigured him.

The injury reduced to an accident from a sinister flower pot—no one can contain your majestic stalk, imagination, was about the sense of the crude news item—our friend would

---

†Laurent Tailhade was the author of *Le Jardin des Rêves* (1880; preface by Théodore de Banville) and several successful satirical collections, like *Au Pays du Mufle* (1894). He fought many duels for his ideas, in particular one with Maurice Barrès over Colonel Dreyfus (from which Tailhade, avid defender of Dreyfus, came out rather badly), and was seriously wounded in 1894 by an anarchist's bomb (origin never determined) while eating in the Restaurant Foyot. Thenceforth he owed his celebrity to his disfigurement, not to his literary works. In this text, Mallarmé probably alludes to Baudelaire's prose poem "Le Mauvais Vitrier," since it is a matter, here and elsewhere, of *verre brisé* (broken glass [*verre*] or broken verse [*vers*]), and since the engine of destruction is a *pot de fleurs* (*du Mal?*).

The essay was written as an introduction to *L'Iconographie de Laurent Tailhade*, by F.-A. Casals (Paris, 1894). "Frontispice" is Mallarmé's own spelling. [—*Trans.*]

come out marked, obligatorily for those myopic people who couldn't see him any other way. He was sewn back up after the incident, but we could find and bless the inner spirit that made him fight, judging from his beautiful knit brow; the Public, which needs a reality, could thenceforth point to one with all the certainty required.

The public has, in addition to his poetry, invented vulgarizers to cast sudden light—to attract attention—on the writer; the signatory of marvels like *Vitraux* [Stained-Glass Windows] and that *Au Pays du Mufle* [In the Land of the Lout].

His head emerged from the statuary gauzes as if it were a study in meditation: very confident, serious, mature, and determined to think virile thoughts.

"So long as nothing happened to the stained-glass window up there!" came the translation of the cloud over his awakening, the moment when life asks questions and bathes in its newness.

Nothing happened, despite the intrusion of political accident on glasswork, I know the one you meant, Tailhade, and it was not hurt: protected by a fragility where pieces of glass are already encased in lead throughout its colored surface, not a single shining piece, colored by passion, gemstones, overcoats, smiles, or lilies, is lacking in your splendid Rose Window, which already itself simulates a stilled explosion, by which is radiated, but to which remains immune, the mind of a Poet.

WHO HAS not regretted the failure to reach sublime heights on the part of the richest and most pleasant of prose works, as if, metamorphosed by its readers, it has in the past been betrayed? A veil covered, the better to bring them out, the political and moral abstractions of the eighteenth century when the ORIENTAL TALE flourished, dressed up in Indian muslins; whereas today, with the help of science, such a genre stirs up the authentic ashes of the histories of cities and men, immortalized in *Le Roman de la Momie* [The Novel of the Mummy] and *Salammbô*. It's true that *La Tentation de Saint Antoine* [The Temptation of Saint Anthony] mixes eras and races into a prodigious festival, the last glow of an Orient gone by, but otherwise if you look for it anywhere, it should be among the old-fashioned books where fantasy and anachronism reign whenever a synthesis is needed, above which floats a cloud of perfumes that has never burst. The cause? many essays and, I have to admit, chance. Perhaps some serene daydream made for our fantasy alone is better attained in poetry: there, rhythm transports it beyond gardens, kingdoms, rooms; where the wings of peris or djinns melting into the climate leave only, as they disappear, the scattered but glittering purity of stars at noon.

These books, their irony at first very little concealed, in most cases keeping to the old tone and, in feeling and authenticity, resembling the modern evocative novel, have often given me pleasure: either as a transition or in themselves. The lack of effort to achieve the type we just talked about does not obsess me as I read these hundred or so pages: most of the oriental novels I read, trying to be both witty and knowledgeable, reveal, on the part of whoever wrote them, a need to satisfy the ability to imagine objects both rare and grandiose.

Well, then, this Tale, quite different from the *Thousand and One Nights*—when was it popular, and what is its origin?

Under the tutelage of lords Chatham and Littleton, who were eager to make him into a notable political man, studied, cherished by a mother who forbade him her presence until his sumptuous education was finished, the son of the late Lord Mayor Beckford (whose proud address to George III adorns the wall of the local Guildhall). But in the silent eaves of the provincial family seat, a genie, from fairy tales and from the East, fixed his choice on the youth. Exiled between the secret knowledge in the paternal library and the door of a certain *Boudoir Turc*, the youth was haunted by the genie all through Switzerland, Germany, and Italy. Knowing the classics, depositories of the civil annals of the world of the past, charmed the adolescent as a duty, even the poets, Homer, Virgil; but the Persian and Arab writers, as a reward; and he mastered oriental languages as well as he knew Greek and Latin. Opinions, entreaties, insinuations, and even blame, along with the friendly confiscation of overly thumbed-through books: reason was no match for the genie's enchantment. Since no other job was on the immediate horizon, William Beckford spent the first hours of his majority—free and able to dream whatever he wanted—throwing down on paper, perhaps at the beginning of 1781, VATHEK. *I wrote it in a single sitting and in French*, our beginner recounted later on, and *it cost me three days and two nights of hard work—I stayed dressed in the same clothes all that time—such intense engagement made me quite ill.* At which point this sensitive creature fell under a curse. Did the subject begin in perfect balance before this? Not at all, be-

lieves the author; omitting here all mention of the ancient adaptation of his latent dream, all grandeur and beauty, to his
daily life. One is also hard pressed to identify the origins of
the main figures of the story, or its setting; it's simple, the
roof of his childhood home sheltered thousands of Arabian
visions; all the people, taken from the real world, were endowed with the seductiveness or the horror required by the
tale. *It would be difficult for you to find anything like it in a
known oriental description* (goes the quotation): *it was the work
of my own imagination. The old mansion at Fonthill had one of
the largest rooms in the kingdom, vast, tall, and full of sonorous
echoes; and its numerous doors led to different parts of the building, along dark, sinuous, long corridors. It's from there that I drew
my imaginary room, Eblis, modeled on my own residence. Imagination colored it in, made it even bigger, and gave it a thoroughly
oriental character. All the women mentioned in Vathek were drawn
after those who lived in Fonthill, with their good and bad qualities, often exaggerated to fit my design.* There follows a series of
remarks confided by a mature eye when it once again plunges
into the early years, which seem almost transparent; but those
are too brief, and they end with the following significant
words: *I made everything up out of my own ideas. I had to elevate, magnify, and orientalize each thing. I soared in my youthful
fantasy on the wings of that ancient Arabian bird, the Roc, accompanied by genies and their charm, no longer living among
men.*

According to what very mysterious influence—the same
one that completely transmuted his time there—was the book
written in French? A parenthetic point that nothing in the
notes he left behind clarifies. Unlike the need to draw on
works by *Herbelot, Chardin,* and *Salé,* recognized in the final
annotation (also on one that isn't cited: *Abdallah, or The Ad-
ventures of the Son of Hanif, Sent by the Sultan of India to
Discover the Island of Borico,* etc., 1723), sources that were in
those days just about all the references that orientalists had at

their disposal, a confident and correct use of our language, first learned in London, then practiced in Parisian society and during three years in Geneva, explains the ease and skill displayed by the writer. In general, there is nothing surprising about choosing a language other than one's mother tongue to free oneself, in writing, from the obsession that hovers over a whole youth: don't try to read into it anything but the kind of solemnity required to sit down to a unique task, different from what was forecast for the rest of his life.

To be obliged to turn one's eyes away from the manuscript, as a second movement, in order to settle a quite considerable fortune (the interest on about two million five hundred thousand francs), also the impact of turning twenty-one: done with the utmost strictness. Since the cycle of voyages was finished—one with a young and very beautiful wife, and others alone, to air out death and memories—it came time to go back, but without the obsessive thoughts of the old days. This vast imagination, as if dispossessed of its spiritual goal, now fulfilled, but nevertheless unchanged, developed an obsession with tearing down the old Fonthill House, reflected in the mirror of a stagnant pool, in order to build Fonthill Abbey, not far away, surrounded by gardens deemed among the most beautiful in England. A resurrection where no expense was spared, similar to those done in all times and places; and dream alone, invited to repopulate the new interior, used the materials of universal art, in this case represented by its marvels: the sky above huge banks of flowers. No false concern, no effort toward social honors: only to finish off that magnificent construction by draping it with silk and filling it with vases, each piece of furniture arranged with a taste hitherto unknown, and *voilà!* Then came the desire, common to all great minds, even the most reclusive ones, to throw a party; at one of them, attended by a Nelson following closely on the heels of the second Lady Hamilton, Nelson had a chance to applaud his muse in a tragic and sculptural performance. Then quiet fell on the group, good for meditating on the pure products of mind; no book belonging to the great generation avoided going through the hands of a bibliophile, eager to fill its noble margins with his judgment. So discreet was this participation in the moment that it wasn't even shown up by the display of books mocking the fashionable cant of the day: *The Elegant Enthusiast* and *Améʒia, rhapsodical, descriptive and sentimental romances, intermingled with pieces of poetry;*† I separate them from this sarcastic and personal vein which, to a boy of seventeen, gives a *History of Extraordinary Painters,* a mystification for country visitors to the paternal gallery; or should, sometime in the distant future, produce a *Liber Veritatis* (that title almost changed to *Book of Folly*), a heraldic pamphlet on the pretensions to ancient nobility on the part of many members of parliament, still in manuscript form. All were private works, but with brilliant verve, and meant to be read aloud to a circle of familiars if the conversation should ever flag; which was rare in the salon of a speaker to whose vivacity we owe the following random remarks: *Important truths have, without exception, resulted from the work of solitary individuals—none has come from the masses, and none is likely to— all of them result from knowledge, joined with reflection on the part of highly gifted minds: mighty rivers flow from solitary sources.* The many fanciful reconstructions of his domicile signified, for the dreamer who had outlived the *Arabian Tale,* imaginary games as good as letting his imagination loose on ruins, or edifices of clouds: in the absence of any immediate object, his great literary talent persisted. Even selling the abbey itself, whose style, after traveling widely, he had simply pointed out to a famous and mediocre architect, was (on a day the patrimony happened to drop in value), the decision of a mere instant: and then, amid his last construction projects, closer to the city of Bath, at Lansdown, still dominated by a remaining tower like a lighthouse, to devote himself, until his

---

†In English in the original. [*—Trans.*]

death, to converting his old familial memories into sparkling pages! *Italy and Sketches from Spain and Portugal, with an Excursion to the Monasteries of Bathala and Alcobaça:*† keep such titles nestled in the repertoire of beautiful works in any language. The young cosmopolitan heir of the 1700s had, thanks to his princely lifestyle and the use of quasi-diplomatic letters of introduction, penetrated deep into the secrets of old Europe; but our dilettante was also able to see, before anyone else, what was picturesque. He was able to achieve, in a short time, the same degree of perfection in the genre of the Voyage as that of some of our poets, equaling their style: the collector collected brilliant and truthful words by handling them with the same prodigality and tact as precious objects found in archeological digs. Whether he brought back from his travels notebooks that he exhausted late in life, or whether he put down on paper next to his will a past that suddenly surged up in his memory, his biography does not say what the origin of these writings might be; in any case, his astonishment, one way or another, grew. Whatever might be the truth of these works from the start or the end of a career, it can be said that they do honor, even in the absence of his major work, which was written in French, to one of the greatest of English writers. At his death, on May 2, 1844, lifting his eyes between the treasures of human thought and the treasures of human work and raising them up, as he had often done, to the vast windows framing the same landscape through which he had seen all the seasons for half of one century and almost half of another, this extraordinary gentleman closed them; apart from his talent, he was a figure like Brummel: but perhaps the dreamer Beckford wins out over the dandy Beckford who fascinated his time, because of his solitary splendor. It is to you, reader, that he shows you here, minus a thousand absurd fables, through his works of imagination, his biography, the ex-

†In English in the original. [—*Trans.*]

istence of him who, to his dying day, was known as the *Author of Vathek*.

Everything here is exceptional, the man and his estate, and the work with respect to the man: but first and foremost, his use of French. . . . Did he send a copy with a dedication to each of the grand figures of the French literary scene? One doubts this, given the total silence about it in the annals of the time. The adolescent who had gone to Ferney with his tutor and had seen Voltaire, ten years earlier, found that the great French author had died, at the very moment when Madame de Staël (whom the mature man later visited at Coppet) was just beginning to emerge from the paternal salons. After digging through many memoirs, one finds that these are the only two French literary figures Beckford encountered; the French society that took him in during his travels was restricted to the high aristocracy. Proudly timid, perhaps he was waiting for others to mention his early work first; but nothing shows that he ever used it in the presence of his noble hosts as a distinctive object; nor as an adjunct to his letters of introduction, nor as a visiting card or gift. Not that the Master of Fonthill was unknown five or six years later, in the midst of political change: accompanying the first revolutionary scenes, our prints show an Englishman on horseback watching everything with curiosity. The fall of the Bastille and the death of the King occurred just before this popular foreigner's return to London and then to his own domains; but it was without any specific reference to the literary glory which his own indifference had denied to his country and conveyed elsewhere that the Commune felt obliged to write in his passport: *Paris regrets seeing him go.*

While we were thus neglecting one of the most interesting works in French, England, at least, with an obstinacy that was not fortuitous, had hardly enough words to praise a translation that chance had made of it. Produced some time before the publication of the original, this work (we know) resulted from an indiscretion; but also from a forgery, since someone presented it as taken not from the borrowed French text, but from the "original" Arabic. Who had done it? The author long remained ignorant of this; only in the fourth edition of his book, at the height of its success, did he finally add a comment, good-humoredly saying that, after all, the fake translation was passable. The impression made by the book on the contemporary generation seems to have been great and to have contributed not a little to the imaginative reawakening of that time. Thousands of paragraphs and essays survive, scattered in English reviews, as an echo of the approval that accompanied the book's career throughout the century. In my quick researches, I haven't come across long quotations; people choose a volume and ask, *What's this?* without really looking closely at it. In the work of Byron, soon to reveal his own Orient, the answer haunts his memoirs and is therefore worth transcribing: *For the exactitude and correctness of the costumes, for the descriptive beauty and the power of imagination, this tale, more oriental and sublime than any other, leaves well behind it any European imitations, and shows such signs of originality, that those who have been to the Orient will have difficulty believing it's a simple translation.* The great genius shared the common belief in some anonymous imitation of Arab parables, a neutral ground but an error from which the figure of Beckford detaches itself more and more. It is interesting that Byron's own hero, Childe Harold, in his very first canto, shouts out the following apostrophe: *It was there* (in Montferrat) *that you, too, Vathek, Albion's most fortunate son, once made yourself a paradise,* etc. . . . *There you lived and drew up plans for happiness under the eternally beautiful brow of that mountain; but now, as if something cursed by man, your fairy domain is as solitary as you are.* . . . *The overgrown plants barely allow a passage to the deserted rooms, and the door stands open: these are new lessons for the breast that thinks, how vain are the pleasures earth offers; and they mingle with the shipwreck on the inclement tides*

of Time.† So strong and lasting was the astonishment inspired in the poet by the prose writer, that the former, on his
travels, continually saw the shadow of the latter; in the very
spots where nothing like a legendary palace built in the course
of a several-months' ramble in Portugal could ever arise.
But enough; nowadays, I don't know a single bookcase that
doesn't have a deluxe—yet thoroughly familiar—edition of
Vathek, nor any reader who doesn't consider this tale one of
the proudest feats of the dawning modern imagination.

This is a special case, unique in my memory: a work that
England claims as its own and that is unknown in France; here
original, there translation; while its author (to make things
even more complicated), from the fact of his birth and training, does not belong in our literature, yet, after the fact, claims
a preponderant place—almost that of forgotten initiator! Our
duty and our intellectual relations are, in this regard, complicated.

Great Britain, waiting, points to the book's faulty and ste-
reotypical French; the very fact of translation makes the original glow with splendor, but doesn't prove the excellence of

---

†There thou too, Vathek, England's wealthiest son,
  Once formed thy Paradise. . . .
  . . . . .
  Here didst thou dwell, here schemes of pleasure plan,
  Beneath yon mountain's ever-beauteous brow.
  But now, as if a thing unblest by man,
  Thy fairy dwelling is as lone as thou!
  Here giant weeds a passage scarce allow
  To halls deserted, portals gaping wide:
  Fresh lessons to the thinking bosom, how
  Vain are the pleasaunces on earth supplied;
  Swept into wrecks anon by Time's ungentle tide!
            Canto I, stanzas 22 and 23 [—*Author*]

the French. The two versions, each in its own idiom and with great difficulty keeping up with the impetus of the other, seem to indicate that the thoughts, subsequently, finding their natural mold, are themselves perfect. There should be a moratorium on external discussion; one should speak only about the particular, with documents in hand. Given the accidents at stake here, no one, casual or interested, demands that its style have that almost eternal flow that comes from the refinement of many generations, century after century forging language anew. But one does expect correct phraseology and even at moments something that equals paintings in luxury, or even some greatness of feeling; the balance between imagination and *act* usually tipped toward the latter among classic prose writers; if it inclines toward the former here, so much the better. A few Anglicisms here and there barely create some unease; others evoke some charm. The only error repeated more than it should be according to our model stylists is a confusion between the *possessive* and *relative* pronouns in *son, sa, ses* and *il, elle, la, lui,* etc. I beg your pardon! And (in closing) such a mistake depends on certain grammatical conditions incompletely forgotten from English, as well as an overly strict obedience that someone from outside might have to our own rules. Nothing absolves the incompetence of the handling of certain connections of the sentence or its dissemination into shadow and vagueness; but what admirable conquests of those evil twins, in the tight control or the glittering of certain words! There is even, I admit, a certain—but pleasant—preciosity in the certainty of choosing, among all possible words, the perfect and only one. Many a passage—veiled or intense, calm and grand—owes its multiplicity to the ever-vigilant author: what can be detached that wouldn't sound like a vain fragment? The subtlety of the whole floats between the lines, and to understand an extract, with all its requisite explanations, you might as well read the whole thing. An imitation of Voltaire (the Voltaire of the first water; it must be painful to be so perfect), a prose, that often anticipates Chateaubriand, can also do honor to that other name, Beckford. Everything flows from the same spring, with a lively limpidity and the shimmering of large periods; and its brightness tends to blend into the purity of its whole course, which carries along many riches of diction that aren't noticed at first: a frequent occurrence in the case of a foreigner worried that some overly daring expression will give him away if the eye stops on it too long.

SINCE everything has already been said for many days now, and even Westminster keeps silent, it may be an act of piety to pin down, even abroad, before they are dispersed, the swirling and flying welter of regrets, judgments, and emotions that surround the great void left by the death of Tennyson. Incompetence, here, is an advantage; it was in a way displayed by the weekly or daily press in its praiseworthy modesty: the press wanted to seem thoroughly in the know—too rapidly, as it admitted when expressing its surprise at the moment. I'm grateful to a paper that announced the fatal event right away, and sent me, as it might have to any other poet, this news along with other news about British literature, speaking of the superb deceased knowingly and indirectly. A piece in the same issue shows his grandeur nevertheless; but what good does it do to recall immediate particular judgments when, for example—doubtless with reference to the colors chosen by the decorator for *Idylls of the King*—the writer invoked chromolithography, whereas he should have thought of delicate frescoes; when Cabanel was cited, perhaps à propos of the gallery of fascinating portraits of women in the early poems, whereas that lone name stuck out and the reference should have been more general. Note that a kind of prudence is required in these transpositions from one art to another—one must know what one is talking about—but we feel obligated to try to compare the British poet to one of ours. Who? All comparison is defective from the start; and also impossible. As soon as one draws closer to another mind, the differences increasingly strike one; and what one thought was familiar is volatilized and flees before one's eyes, all the way down to the most obvious traits. Nevertheless, in order to cater to a public that perceives something only when one offers easy equations, or when one side is known in advance, I shall (and may time dissolve quickly these fugitive words!) throw out some names on the subject of Tennyson: that of Leconte de Lisle tempered with Alfred de Vigny, with a little Coppée thrown in; but it's so false!

One nation has the right to remain unfamiliar with the poets of another; it so badly neglects its own! That misunderstood title of poet laureate, in addition, sounds like a license to engage in boosterism, seems almost to designate some sort of versifying comrade, inferior to the gossip columnist.

The judgment of literary friends is the only thing to consult here; the fact is, though, that poetry is very different in France; these would-be recluses find in their language meanings or sonorities particular to French, whose instinct they glorify while they secretly abhor admitting anyone else to their company; they are, and remain, farther than anyone, patriots. They suffer, perhaps, from a necessary infirmity that reinforces, for them, the illusion that an object proffered— i.e., named—surges up, at home in the language; but actually—don't you agree?—this *is* a very strange thing. A translation, to render false all I've just said, appeared, in verse, as an exquisite funereal offering, last week: parts of *Vivien*, rendered by the acute Jean Lorrain. Yet this remains a special case; it seems to me that in his own poetry, where Melusine and the fairy princesses are constantly coming back, the works are studded with Tennysonian influences, though spontaneously.

The reading public, to whom we should limit our survey, will recall a monumental page in Taine's *History of English Literature* on Alfred Tennyson in his maturity; but it does not allude to where anything originated. In every school we teach *Enoch Arden,* with grammatical notes at the bottom of the page. The fashion, twenty years ago, for lavish books in the manner of the illustrator Gustave Doré, meant that every living room had its leather-bound copy of *Idylls of the King.*

My own preference is for *Maud*—romantic and modern, full of dreams and passions—but I know it's not typical of the master in the way that the much-recited *Locksley Hall* is, or enchantments like *The Lotus Eaters* or *Oenone*—in fact, all the pages that serve as tombs, the same thing buried there or haunting every step away. *In Memoriam* is an entire cemetery for a single corpse. Really, from his early *Poems, Chiefly Lyrical* all the way to *Demeter,* there are so many diverse pages of perfection, each one a model of its type, that separate from the rest and enter our reveries!

All that I have gathered and summarized here would occasion only idle, parochial chitchat if it were not possible, relative to an author, by amassing vague feelings, to induce those that Time would establish. Distance, in any case, can play for centuries. To get away by coach or by sea for even a couple of hours is the beginning of immortality. There, especially, in an indifferent country, is the case that is analyzed in the following passage:† "Indeed, literature properly speaking existing no more than pure space does, what one remembers from a great poet is the so-called sublime impression that his work leaves on one, not the work itself. This impression, beneath the veil of human languages, comes through even in the most vulgar translations. When this phenomenon is formally attested about a work, the result for that work is eternal GLORY!"

The name of the poet mysteriously blends with the totality

---

†Villiers de l'Isle-Adam, "The Glory Machine," in *Contes Cruels.* [*—Author*]

of his work, which, by uniting words among themselves, ends up with only one, the summary of an entire soul, deeply significant, conveying it in passing. He steals whole pages spread open in the book, henceforth vain; for, finally, genius has to take place, known by each person, in spite of everything, and even if no one is really reading him. This chaste arrangement of syllables, *Tennyson,* said this time with solemnity, *Lord Tennyson*—I know that he already summons and awakens, even through the misunderstandings of translation, or through gaps and stupidity, and will do so more in the future—he will appear as a lofty but tender figure, strong-willed but introverted and abstemious about anything owed; his nobility and his seignorial manner bringing something to the spirit; unsuspecting, taciturn; and I would almost say that death establishes for the crowd something serene, isolated, and complete; the proud withdrawal of physiognomy.

None of these terms . . . you can't use one without its seeming to be the illustrated repetition of recent coronations or obsequies; but, better than any flourish, by designating with a sweeping line or two the vanishing of that lyric wing, one hopes to raise a sketch to the proper level.

If I may speak personally, after all these observations or reports that derive their dignity from their subject, let me offer an opinion. Everything in literary culture raised to its highest degree, that of an art form—originality, taste, certainty— along with a delicious primordial poetic gift, can, beautifully amalgamated, produce in one of its elect, and Tennyson had all of it, without giving in to anxious variety: that is not common; what more could one want? Unless it could be unknown gods with peremptory brevity, dropping down into the ages? But to have given the language some intonations never heard before (without Tennyson, a certain music proper to him would not exist in English) to give the national instrument new chords that are recognized as inherent in it, constitutes a poet, as one extends his task and his prestige. The man, who summed up so much exceptionality, has just died, and I think a considerable sense of mourning is floating around the suave columns of the temple of Poetry, whatever one might say about the building. Let his shade be received there with the very terms used in the affectionate hyperbole, well known in his youth but heralding someone who was still in the future, consecrated to him by the enthusiasm of Poe: "the noblest poetic soul that ever lived."

THE SUNNY immortality of a poet solves all questions, dissipates all vagueness, with a bright ray. This is what happened around noon the other Sunday—a rather autumnal day—when some of us, who observe the Master's cult of poetic rhythm and honor his memory, were dedicating a monument, in the middle of a garden, to Théodore de Banville. The real tomb contains the remains, and presents a hard stone to the grieving widow or other intimates; I imagine—and here I anticipate the decision made with regard to a fraternal resurrection via marble or bronze, attributed to Baudelaire—that what befits that daily apotheosis is a disinterested cemetery, profane and glorious, like the Luxembourg Gardens: open to the sky particular to the tall urban trees, the decorative vases, the flowers; loved by the passers-by. It may be a detail, but the man being memorialized was, barely eighteen months ago, our host, almost every day. His traditional yet new spirit introduced, beforehand, a modern mythological evocation:

> One June evening which the waves caressed,
> When pale irises grew along the stream;
> And in the Luxembourg, as heavenly as a dream,
> The Attic statues, their love for Paris scarce expressed,
> Could see the air, the sky, and the earth, with flowers
>   blessed.

("Malédiction de Cypris")

Always, when this close to the Pantheon, one begins to regret that Hugo (though scholars and politicians get used to the empty dome under which Death proceeds with its parliamentary and institutional sessions) inhabits a chilly crypt; when the occasion seems to push toward a season of rebirth among the woodpigeons, or just space.

Affection aside, if I may speak of poems themselves while omitting the memory of that fine, dignified head which this monument evokes in the minds passers-by and friends, I dedicated many years of my youth to worshiping Théodore de Banville. The exceptional clarity I admire in him—a unique and almost absolute trait—will be enhanced by the brevity of my remarks. Not that it's irrelevant to point out his widely diverse gifts, but they blend into one another as if they were elements in a miracle. Just in order to prove that I see like everyone else, only less well, I'll exhume, without pity for myself, one of the very first pages I wrote as a schoolboy, which I dedicated to him in solitude, as to a god; and even though today I would put it in different words, I'd express the same thing, or would imitate his manner or his turn of phrase or his voice, and say: "If the spirit is not gratified with a mystical ascension: tired of contemplating tedium in the cruel metal of a mirror, and yet during those hours when the rhythmic soul aspires to the antique delirium of song, my object is Théodore de Banville, who is not a person but the very voice of the lyre. With him, I feel Poetry intoxicating me, I see that all eras have uttered this call and that I'm drinking at the fountain of lyricism. With the book closed, large tears of tenderness in my eyes, and a new kind of pride. What fills me with enthusiasm, and musical goodness, worthy of kings, is singing, and I love! I love being born, I love the luminous sobs of long-haired women, and I'd like to embrace it all in one poetic kiss. These days, no one better represents the Poet, the invincible, classical Poet, who submits to the goddess, and lives amid the forgotten charm of heroes and roses. His indefatigable speech is like ambrosia, which dries up only at the sound of the drunken shouts that always accompany fame.

The whistling winds that speak of fright and darkness and the picturesque abysses in the region are things he wishes neither to hear nor to see. He walks in a cloud of Edenic enchantment, forever designating the nobility of rays of light and the stunning whiteness of an unopened lily—the happy earth! That must have been the feeling of the very first person who received voice from the gods and uttered, dazzled, the bright ode, even before our ancestor Orpheus. Instate, O dream, the ceremony of a triumph, to be evoked in those hours of splendor and magic, and call it the Festival of the Poet: the Chosen One is that man predestined by his name, as harmonious as a poem and as charming as a lovely setting. In the heavens, he sits on an ivory throne, dressed in the royal robes that he is entitled to wear, his forehead shaded by the giant leaves of the Turbian laurel. I can hear stanzas somewhere: the Muse, wearing only the smile that surges up from her young torso, fills him with inspiration—as a grateful nude lies dying at his feet. The great lyre grows ecstatic in his hands."†

A poor construction, out of date; I beg your forgiveness.

Nevertheless, I take a certain pride, a reflection of the gratitude conceded by the prince of letters to his true admirer, in the fact that, after a quarter-century, the feeling is still recognizable; I'm going to say what remains the same and what has been refined until it is almost painful, and try to define the difference, perhaps, very subtly.

Poetry, or what has existed for centuries under that name, attaches to earth, with faith, through the dust that everything is; like huge buildings, whose serious shadow augments their substructure, connects and blends with it. This call of the

---

†The quotation is a highly rewritten version of the Banville section of Mallarmé's youthful "Symphonie littéraire," one of his first prose works. [—*Trans.*]

stone coalesces, as it ascends toward the sky, into interrupted columns and arches having an audacious spurt in prayer; but, finally, a certain immobility. I'm waiting, as for a dazzling bat and a breeze of gravity, for him to escape, suddenly, with an autochthonous wing sweep, the insane, adamantine, angry, whirling genius, striking the ruin and flying away, the personification of flight, which he alone is.

Théodore de Banville at times becomes this supreme sylph.

When everything is going out or down, he is the last—or the first—to wait patiently beside the inner source while the grandiloquent thunderbolts and the brutal fragments, very far away from the simple fact of singing, finish striking down their colossus, in order—yes!—to appear, like the crown of mocking laughter without which everything would be in vain.

If I may resort, in an attempt at clarifying or generalizing, to the functions of the Orchestra, before which our musician of words remained candidly, knowingly closed: note how the instruments separately bring out, according to a magic easy to surprise, at the summit, in order to see better, natural landscapes; they dissolve them and restore them higher up. Thus it is that, to express a forest blending into the green horizon at dusk, it suffices to find a chord almost totally devoid of associations with the hunt; or a meadow, its pastoral fluidity flowing away in the late afternoon, is reflected and disappears in recollections of the river. A line, a vibration, a few summary details, and all is indicated. In contrast to lyric art the way it was, full of eloquence, because of the strict need for meaning. Although it contains a supremacy, or a rending of the veil, a lucidity, the Verb remains, along with subjects, and means, only more massively linked to nature.

The divine transposition, for the accomplishment of which man exists, *goes from facts to ideals.* Thanks to scintillating qualities, which were developed over two aristocratic French centuries, and which Banville summed up in one word: *wit* (for he was the only witty person his—ahem—friends could stand, and he was witty in a lyrical way, or like thunder), we had the impression of something rare, extreme, and superlative. His own poetry gave off a strong whiff of the beyond, but there was nothing second-hand or artificial about it. He knew himself so well as the heir to the tradition, cherished and incapable of anything underhanded, that he could explode, closely grazing Hugo himself and illuminating his enormous beauty, while giving the tenderest and most respectful of testimonies, his weapon of clear laughter. And thereupon he would play his characteristic secondary games. Who, among the moderns, is remotely comparable to him? They live in a time that absolutely refuses to say goodbye to eternal art, as old as life itself; but wants to derive it, in all its purity, by vocalizing everything to pieces! I'm speaking of Heine, his favorite bedside volume, so different, and so unified, that the local men of letters want to claim him as their own, just as they want to appropriate Poe, whom he resembles through certain crystalline airs, brief and young. Did I say that? Precisely, I had to; in order to mark the fact that it was not through the sparkling of gaiety (although, in his *Odes Funambulesques,* he invented comedy that is versified or stems from prosody, with humorous use of rhymes and breaks), nor through his irony, even though it was very precisely and masterfully pointed, but rather through his assumption of the need for a virgin role previously unknown, that the author of *Caryatids* and *Exiles,* of *Blood in the Cup,* the *Odelettes,* the *Amethysts,* and *All of Us,* of *Cowbells and Jingle Bells, In the Oven,* and finally a whole prestigious theater, to say nothing of his magnificent prose, equaled only by his conversation, represents, through his splendors, his ingenuity, and his piety, the very being of joy and gems, brilliant, dominant, effulgent.

Edgar Poe

Edgar Poe appeared to me in person only since Whistler. Before then, I had known that forehead which defies marble, those eyes like stars negated only in their distance, that mouth stung by every serpent except laughter—all as sacred as a portrait on the first page of someone's works; but to see the life-size demon! His dark, tragic coquetry, anxious and discreet: his bearing similar to that of the painter, whom I met once at my house, and in whom I sensed that same preciosity, that same American refinement, tending almost toward beauty. Villiers de l'Isle-Adam, in his frock coat, some evenings, young or at the height of his powers, evoked that Shade with a gesture in total silence. Nevertheless, after gazing at engravings and daguerreotypes, I must admit that a unique kind of piety enjoins me to represent the purest of pure Spirits as an aerolite; interstellar, thunderous, projected from final human designs, very far from being our contemporary, someone we could only see burst into a sparkling cloud, creating a crown that fits no one now, meant for centuries hence. He is indeed that exception: the absolute literary case.

Whistler

WHILE he seems externally to be the man of his paintings, the question is wrongly posed—just the opposite, insofar as an innate, eternal sense gives the secret of beauty; plays at miracles, and negates the signer. A rare Gentleman, some sort of prince, an artist certainly, pointed Whistler out to me, and at once, his entire person resembled his paintings—small in stature, if one wishes to use such measures, haughty, his head tormented, knowledgeable, attractive; and lost in the obsession of his canvases. Time to provoke the viewer! The master enchanter of a work of mystery as closed as perfection, which the crowd passes by without hostility, has understood the duty of his presence—to interrupt all that with some mad bravura until the admiring silence around the work is broken. That discretion refined through gentleness, in leisure, constituting his bearing almost entirely, without losing the slightest grace, explodes in vivid sarcasm increased by his black suit and reflected in his underclothes, as laughter breaks out, and presents, to contemporaries facing the sovereign artistic exception, just what they need to know about the author, the shadowy yet all the more visible guardian of a genie; a chaperone, bodyguard, fighter, worshiper, able to be both precious and worldly.

Edouard Manet

WHENEVER a tragic destiny—other than death, which stalks everyone—marks the joy and grace of a famous man, hard and hostile, it bothers me; not the alarm raised a while back when he refreshed the grand tradition, nor all the posthumous tributes; but rather, in the midst of all this, a virile, goat-footed innocence wearing a beige raincoat, his beard and sparse blond hair graying with wit. As mocking and elegant as any habitué of the Café Tortoni; in his studio, a fury bent him over the empty canvas, dazed, as if he had never painted before—with his precocious gift, worrisome then, now rolled up with a nose for solutions and a sudden calm trainedness: so says his unforgetting daily student-witness, myself, as we wagered ourselves entirely, every time, being the same as everyone else without staying different, as long as we wished. In one of my most vivid memories, I can picture him saying, "The eye, a hand . . ." That eye—Manet himself—from a long line of city dwellers, could impart newness to any object and, when subjects posed for their picture, could give every painting the freshness of a new encounter, virgin and abstract; he had crinkles at the corners of his eyes that would wipe out the fatigues of the twentieth sitting. The clear, ready pressure of his hands as he clasped those of his subject told of the mystery into which the limpidity of his sight would plunge, in order to produce, lively, clean-washed, deep, acute, or haunted with a certain blackness, his masterpiece, which was both very new and very French.

So many light, iridescent canvases, spontaneous and exact, can await the smile to come, and will consent to the use of a Name for the book that contains them, before their fine quality is acknowledged, a name pronounced for its own sake or for the extraordinary charm with which it was borne, evoking a figure from a pure bloodline, in life and in person extremely elegant. Paris hardly knew her, so much herself in her lineage and her grace, except through gatherings like this; but usually the exhibits are of Monet and Renoir, with a Degas in front of a Puvis de Chavannes or a Whistler, many of them evening guests of some high-toned salon; in the morning, she could be found in her discreet little studio, whose Empire wainscoting framed paintings by Edouard Manet. When, in turn, the lady painted herself, with fury and nonchalance, over the years, preserving the monotony and profusely releasing a freshness of idea, one must admit—always—with the exception of those intimate receptions where, the materials of work put away, art itself seemed far away though immediate, in a conversation equal to the setting, ennobled by the group: for a Salon, especially, imposes, with the presence of some regulars, the absence of other people, the room, then, explains its elevation and confers, from its high ceilings, superiority on the hostess, there, the guardian of the space, so (as was true then) enigmatic, appearing cordial or mocking or welcoming depending on the expectations of the scrutinizing witness, who, on some low piece of furniture, awaits, fervently, the distinguished woman. Prudence is required of those who would bring some ordinary jollity to the gathering, like comrades who know that here, on this occasion, imbued with friendship and beauty, something strange hovers, which their small numbers point to and came for: the luxurious and unconscious obliteration of everything outside.

These qualities of a great artist, who, also as the mistress of a grand house, possessed nothing banal, caused, during ceremonies of presentation, something close to discomfort. Why I concede, in order to defer my evoking of a perfect memory, good but defunct, to the summary we came up with, as we went down the avenues of the Bois de Boulogne or the Champs-Elysées, which brings up my memory again; one midnight, the satisfaction I felt, when I read in a book by an elegant comrade, that he suffered from the same shyness which long afflicted me before the friendly Medusa, especially when it came to stopping the playing and showing one's devotion. "Next to Madame Manet," said the paradoxical confidant, a refined conversationalist at ease with great young poets, "I feel like a rustic and a brute." Such a quip, which the person concerned never heard, will never be uttered again. Just as every subtle remark understood in the context of frequent encounters is hard to lay properly before a reader, even fleshed out with a portrait and a description of the context; that's what makes her silent election in spite of oneself so magnificent—a woman of the world, her sincerity known only through her withdrawal, a great painter, without ceasing to be a fabulous hostess and a fact of society, it seems, even now.

The few sexual dissidents who present aesthetics otherwise than through the individual run the risk, I won't say of treating with summary ardor a cult which, perhaps, we also have with learning and reverie, and I'll skip over the high-priestess contests; but, when the topic is art, of disdaining our caution in matching each one's aim and gifts, and of leaping directly to the sublime—far away, it's true, from the coarse and brutal:

they give us a lesson in virility, and also take over from the State, by taking good care of the notion of vast eternal models, among which is taste, very well behaved, unless there is special lighting.—A constant juvenility absolves emphasis.— This practice, which is effective, would be pleasing if it elevated things to greater rarity and, again and essentially, forms of delicacy, which we limit ourselves to having almost as feminine traits. According to the tact of a great-grand-niece, descended from Fragonard, Madame Berthe Morisot was a devotee of this game, and was related to the man who gave new life to the French tradition in his day—since she married his brother, Monsieur Eugène Manet, whose mind was very perspicacious and correct. She always slipped in, among the Impressionists[†]—in 1874, 1876, 1877, 1883—a canvas, shivering with carnations, orchards, skies, with all the lightness expected, plus a blend of the eighteenth century and the present in the scene; the critics, moved by something less peremptory, made the mistake of excluding, in their acuity, this or that bouquet, and lost the viewers' goodwill. At least, one has to believe that the fascination one would like to profit from, however superficially and presumptuously, operates only on conditions of strict integrity and even, for the viewer, hostility. Any mastery casts a chill: a fragile tint defends itself with a stained-glass window, which for some is a divination.

Thus, with bravura, an existence expected to continue, without cares, after the victory and the homage[††]—when the prophecy failed during the winter of 1895, with its late frosts, and now it's almost a year later. The city learned then that the absent woman, far from being called away by some

[†]In addition to those already mentioned: Mary Cassatt, Cézanne, Pissarro, Rouart, Sisley, Caillebotte, Guillaumin, before their consecration. [—*Author*]

[††]The entire exhibition was on view at Boussod and Valadon in June 1895. One of the paintings was acquired for the Luxembourg Museum. [—*Author*]

magic, had withdrawn more than usual—had withdrawn supremely—carried off by a seasonal malady. It was not the reticence of a sober decision or an attempt to disappear as her half-century approached: her vigorous caprices and resolute nature were well known, but she doubtless did not welcome this caprice of death and would rather have preserved her faithful circle, because of her passionate maternal ardor, which the creative artist shared whole-heartedly. She certainly felt the pity or torture of abandoning, despite her strength of soul, unless there was a motive for separation on either side, with the easel nearby, a very young daughter, offspring of two illustrious lines, joining to her own hopes the happy destiny of her mother and of the Manets. Let us simply record our astonishment that the journals themselves reported, as a detail well known to their readers, on the emptiness, in art, left by such a discreet departure. All of a sudden, everyone they interviewed acknowledged—and saluted—her tacit fame.

If I have inopportunely brought to this celebration of her work, on the anniversary of her death,† the mournful face of sorrow, when I should have tried to recreate for you the noblest of physiognomies, I bear witness to a wrong, and plead the usual exigencies of mourning: the impartial visitor of her own work, among all the portraits, does not wish to intercept, her hair whitened by her search for the beautiful rather than by age, a judgment, the serene focal point of vision, or not needing, in these circumstances, the distance of death: not to mention the fact that it would be, for the artist, to spill into a room full of celebration, flowers, and joy the only shadow she ever painted, and which, indeed, her brush shied away from.

Here, even as her pictures seem to vanish in the act of dispersing a radiant, idyllic, delicate, powdery, iridescent caress,

---

†Mallarmé wrote this essay to introduce the catalogue of Berthe Morisot's works (almost four hundred of them) which were exhibited on the first anniversary of her death. [—*Trans.*]

leaving in their armature many superb designs, no less learned, evidence of a science behind the apparent willfulness of her canvases, apart from colors, on a subject—altogether more than three hundred works, approximately, as well as studies, delivered to the public's appreciation, all bathed in sense—unknown, untouched, virginal, inspired by this mother-of-pearl or silvery luster: should one, haunted by suggestiveness trying to translate itself on this occasion, keep silent, in a shimmering suspension of perpetuity? Silence, except when there appears a spectacle of modern enchantment. Far away or right outside the window, in a greenish hush from the Hesperides, there are simple oranges against the pink brick of Eldorados, when suddenly a carafe erupts, sparkling with daylight, and propagating its many colors on the people and rugs, the genius, distilling the Crisis, and cutting the chimera off at the furniture, is, first and foremost, painterly. To poetize about this plastic art, a means of being attuned to direct prestige; it seems, without weighing these works down, to be an effect of the atmosphere awakening from each surface its luminous secret: or, to analyze richly yet chastely, to restore mobility and illusion—life—by means of an unknown alchemy. There is no intrusion of the perspective of dreams, but, suppressed, the common or professional aspects of the spectacle are, too. So be it; let humanity simply exult in the everyday, the flesh, preferably of children, fruit, all the way to its nubility; that's where this tender celebration of the nude ends; our contemporary approaches her sisterly double, her fellow artist, who can't be omitted; dressed up, readied for unknown eyes, curved or finished like the work of a calligrapher, unless the image attracts the attention, literarily, of a novelist. Miraculously, she brings them alive, the satin animated through contact with skin; the Orient through pearls; or shows them in undress, puts them in ideal négligés, their worldliness formerly not susceptible to style, so that what becomes visible is a relation to gardens and beaches, a greenhouse or a gallery. And back to the classic relations between fluidity and luminosity.

The daily magic of the quotidian—without distance, through inspiration, something more than open air slipping us, some morning or afternoon, an airborne swan; even the beyond becomes habituated, and wings aimed at heaven turn around, to the enthusiastic innateness of youth in the depths of a day.

Let's recall, independent of her magic, that her dearest wish was for an exact correspondence between how she was perceived and how she felt she was: one can at least say that she never lacked for fans or for solitude. Then let's ask, looking at the walls, why she whose gifts were so commonly said to be those of a woman—and of a master—why the pronouncements of those great originals, who after all counted her among their friends, carries so much more weight than anyone else's for her, and links her to the history of the paintings produced in a certain half-century.

Richard

Wagner

Richard Wagner • The Reverie of a French Poet

A CONTEMPORARY French poet,† excluded, for various reasons, from any participation in official celebrations of beauty, likes, whether from his practical task or from the mysterious refinement of verse he keeps for his solitary rites, to reflect on the nature of a public ceremony paying tribute to Poetry, and on the possibility that this could exist alongside the flow of banality carted around by the arts in the semblance of Civilization.—Ceremonies of a day that resides in the unconscious heart of the crowd: almost a religion!

The certainty of not being implicated, neither he nor anyone alive today, in any such enterprise, frees him from having to apply to his dreams any restriction stemming from his fear of incompetence or from a neglect of facts.

His vision of untroubled uprightness extends very far.

At his ease, and it's the least he would consider doing as an exploit, he contemplates, alone, in the proud billowing folds of consequences, the Monster-Who-Cannot-Be! Fixing on its flanks the wound of a look both affirmative and pure.

If we leave out the many glances at the extraordinary but unfinished splendor of sculptural figuration and concentrate on its one successful outgrowth, Dance, capable of translat-

†Baudelaire. [—*Trans.*]

ing, in the perfection of its rendition, the fleeting and the sudden up to the Idea—such a vision comprehends all, absolutely all, of the Spectacle of the future—our enthusiast, even if he envisages the contribution of Music to Theater, made precisely to mobilize its magic, does not really think about it enough in himself . . . already, with whatever leaps his thought takes off, it can feel the colossal approach of an Initiation. Your wish, rather, let's see if it isn't reciprocated.

What a challenge is inflicted on poets, whose duty is usurped, with the most candid and splendid bravura, by Richard Wagner!

The feelings—transports, veneration—grow complicated toward this foreigner, also uneasiness that everything has been done, and it hasn't illuminated, through some direct path, the literary principle itself.

In order to pronounce a judgment, to integrate doubts and necessities, one should start by discerning the circumstances encountered by the efforts of the Master. He appeared at a time when, in Theater—the only theater that can really be called passé—Fiction imposed itself directly and right away and was composed of gross materials, demanding belief in the real existence of the character and of the story—just belief, mind you, nothing more. As if the faith demanded of the spectator should not have been the result of the co-presence of all the arts that call forth the miracle, otherwise inert and null, of the stage! You should be falling under the power of a spell, for the accomplishment of which no kind of enchantment implied by musical magic is too much, so that your reason, struggling with a simulacrum, is shocked, and suddenly you hear: "Suppose that this is really taking place, and you are there!"

Modern man disdains the imagination, but, expert at making use of the arts, waits until each one carries him up to the point where a special power of illusion gleams out, then consents.

He didn't have any choice, since Theater before Music was grounded in a simple, naïve, but authoritarian concept, not having at its disposal the new evocative resource, its masterpieces couched, alas! in the pious pages of a book—without hope, for any of them, of rising up to our kind of solemnities. Its type of play-acting remains inherent to the past, or to what popular representation repudiates, because of that same intellectual despotism: the crowd, following art's lead, wanting to remain in charge of its beliefs. The mere addition of an orchestra completely changes things, annulling the former theater's very principle, and it is as strictly allegorical that the theater now is experienced; the stage, empty, abstract, and impersonal, now needs, in order to come alive with plausibility, the life-giving flood dispensed by Music.

Music's presence and nothing more constitutes a triumph, so long as it doesn't apply itself to antique conditions, but bursts out, the fountain of all vitality: an audience should feel the impression that, if the orchestra stopped playing, the mime would immediately become a statue.

Could the Musician, privy to the secrets of his Art, simplify its description down to this initial aim? Such a metamorphosis requires the disinterestedness of a critic who does not feel pressing against him, ready to burst with impatience and joy, the abyss of musical execution here—the most tumultuous that any man could contain by his limpid will.

He alone did this.

To take first only the most urgent thing: he reconciled a whole intact tradition, just about to fall into decadence, with the virginal, occult energy surging up from his scores. Outside of some sterile perspicacity or suicide, this creator's gift for assimilation was so life-filled that, of the two elements of beauty that exclude each other, or at least remain unknown to each other, personal drama and ideal music, he brought about the Hymen. Yes, with the help of a harmonious compromise, calling forth a specific phase of theater, which corresponds, as if it were a surprise, to the fundamental character of his race!

Although, philosophically, they are still only juxtaposed, Music (I command that one say where it comes from, what its first meaning was, and what its destiny is) penetrates and envelops the Drama through its dazzling will, and allies itself with it: there is no innocence or depth that it doesn't throw itself into, as if awakening into enthusiasm, except for the fact that Music's very principle still escapes.

It takes a prodigious sense of tact to bring about, without transforming any of them, the fusion of very different forms of pleasure.

Indeed, these days, a music that possesses of that art only the observance of some very complex laws, at first only the variable and the innate, mixes the colors and lines of a character with timbres and themes into a richer ambience for Dreams than any song here below, a god dressed in the invisible folds of a fabric of chords; or else he takes from the wave of Passion, from an unfurling too vast for a single individual—he is thrown and twisted—the adversary is superhuman—only in order to give it to man again when he dominates everything through song, pouring through a tear ripped in inspirational thought. Always, the hero, who walks on the mist as one walks on earth, will be seen in the distance, covered by the stream of complaints, of glories, of joys emitted by the instrumentation, thus rolled back to its beginnings. He acts only when surrounded, Greek-style, with the blend of stupor and intimacy that an audience feels in front of myths that have almost never been, so much does their instinctual past blend in, without ceasing to benefit from the familiar appearance of the human individual. Some even satisfy the spirit by making it feel knowledgeable about what are some rather chance symbols.

And thus the Legend is enthroned on the stage.

The public, with a piety that belongs to former times, first Hellenic, now German, considers the representation of origins. It sits calmly, with an odd kind of happiness, fresh and barbarous: the subtlety of the orchestration ripples the veil, and decorates the magnificence of the origin.

Everything bathes again in the primitive stream: but doesn't go all the way back to its source.

If the French spirit, which is strictly imaginative and abstract, and thus poetic, ever projects a glimmer of Truth, it won't be like that: it rejects, and is thus in agreement with Art as a whole, which would rather invent, any existing Legend. Look at it keeping no enormous, unpolished anecdote from bygone days, as if made to be a source of anachronism in what it foresees as a theatrical event, the Feast of one of the acts of Civilization.† Unless it should be that the Fable—virgin of anything: place, time, or known characters—reveals itself to be borrowed from the sense which is latent in everyone's striving, the one that is written on a page of the Skies, and of which History itself is just a vain interpretation, a Poem, an Ode. One century, our country, which exalts myths, dissolved them through thought, in order to make them anew! Theater calls for them—no! not fixed ones, neither ancient nor famous, but one, stripped of all personality, for it is based on our multiplicity: any local prestige corresponds to a national functioning, the single one evoked by Art and reflected in us. A type without a prior designation, so that he can provoke pure surprise: his gesture encompasses toward himself

---

†Exposition, Transfer of Powers, etc. Can I see you in it, Brünnhilde, or what would you do there, Siegfried!? [—*Author*]

all our dreams of places or paradises, which the antique stage submerges with its pretense of containing or depicting them. He is Everyman, and this stage is anywhere (a correlative error is a stable décor and a real actor in a Theater that lacks Music): Does a spiritual fact, the unfolding of symbols or their preparation, need a particular place to develop, other than the fictive focal point of the eyes of a crowd? Holy of holies, but mental . . . then everything moves toward some supreme bolt of light, from which awakens the Figure that No One is, whose rhythm, taken from the symphony, comes from the mimicking of each musical attitude, and liberates it! Then, at the feet of the incarnation, not without a link thereby to its humanity, expire the natural rarefactions and solemnities that Music renders, the farthest vibratory prolongation of everything, or of Life.

Man and his authentic stay on earth exchange a reciprocity of proofs.

That is the Mystery.

The City, which gave, for this experience of the sacred, a theater, imprints on the earth its universal seal.

As for its people, at least they testify to the august fact, and I attest that Justice has no choice but to reign there! since this orchestration, from which, a minute ago, we saw the evidence of a god, never synthesizes anything but the innate, immortal delicacies and magnificences, unbeknownst to anyone, that reside in a mute, attentive audience.

That is why—Genius!—humbly enslaved to an eternal logic, O Wagner, I suffer and reproach myself, in those minutes marked by lassitude, for not being among the number of those who, bored with everything and looking for definitive salvation, go directly to the edifice of your Art, for them the endpoint of the road. And the incontestable portal does open onto a jubilee time for no particular people, offering hospitality against the insufficiency of oneself and the mediocrity of nations: it fills the fervent all the way up to certainty: for them, it's not the biggest step that has ever been taken by a human sign, with you as a guide, but the complete progress of humanity toward an Ideal. At the very least, wanting my share of delight, I hope you'll permit me to take a taste, in your Temple, halfway up the sacred mountain, whose ability to elevate Truths trumpets the attractions of the summit, and invites one, out of sight of the base, on the lawns that the feet of your elect have trampled, to rest; for the spirit, it's like the isolation of our incoherence, which has been hounding it, as well as a shelter from the too lucid and too threatening absolute of the summit that has been haunting it, which can be guessed at from the departure of clouds up there: a dazzling, stark, isolated summit that no one seems about to scale. No one! The expression does not obsess with remorse the passerby who drinks from your convivial fountain.

Scribbled at
the Theater

Mʏ ɪᴅᴇᴀ's last despair, after leaning on a balcony covered with glue or pasteboard, her eyes lost in thought, her features in advance tired of nothingness, it's that—not at all!—
after a few words on the stageboards, disdained by her if they
didn't strike up the rhythm of her only trick, unfailingly here
she is whispering in a tone of muffled anguish, and holding
out to me her renunciation of flight, which she had long
waved in my face as if by caprice. "But it's fine, perfect—
what are you still claiming to do, my love?" Then, with a hand
empty of any fan: "Let's go [she gestures] nevertheless—we
wouldn't even be bored for a short time, and I would fear that
I couldn't dream of anything else.—The author or his substitute has done exactly what he set out to do, and I defy anyone
at all to execute it better or differently."

What did they hope to accomplish, O my soul? I replied
once, still dumbfounded, then eluding the responsibility of
having brought here so exquisite but abnormal a lady: for
surely it wasn't a soul or an idea (that is, the divinity present
to the spirit of men) who proposed so despotically: "Come!"

But a habitual and inconsiderate lack of foresight.

"What they set out to do?" She didn't take pains to prolong her feigned curiosity, "I don't know, or maybe . . . ,"
stifling—the worst torture being to find everything "fine,"
and not be able to abominate what one has been stuck in front
of—a yawn, the innocent, solitary, supreme protest, which is

echoed in the chandelier [*le lustre*], suspending thousands of cries of radiant and visible horror.

". . . Maybe this."

She explained and indeed approved of the attempt by people of indisputable talent and even bravura, and conscious of their emptiness, but with an admixture of mediocrity from their concept of the crowd, to fill the magnificent hole or hunger or anticipation dug every night as the sun is setting—the opening of a Chimera's maw, carefully frustrated by the current social system.

Anything else seems inexact—and besides, what can one say? The current mental situation is like the meanderings of a drama, and their inextricability dictates that, in the absence of the topic that is never talked about, or Vision itself, whoever ventures into a real contemporary theater will be punished by all the compromises that are required: if he's a man of taste, for instance, by his inability not to applaud. I think, besides, however interesting it might be to research the reasons behind a character's placidity—some We or I—that the initial mistake was to come to the spectacle accompanied by one's Soul—*with Psyche, my soul*[†]: What can one do? if everything is magnified by the banal misunderstanding, to use one's pure faculty of judgment in evaluating things that have supposedly already entered Art (have become second-hand), in short, have become Works.

Criticism, in its integrity, is not, doesn't have, or doesn't equal Poetry, to which it brings a noble complementary operation, unless it aims, directly and superbly, also at phenomena or at the universe: but in spite of that, perhaps because of its quality of primordial instinct placed at the heart of our billowing folds (a divine unease), it gives in to the attraction of a

[†]Edgar Poe, "Ulalume," stanza 2. [—*Author*]

theater that offers a mere representation for those who can't see the things themselves! of the play written every night in the folio of the sky, and mimed in the gestures of his passions by Man.

Besides lazy errors that are cause for debate, you see, our epoch is already getting ready for a plausible transformation: what was called drama criticism or serial articles, which one cannot go back to, is very correctly left to telegraphic reports of opening nights, without eloquence other than the fact of speaking for a unanimity of mutes. Add to that whatever gossip one can pick up from the wings, from beings of gauze or of flesh caught on their way to their trailers, whose canvas tops were hastily put up for rehearsals (openings are always a relief, even if they say only what has been said before): so far as the theater is concerned, all this falls to the tabloid press, concerned with small or quirky news items. The paradox for the more ambitious writer, for a long time, was, with imaginative fugues and organ tones—we remind you—to take over the creative literary genre from which we get prose, Criticism, and to note the fluctuations in some article of wit or fashion.

So when nothing is announced for the evening that tempts one to march eagerly up to the monster and throw oneself into its jaws, and thus lose any right to mock it, being oneself the only one who deserves ridicule, isn't there at least the occasion to proffer some words in front of the fire; given that the ancient secret of ardor and splendors twisting there, beneath our fixity, evokes, in the warming rays of the hearth [âtre], the obsession with a theater [théâtre] still reduced and small in the distance, here an intimate celebration.

Meditative:

There is (we're poking at the fire) an art, the only or pure art, according to which uttering signifies producing: it shouts out its demonstrations through its practice. The instant the miracle happens, to say even that it was that and nothing else, will invalidate it: so intolerant is it of any evidence other than existing.

I would have liked, constrained by circumstances rather than idly, to note here some of its fundamental traits.

The ballet gives but little: it's an imaginative genre. When a sign of scattered beauty is isolated for the eye—flower, wave , cloud, jewel, etc.—if our only way of knowing it is to juxtapose it with our spiritual nudity so we can feel that it is analogous, and adapt it in some exquisite confusion of ourselves with this fluttering form—even if it's through a rite, the utterance of the Idea1. Doesn't the dancer seem to be half the element in question, half humanity eager to melt into it, floating in reverie? The operation, or poetry, par excellence, and theater. Immediately, ballet becomes allegorical: it will bring together as well as animate, to mark out each rhythm, all the correlations or Music, latent at first, between its attitudes and such-and-such a character, so much so that the figurative representation of earthly props by Dance contains a test of their aesthetic merit, and a consecration results, which is the proof of our treasures. We have to deduce the philosophical point where the dancer's impersonality is located, between her female appearance and a mimed object, destined for what Hymen: she sews it with her unerring points, and puts it in place; then unrolls our convictions in a writing of pirouettes extended toward another motif, it being understood that everything, in the whirling through which she illustrates the meaning of our ecstasies and triumphs, also being played in the rumblings of the orchestra, is, as art itself would want it, in the theater, *fictional or outside time.*

Sole principle! And just as the chandelier [*le lustre*] shines, that is, by itself, and exhibits at once our adamantine look, a dramatic work shows a succession of exteriors of an act without any moment's having any reality, and what happens is, finally, nothing at all.

Old-style Melodrama, occupying the stage together with Dance, under the reign of the poet, satisfies this law. Moved, the perpetual suspension of a tear that can never be completely formed or fall (*le lustre* again) shines in thousands of gazes, and, at the same time, an ambiguous smile crosses one's lips at the perception of mockery among the strings or the flutes, which refuse complicity with the emphatic sorrow marked in the score, and open up fissures of hope and of daylight: an announcement, even if maliciously silenced, that I consent to await or to follow, along the labyrinth of anxiety that art creates—truly not to hit me over the head, as if my fate were not enough, as a spectator attending a festival; but to plunge me back among the people, to liberate me there according to some naïve melodic source, audience and saint of the Passion of Man. A similar use of Music considers it the strongest magic, since it tangles and snaps or conducts the divining thread—in short, controls the audience's interest: it would illuminate the composers so lavish with chords and melodies, indiscriminately, and without knowing the precise sense of the sonorities they work with. No inspiration would be the loser for knowing the humble and profound law that rules, by virtue of a popular instinct, the relations between orchestra and stage in this instance of French genius. Axioms can be read in it, written by nobody; one above all! that every insoluble situation, which seems likely to remain that way, assuming that the drama is something other than mere appearance or trap for our inattention, represses, dissimulates, and always contains the sacred laughter that will untie it. Even a funereal imagination like Bouchardy's† cannot drape itself in ignorance—that the enigma behind the curtain exists only

†Joseph Bouchardy (1810–1870), writer of melodramas in the mid-nineteenth century. [—*Trans.*]

through a revolving hypothesis that our lucidity, little by little, solves: lit by gas or electricity, the instrumental accompaniment is graduated, and, somehow, the Mystery dispensed.

The opportunity to keep quiet has not arisen, and I'm not going to make the usual excuses about the nullity of the year to explain the emptiness of this study, or of all the ones I've done (discreet complaints!); but rather, the lack of a glance over the whole enterprise by a writer who has forgotten that between himself and his era there remains an incompatibility. "Do you go to the theater?"—"No, almost never": when I ask anyone of note, this is what they say, and it suffices, whether from a man or a woman of the world, with the hangings of their dreams even in their daily life. "Now that you mention it, neither do I!" I could answer, if most of the time my lack of interest weren't perfectly obvious from what I write here, down to the final blank.

So why . . . ?

Why! Other than at the instigation of the irreducible Imp of Perversity, which I summarize thus: "Do what is expressly forbidden, with nothing to gain but embarrassment before the productions (to which you are, by nature, foreign), while pretending to pronounce a judgment upon them: while a link, having to do with appreciation, escapes, or you are silenced by shyness about exposing supreme, untimely principles in a false light." To wager, in one's efforts to achieve a gratuitous mediocrity, always to fall short of it; besides, nothing drives one toward this contradiction except the charm, perhaps unknown in literature, of strictly extinguishing, one by one, any view that could burst out with purity—just as one crosses out certain words that, in me, take the place of what once was a heart; it would thus be a mortal sin to serve them badly. A fool blabbers on without saying anything, and to do the same without any notorious taste for prolixity and precisely in order not to say something represents a special case: mine. I exhibit myself as an exception to that particular ridicule. It is not even

appropriate to denounce, by spewing verbiage, the role of the
formidable omnipotent Plague . . . our era has let loose, legiti-
mately seeing that in the crowd or majestic amplification of
each one of us the dream lies hidden; in a multitude lies the
awareness of its sovereign judgment or supreme intelligence,
without preparing a place for it in new circumstances or a
mental milieu that equates the stage and the house. In any
case, before the celebration of the poems that were stifled in
the egg under some missing future dome (if a date can be as-
signed to the incubation period, which we doubt) it was necessary to erect in haste, for contemporary infatuation, between
the pit of vain hunger and successive generations, a simulacrum appropriate for the immediate need, also known as official art, which can also be called vulgar; ready to contain
through the basaltic veil of the banal the surge of the crowd,
jubilating so little that it notices the coarse imagery of its divinity. A machine we thought was provisional in order to so-
lidify—what!—a durable and empty institution convincing by
its timeliness: the call has gone out to all artificial and man-
nered cults; that's what gives us the annual salons of Painting and Sculpture when the theatrical schedule is idle. Falsi-
fying, as creative refuse, both the delicate, virgin outpouring,
and the twin clairvoyance that comes directly from simplicity;
which, perhaps, still had to be brought into tune. It's simply
heroic, when today's artists, rather than painting a cloistral
solitude by the light of their immortality, or sacrificing before
the idol of themselves, put their hands on this monument, an
enormous sign, no less than the boulders of abstention scattered about by former ages, which could only deposit on the
ground a considerable negative vestige.

In the distance, Nature, in autumn, prepares its sublime and pure Theater, waiting to illuminate, in solitude, some prestigious significance, whose meaning the unique, lucid eye can penetrate (notorious, it's man's destiny), it's too bad a Poet should be called back to mediocre pleasures and worries.

Here I am, oblivious to the mournful mood of dead leaves, back and all ready to jot down, for myself and a few friends, our impressions of banal Nights Out, which the loneliest of loners cannot, since he's wearing the uniform of Everyone, neglect to consider: if only to keep up the unease and, knowing, because of certain laws that have not been satisfied, that it is no longer, or not yet, the extraordinary hour.

. . . . .

And nevertheless, weaned on glory,
You feel run through the darkness derisory,
Across your pale forehead, milky white,
The breeze lifting your black plume, mandatory
For the young Prince of Denmark, and caressing you,
    O Hamlet!

(Théodore de Banville)

Our adolescent self, who vanished at the beginnings of life, and who will continue to haunt high or pensive spirits through the mourning-clothes he always wears; I recognize him struggling to appear: for Hamlet externalizes, on the stage, the lone character of an intimate, occult tragedy; if his name alone is posted, it exerts on me, or on you if you read it, a fascination, akin to anxiety. I'm thankful to the fates for having pulled me away from the imaginative vision of the theater of the clouds and of the truth down to some human theater, only to present me, as my first assignment, with the play I consider The Play par excellence, when they could have counted on easily obfuscating eyes too quickly grown unused to the scarlet, violet, pink, and always gold horizon. The encounter of skies I identified with ceases, without my being replaced by a brutal contemporary incarnation behind their shield of fame (farewell to the splendors of a holocaust of the old year, enlarged to fit all times so no one can equal its vain celebration); but there steps forth *the latent lord who cannot become,* the juvenile shadow of us all, and thus partaking of myth. His solitary drama! and who, sometimes, so much does this wanderer of his labyrinth of trouble and grief lengthen its circuits through the suspension of an unaccomplished act, seems to be the very spectacle for which the stage exists, the footlights defining and defending a golden, quasi-moral space. For there is no other subject, note it well: the antagonism created by dreams within the fate of Man's daily existence, fate distributed by bad luck.

All curiosity, it's true, in today's case, centers on the interpretation, but one cannot speak about it without comparing it to the idea.

The actor sets the tone.[†]

All by himself, as if by magic, with his incomparable mastery of technique and also a literary man's faith in the always certain and mysterious beauty of the role, he has known how to conjure away the evil spirits that have slipped into this imposing representation. No, I don't criticize the production for

---

[†]Monsieur Mounet-Sully (October 1886). [—*Author*]

its lavish use of plants in its magnificent sets, nor for its sumptuous costumes, although, according to today's learned mania for detail, the production is dated, too *certainly;* and the precise choice of Renaissance costumes, spiritually darkened with a hint of northern furs, takes away the distance of primitive legend, transforming, for example, the characters into contemporaries of the playwright. Hamlet himself avoids this problem by wearing his traditional black clothes, almost a dark nakedness, as if out of a Goya painting. The work of Shakespeare is so well modeled on the sole theater of the spirit, the prototype of the rest, that it adapts to a contemporary staging, or does without it, equally well. Another thing that disconcerts me comes from tiny details hard to pin down: a particularly Parisian mode of intelligence in the place where Elsinor is installed, and, as philosophical language would have it, *the error of the Théâtre Français.* This plague is impersonal, and the much-heralded troupe, under the circumstances, multiplied its zeal for minutiae: to act Shakespeare, they can very well do, and they aim to do it very well. In which talent is not quite enough, but gives way before certain inveterate habits of comprehension. Here, for example, Horatio, not that I single him out, has something classical and Molièresque in his bearing; but Laertes, I'm getting into my subject, stands in the front and acts on his own account as if his voyages and his pitiful double mourning were of particular interest. What do the most beautiful of qualities (all of them) matter in a story that extinguishes everything but an imaginary hero, half mingled with abstraction? To refer to the real is to break through the ambience, using reality as a battering ram to punch through a vaporous canvas, around the emblematic Hamlet. Comrades, admit it! For in the ideal image of the stage, everything moves *according to a symbolic reciprocity of types, among themselves or relative to a single figure.* Thus, masterfully, one actor infuses his frank vigor into Polonius, with the fussy, senile dottiness of some old servant in an amusing story; I laugh, but have already forgotten the completely dif-

ferent minister who also made me laugh, a figure out of a
worn tapestry like the one he'll go back into, to die: a dreary,
inconsistent old buffoon, whose weightless corpse, left lying
halfway through the play, implies no other importance than
the brief, haggard exclamation, "A Rat!" He who wanders
around a type as exceptional as Hamlet can only be a part of
Hamlet: and the fateful prince who will perish in his first steps
toward virility, gives a melancholy shove, with his useless
sword tip, out of the path that will be forbidden to him, to the
lump lying there—a bundle of loquacious vacuity that, later,
he would have risked becoming in his turn, if he had aged.
Ophelia, the objectified virgin childhood of the lamentable
royal heir, remains in agreement with the spirit of modern
conservatories: she has naturalness, as ingénues understand it,
preferring, over abandoning herself to ballads, to introduce
daily life and the everyday acquirements of an erudite among
actresses; from her bursts out, not without grace, some perfect
intonation, in the performance of days and of life. And then
there swirl around in my head, in addition to the letters that
spell the name of Shakespeare, other names it's a sacrilege
even to avoid saying, since everyone guesses them anyway.

Such is the power of Dream!

The—I don't know what kind of subtle and faded effacement in yesteryear's imagery, which is lacking even to the
master artists of our time, who like to present events similar to
those that actually happen—clear, striking, and new!—Hamlet, foreign to all places he's dropped into, impresses these living people, who stand out too much, with the invasion of
his mere funereal and ominous presence. The actor, on whom
the French version was perhaps fitted too closely, puts everything back in place exclusively through the double gesture of
annulling the pernicious influence of the House and spreading around him the atmosphere of genius, with a dominating charm, and from the fact that he mirrored himself in the
centuries-old text; then there is the nostalgia for primal wis-

dom, after all the storms that have battered the delicious plume of his hat. this is the character and perhaps the performance of our time, drawing out, in an instinctual way sometimes undecipherable even to him, the illuminations of an annotator. Thus the morbid duality that makes up the case of Hamlet seems to me to be rendered: yes, mad on the outside and flagellated by the contradictory demands of duty, but if he fixes his eyes inside him on an image of himself preserved intact, like an Ophelia never drowned, always ready to come alive . . . An intact jewel under all the disasters.

A mime and a thinker, the tragedian interprets Hamlet as a mental and material sovereign of art, and especially as Hamlet's heredity hangs over the minds of this fin-de-siècle: it was appropriate, after the agonizing romantic vigil, to hand down to us, all summed up, an image of the beautiful demon, perhaps tomorrow incomprehensible; now that's done. With solemnity, an actor leaves us, elucidated, somewhat composite but all there, as if authenticated by the seal of a supreme, neutral epoch, to a future that probably won't give a damn, but at least can't change it, an immortal resemblance.

LA CORNALBA enthralls me—she dances as though un-
clothed; that is to say, without the semblance of aid offered to
an abduction or a fall by a rising or settling presence of gauze.
She appears, called into the air, to float there, from a very Italian blend of tension and mellowness in her person.

The whole memory—no! not the whole!—of the show at
the Eden, for lack of Poetry: what is called thus, on the contrary, proliferates there, a pleasant debauchery for the spirit
liberated from frequenting only people in robes or suits and
famous words. Except for the fact that the charm of the book
doesn't pass into the representation. The stars themselves,
which I believe one shouldn't often disturb without good reasons or meditative gravity (here, according to the explanation,
Love moves and arranges them), I flip though the program
and see that they will join in; and the haughty, incoherent lack
of signification that shines in the alphabet of Night will consent to spell out the word VIVIANE, the enticing name both of
the fairy and of the poem, stitched into the stellar surface on a
blue backdrop: for the whole chorus of dancers will not,
grouped around the *star* (could it be better named!), dance the
ideal dance of the constellations. Not at all! from there one
would take off, you see through what worlds, straight into the
abyss of art. The snow also, each flake of which doesn't come
back to life in the comings and goings of a white bauble, or
according to a waltz, or a floral tuft sending up shoots in the
spring: everything that is, in effect, Poetry, or Nature ani-

mated, comes out of a text to fix itself in maneuvers of card-board and the dazzling motionlessness of chiffon, fire, and ash. Thus, in the order of the action, I saw a magic circle drawn by something other than the continual turns or the bends of the fairy herself; etc. There were many inventive, pi-quant details in the rendition, without any of them attaining the importance and function of an actually stated norm. Did anyone ever, notably in the sidereal case cited above, with suf-ficient heroism, go beyond the temptation to recognize both solemn analogies and the fundamental law of dance toward its first subject? For dance, in its ceaseless ubiquity, is a moving synthesis of the attitudes of each group; just as each group is only a fraction, detailing the whole, of the infinite. There re-sults a reciprocity producing the *un*-individual, both in the star and in the chorus, the dancer being only an emblem, never Someone . . .

The judgment or axiom to be affirmed in the case of ballet!

Namely, that *the dancer is not a woman dancing,* for these juxtaposed reasons: that *she is not a woman,* but a metaphor summing up one of the elementary aspects of our form: knife, goblet, flower, etc., and that *she is not dancing,* but suggesting, through the miracle of bends and leaps, a kind of corporal writing, what it would take pages of prose, dialogue, and de-scription to express, if it were transcribed: a poem indepen-dent of any scribal apparatus.

After a legend, a Fable unfolds, as classic taste would dic-tate, or as the celestial machine requires, but here in the re-stricted sense according to which *human* characters and man-ners are transferred to simple animals. An easy game would consist in *re*-translating, by means of characters, it's true, more instinctual in their mute boundings than anything a con-scious language permits one to express on stage: the human feelings the fabulist has given to his amorous avians. The dance is all wings: after all, it's about birds; departures in the forever and returns like a well-aimed and vibrating arrow. Anyone who studies the show called *The Two Pigeons,* will see, by virtue of its subject, an obligatory series of Ballet's fundamental motifs. The effort of the imagination is not predicted to be arduous, but it's something to see even a mediocre parity between things, and make the results interesting to the audience, in art. It's a trap! except in the first act, where human dancers prettily incarnate the birds who act like humans.

Two pigeons loved each other with a tender love

Two or several, on a rooftop, in pairs, just as one catches a glimpse of the sea from an archway in a Thessalian farmhouse; they are alive, which means, better than painted, they plumb the depths of correct taste. One of the lovers shows the pairs to the other, then shows himself, initial language: comparison. Gradually, the couple's manners begin to reflect the influence of the dovecote: amid peckings, flutterings, swoonings, we see this invasion of aerial sensuality slide onto him, with uncontrolled resemblances. From children, they have become birds, or the opposite, from birds they have become humans, depending on how one wishes to view the exchange, and they will from then on, him and her, have to play this double game: perhaps the whole adventure of sexual difference! But I'll stop trying to raise myself up to any consideration suggested by the Ballet, to aid me to reach the paradise of all spirituality, because after this innocent little prelude, nothing takes place, except the perfection of the dancers' skills, that deserves the exercise of a backward glance, nothing . . . It would be tedious to put one's finger on the precise type of inanity that grows out of such a graceful beginning. Here, the flight of the vagabond, which at least contributed to the type of ecstatic inability to disappear that attached the ballerina deliciously to the stageboards; then, when the recall to the hearth comes, when the poignant and admired hour of going home arrived, with the intervention of a festival around which everything under the storm turns, and when the two lovers, torn apart, forgiving and flighty, reunite, it will be . . . You can imagine the triumphal hymn in the final dance, where one sees, as it shrinks down to the source of their intoxicated joy, the dimension of space placed between the lovers by the necessity of the voyage! It will be . . . As if the thing were happening, Sir or Madam, at your house, sealed with a kiss which is completely indifferent to art; all of Dance being only the mysterious sacred interpretation of the act. But to let oneself fantasize like that is to be summoned by the sound of a flute to remember how ridiculous one's visionary state is to the average banal contemporary that one must, after all, represent, to show one's respect for the Opéra's seats.

With the exception of a relation clearly perceived between flight and the choreography of dance moves, and the transposition to the Ballet, not without trickery, of the Fable, there remains, at bottom, a love story. But in the interval, which is supposed to be light and entertaining (and where everything is just pieces stuck together), one needs the marvelous Mademoiselle Mauri, an unparalleled virtuoso, who sums up, with her incomparable divination, an animality both earthy and pure, always designating unfinished allusions, as when, before taking a step, she invites one, with two fingers, into the trembling folds of her skirts, and simulates an impatience of plumes toward the idea.

An art fills the stage, historical with Drama; with Ballet, something else, emblematic. They should be allied but not mixed; it is not right away and through a common treatment that one should join two stances so jealous of their respective silences: the mime and the dancer, suddenly hostile to each other if one forces them together. Here's an example that illustrates this incompatibility: Why did one not imagine, when asked how to impersonate a unique essence, that of a bird, by

using two different interpreters, the election of a mime beside
a dancer? It would be to confront too great a difference! the
other, if one is a dove, becoming I don't know what—the salt
spray, for example. At least, very judiciously, at the Eden, or
according to the two exclusive modes of art, a theme marks
out the antagonism which, in the hero participating in a double game, a man already, yet still a child, sets up a rivalry between the woman who *walks* (even if toward him on carpets
of kings) and the one, not less cherished from the fact of her
leaps alone, the primitive woman or fairy godmother. The
trait distinct to each theatrical genre, juxtaposed or opposed,
takes charge of the whole work, whose architecture depends
on the discrepancy; it remains to find a communication between them. The librettist is usually oblivious to the fact that
the dancer, who expresses herself through steps, understands
no other form of eloquence, not even that of gesture.

Unless there is a genius saying, "Dance represents caprice
taking flight according to rhythm—here, with their numbers,
are the few summary equations of all fantasy—the human
form as mobile as it can be, in its true development, cannot
transgress them, since they are, I know, the visual incorpora-
tion of the idea": that, plus a glance at a whole choreography!
There is no one moved by this to establish a ballet troupe. On
the contrary, one knows the contemporary frame of mind,
even in these founders, which looks for faculties that have as
their function to produce themselves miraculously: one would
have to substitute I don't know what impersonal or dazzling
absolute look, like the lightning that has enveloped, for several
years now, the dancers at the Eden, blending an electric crude-
ness with an extra-carnal whiteness like that of makeup, forc-
ing the prestigious presence to step back beyond any possible
life.

The only imaginative training consists, during the ordinary
hours of attending Dance without any particular aim, in pa-

tiently and passively asking oneself about each step, each strange attitude, these *points* and *taquetés,* these *allongés* or *ballons,* "What could this mean?" or, even better, from inspiration, to read it. For sure, one would operate fully in the midst of reverie, but appropriate; vaporous, clear, and ample, or restricted, so long as it is similar to the one enclosed in her spins or transported in a fugue by the unlettered ballerina lending herself to the play of her profession. Yes, that one (if you're lost in a hall, very foreign spectator, Friend), so long as you submissively place at the feet of this unconscious revealer, like the roses taken and thrown into the visibility of the upper regions by the dizzying play of her pale satin slippers, first the Flower *of your poetic instinct,* expecting nothing but the display, in its proper light, of the thousands of latent imaginations; then, through an exchange of which her smile seems to hold the secret, she hastily delivers up, through the ultimate veil that always remains, the nudity of your concepts, and writes your vision silently like a Sign, which she is.

Aʙᴏᴜᴛ Loie Fuller, insofar as she spreads around her the fabrics she then brings back to her person, through the actions of dance, everything has been said, in articles, some of which are poems.

The exercise, as invention, without being put to use, encompasses an intoxication of art, and, at the same time, an industrial accomplishment.

In the terrible cascade of cloth, the figure swoons, radiant, cold; illustrating many a spinning image tending toward a distant unfolding: a giant petal or butterfly, uncrumpling, all according to order, clear and elementary. Or she fuses with the rapid nuances transmuting their crepuscular or grotesque phantasmagoria of air and water into a rapidity of passions—delight, mourning, anger. One needs, to set them off, prismatic, violent, or diluted, the vertigo of a soul that is as if cast into the air by an artifice.

That a woman would associate the tossing of clothing with dance, powerful or vast enough to sustain them, to the infinite, like her expansion—

The lesson lies in this spiritual effect—

A gift with innocence and certainty given by the phantom stranger to the Ballet or theatrical form of poetry par excellence: one recognizes it wholly through its consequences, later, with distance.

A banality always floats between the danced spectacle and you.

To protest that this dazzling illumination satisfies a pensive delicacy like that attained, for example, by the reading of verse, shows one's ignorance of the subtleties included in the mysteries of Dance. A fully restored aesthetic will surpass the notes scribbled in haste, where, at least, I denounce, taking a closer look, an error common to any staging: aided as I am, unexpectedly, by the sudden solution given by my muse with a tiny shiver of her dress, my almost unconscious, or not voluntarily in question here, inspiration.

When the curtain rises in a festival hall, a local place, there appears, like a snowflake—blown in from where?—the furious dancer. The floor avoided by her leaps or hard on her points acquires a spatial virginity undreamed of, isolating a site that the figure will, all by herself, build and make flower. The décor is lying about, latent in the orchestra, treasure of the imagination; to come out, with a big splash, according to the views dispensed by the dancer, now and then gives the audience the Idea on stage. As it happens, this transition from sounds to fabrics (is there anything resembling gauze more than Music?) is, alone, the spell cast by Loie Fuller, by instinct, with excesses and retreats, of skirts or wings, instituting a place. The enchantress makes up the ambience, pulls it out of herself and puts it back in, in a silence rustling with Chinese silks. Soon an imbecility, as in this case, will disappear; the traditional permanent or stable stage-set, as opposed to the choreographic mobility. Opaque vehicles, intrusive cardboard—to the scrap heap! Here we find given back to Ballet the atmosphere or nothingness, visions no sooner known than scattered, just their limpid evocation. The stage is freed for any fiction, cleared and instated by the play of a veil with attitudes and gestures; the site, all movement, becomes the very pure result.

If such changes are imported by this creation to a genre without props, except for the human presence—one dreams of scrutinizing its principle.

All emotion comes out of you and expands into a milieu; or comes upon you and incorporates one.

Thus this peeling away of multiple layers around a nudity, enlarged by ordered or tempestuous contradictory flights, circling, magnifies it until dissolution: a central nothingness, all volition, for everything obeys a fleeting impulse to disappear in whirls; it sums up, in the will and dizziness of each wing tip, and hurls her strict, upright statue—dead with the effort of summing up—beyond the liberation almost from herself, the last decorative leaps evoking oceans, evenings, perfume, and sea foam.

So much is understood—but not spoken!—that to proffer a word about her, while she is performing, very softly and for the edification of the immediate vicinity, seems impossible, because, firstly, this sows confusion. But the memory, perhaps, won't be drowned out by a bit of prose here. In my opinion, wherever fashion wishes to range this miraculous contemporary phenomenon, it was important to extract the summary meaning and the explanation that emanates from it and acts on a whole art.

T HE ONLY one would have to be as fluid as the sorcerer in *Vies Encloses* [Enclosed Lives], and piercing—someone who, exceptionally, once wrote about Dance, Monsieur Rodenbach, who easily writes absolute sentences, and whose choice of a virgin subject makes his writing like gauze, like his clairvoyance—with regard to a statue, exposing, before she is dressed, a dancer—he gathers, lengthens, and creases the cloth, holds it out like living folds; then notes the particular care ballerinas have taken, in every age, "to complicate with all kinds of vaporous spins the enchantments of Dance, *in which the dancer's body appears solely as the rhythm everything depends on but is hidden by what it makes possible.*"

Luminous, to the point of being dazzling.

An armature, which is of no woman in particular, from which it derives its instability, through the veil of generality, draws the lightning bolt down on a fragment of form and divinizes it; or breathes out, in turn, through the undulation of the fabrics, the floating, palpitating, scattered ecstasy. Yes, the suspension of Dance, the contradictory fear of seeing too much and not enough, requires a transparent extension.

The poet, in a rich and subtle page,† has, in the process, given the ancient function back its character, so that it fills out. And without delay, he invokes Loie Fuller, inexhaustible

†*Le Figaro*, May 5, 1896. [—*Author*]

fountain of herself, next to whose development the network of imaginativeness—poured over her like atmosphere by the leaders of the chorus of ballerinas, their costumes much too short—lacks ambience, except for the orchestra, and one could wish that their costumes were simplified for the spiritual acrobatics that follow the smallest indications in the text, rather than that the fundamental thing exists, invisibly, in the pure movement and silence displaced by their leaps. The central near-nudity, except for a brief halo of skirts, either to cushion the fall or to lift up the points, shows merely her legs—with a significance other than personal, like a direct instrument of the idea.

Theater always alters, from a special or literary point of view, the arts it appropriates: music cannot participate without losing some of its depth and darkness; neither can song, which ceases to be a solitary lightning-bolt; and, strictly speaking, neither can one recognize in Ballet the name of Dance—which is, if you will, a hieroglyphic language.

I enjoy attaching these studies to each other by means of a running commentary, especially when invited to do so by a wise comrade who can think of the plastic rendition, on the stage, of poetry—whereas others turn their heads away so as not to admit to the public or to themselves that they could ever, given the right metamorphosis of images, use a Ballet for their own purposes, even though the function of space in their stanzas should suggest some analogy between leaps on the stage and verse on a page.

Silence! sole luxury after rhymes, an orchestra only marking with its gold, its brushes with thought and dusk, the detail of its signification on a par with a stilled ode and which it is up to the poet, roused by a dare, to translate! the silence of an afternoon of music; I find it, with contentment, also, before the ever-original reappearance of Pierrot or the epitome of poignancy and elegance, Paul Margueritte.

Such is this *Pierrot Assassin de sa Femme* [Pierrot Murderer of His Wife], composed and set down by himself, a mute soliloquy that the phantom, white as a yet unwritten page, holds in both face and gesture at full length to his soul. A whirlwind of naïve or new reasons emanates, which it would be pleasing to seize upon with security: the aesthetics of the genre situated closer to principles than any! nothing in this region of caprice foiling the direct simplifying instinct! . . . This: "The stage illustrates but the idea, not any actual action, in a Hymen (out of which flows Dream), tainted with vice yet sacred, between desire and fulfillment, perpetration and remembrance; here anticipating, there recalling, in the future, in the past, *under the false appearance of a present.* That is how the mime operates, whose act is confined to a perpetual allusion without breaking the ice or the mirror: he thus sets up a medium, a pure medium, of fiction." Fewer than a thousand lines, the role, the one that reads, will instantly comprehend the rules as if placed before the stageboards, their humble depository. Surprise, accompanying the artifice of a notation of sentiments by unproffered sentences—that, in the sole case, perhaps, with authenticity, between the sheets and the eye there reigns a silence still, the condition and delight of reading.

Of Genre and the Moderns[†]

L ET ME insert here a succinct parenthesis.

Theater is, by essence, superior.

Otherwise, evasive servant of a cult that one needs the authority of a god or the acquiescence of a whole crowd to instate according to principles, one would hesitate to devote these notes to it!

No poet could think himself foreign to such objectivity of the play of the soul: admitting that sometimes by traditional obligation the mantle of the critic falls on him, or he is very singularly summoned from exile; it would be precipitous to go see what is happening with him in his palace.

The attitude, from yesteryear to today, is very different.

In front of the immediate and frantic success of the monster or Mediocrity parading around in the divine space, I like the image of Gautier putting the black opera glasses over his exhausted eyes like a voluntary blindness, and murmuring, *"It's such a crude art . . . so abject,"* in front of the curtain: but since it wasn't up to him to let any disgust cancel out the prerogatives of the visionary, he continued, ironic, *"There should*

[†]Incomplete without Augier, Dumas, etc. [—*Author*]

be only one vaudeville—it would be changed somewhat from time to time.[†] Replace "vaudeville" by "mystery," that is, a tetralogy itself multiple unfolding parallel to the cycle of the seasons, and insist that the text be as incorruptible as the law: there, you have it! Almost.

Now that one has heard its skeleton creak supremely through the carpentry and cardboard of the beast, it is true, flourishing—a last panicked illumination of the paradox of flesh and song; or with lesser and more cynical imagination, assuring everyone that nothing exists but them, that what remains onstage is merely a group of people just like the spectators: now, I think, by avoiding confrontation with the monster face to face, considering his feigned candor, and even suggesting what might possibly replace him (for the new vision of the idea would just be, for him, another costume: he would put it on in order to deny it, just as the acrobatic trick is already starting to show through in the Ballet), veritably, I think that's enough to harass folly with! along with a rapid, clear glance at one difficult point or another. To try for more would be to lose one's force, which lies in shadowy beings who clam up as soon as they are half divulged, where thought takes refuge; or to declare abject a sublime medium just because our era shows it debased: no, I would feel too rich with regrets, and it's no sacrilege, to suggest the unsuspected splendor of the stage.

The stage, our only magnificence, to which the participation of diverse arts sealed by poetry contributes, according to me, a religious or official character, if one of these words has a meaning, I note that the century now ending couldn't care less about them, thus understood; that miraculous assembly of everything needed for the divine, except for human clairvoyance, will end up being for nothing.

---

†See volume 1 of the Goncourts' precious *Journal.* [—*Author*]

In the course of this kind of interregnum for Art, the sovereign, in which our era lingers, a genius must discern—but what? if not the unexplained but invading flood of exact theatrical forces: mime, juggling, dance, and simple acrobatics. This doesn't prevent people from coming to, living in, and going about in the city—a phenomenon that only hides, apparently, an intention to go occasionally to a show.

The stage is the obvious focus of pleasures taken in common, so, all things considered, it is also the majestic opening to the mystery whose grandeur one is in the world to envisage, the same thing that a citizen, having an inkling of it, expects from the State: to compensate him for his social diminishment. Can one imagine the governing entity (from the royal puppets—responding, with a mute come-on, to what was laughable in their beribboned persons—to the simple generals of today) being anything but disturbed before an ignoramus' pretension to the pomp, the splendor, the worship of the god he knows himself to be! After looking around, go back along the path that brought you to the mediocre city and, without tallying up your disappointments or blaming them on anyone, take the train back, presumptuous guest of the hour, to your little corner of un-heard-of reverie; or else stay; you'll never be as far away as here: then begin, all alone, according to the sum of expectations and dreams built up, your necessary spectacle. Satisfied to have arrived in a time when duty links the multiple actions of men, but at your exclusion (that pact torn up because it didn't exhibit a seal).

What did the Sirs and Madams do when they went out, in the absence of majesty and ecstasy according to their unanimous desires, to a play: they had to amuse themselves nevertheless; they could have, while Music surged up, taken a few monotonous steps into a salon. The jealous orchestra lends itself to nothing but ideal meanings expressed by the sylphide on stage. Conscious of being there to see, if not the miracle of Self, at least its Feast! or at the very least themselves as they know themselves in the streets or at home, look, as soon as the pitiful painted-canvas dawn rises, how they invade the stage, impatiently, agreeing to behave as they do every day and everywhere: they call to their friends and chat in a superficial voice about the nothings that, with precaution, make up their lives, while others, still in the hall, turning their heads to make sure their diamond earrings sparkle, as if saying, *I am pure of all that happens here,* or sporting sideburns whose dark line across the cheek says, *It's not about me,* conventionally and distractedly smiling at the intrusion onto the divine stage: which cannot endure this with impunity, because of a certain subtle glow of veracity and brutality, contained by its poorly concealed gas jets, now illuminating, in general postures of adultery or theft, the imprudent actors in this banal sacrilege.

I understand.

Dance alone, because of its twirls, along with mime appears to me to necessitate a real space, or stage.

At the limit, a piece of paper suffices to evoke every play: with the help of his multiple personality, everyone can act it in his head, which is not the case with pirouettes.

Thus, I make little distinction, to take an unexpected example, between the admiration I remember feeling upon reading Monsieur Becque and the pleasure I get from a live show. Whether the actor is reviving the beautiful text or whether it's my vision derived from my reading, what results (as in all the other works of this rare author) is a modern masterpiece in the style of classic theater. The sentences may espouse the voices as well as those of the Théâtre Français declaiming bitter or frank words; nevertheless, I perceive them written, in the immortality of a brochure: but with an aficionado's delight in seeing that the notation of truths or of sentiments done with an almost abstract—or simply literary, in the old sense of the term—precision, come, on stage, to life.

If I put off, when speaking of gestures and steps, outlining a new aesthetic, I shouldn't leave, for instance, this act,[†] perfect in its way, without noting that it has, like all products of the imagination, even exquisitely average or with a rather pedestrian story line, its own powerful touch of poetry somewhere: in the instrumental conduct of the timbres of dialogue, for example, or the repetitions, interruptions, and a whole technique that recalls the execution in chamber music of some fine concerto with a somewhat neutral tonality; plus (I smile) in the fact of the symbol. What could it be but a bourgeois allegory, delicious and true—pick up the play or go see it!—this apparition, to the marriageable young man, of a young woman surrounded by someone else's children, hastening the dénouement through a tableau of future maternity.

In opposition to any theater falsified by a thesis or enfeebled down to chromolithographs, there is its contrary; this dramatic author par excellence, for example (to anticipate any mention of the busts in the foyer), finds harmony in the opposition of types to actions. Thus, for the ugly, pretentious furniture that indicates this century's form of intimacy, a bourgeois tone and furniture from the last pure style before it—Louis XVI—is substituted. Suggestive analogy: in not seeing anything better or more contemporary than the silk that hangs from easy chairs, inside a mahogany trim, discreet, noble, and familiar, where the eye, never fooled by similarities recalling some blinding decorative allusion, does not risk fixing upon their crudenesses, then confusing, because of their twists, the bizarre luxury of its own chimera. I feel a certain sympathy for the workman who has crafted a minor but perfect work, a work nevertheless because a whole art inheres in it, a work

---

[†]*Les Honnêtes Femmes* [Virtuous Women]. [—*Author*]

that charms me through its fidelity to all that belongs to a simple and superb tradition, and neither obstructs nor obscures the future.

The misunderstanding that can exist between the gawkers and the master, if no one cuts it short by admiration, for example, comes from the fact that, in a problematic hope for newness, one expects something entirely made up. Whereas here we see a new, unexpected, and glorious extension of a classic genre right in the middle of modernity, with our own experiences, or I don't know what form of disinterest amounting almost to cruelty, that has never appeared so clearly before this century. Another thing about *La Parisienne* especially: it's to aim at something better than a masterpiece, so brightly does the writer's wisdom shine in this product of his sprightly maturity: Will he surpass *Les Corbeaux?*† I hardly wish for it and would be suspicious of it. Performed, one by one, on some official stage, a reprise of all the plays that, the first night, have seemed obvious, so that the scholar can cluster around them some examples of the genre from which he alone, from a very particular point in history, rather late in our literature, has extracted the lively or sober beauty. Don't feign impatience to be surprised; the fact takes place, finishing off with a stricter illumination than the former geniuses could have lit, its revelation or our French comedy of manners.

Since I have a taste, in addition but differently, for light farce, just as profound as other genres without ever taking on a heavy tone, given that it's already enough if life affects such a tone toward us, nothing deserving the swell of the orchestra with angers, blame, complaints! a score here kept silent according to a rhythmic balance in the structure, in which contrasting or inside-out scenes appear opposite each other from

---

†*La Parisienne* (The Parisian Woman) and *Les Corbeaux* (The Crows): both are plays by Henry Becque. [—*Trans.*]

one act to another, or else in the leaps or comings and goings in all directions of Fantasy, a pinch of whose skirt erases, or whose gauziness reveals, a transparency of allusions to any ridicule; for example, in the case of Monsieur Meilhac.†

Some novels, from their former mental state, have taken on body, voice, and flesh, and given up their base of immaterial coloring to canvas and gas.

The novel—I don't know how to consider it in the hands of masters who have brought to it such vast changes (when formerly all one had to do was pin down its aesthetic), without admiring it for single-handedly sweeping the modern completely off the stage as being disastrous and empty and abstaining from action above all.

The perfect text refuses all adventure, to restrict itself to its chaste evocation, on the tain of memories, like that extraordinary figure, both eternal phantom and breath! when nothing immediate or external happens, in a present that plays at its own effacement in order to cover up the most hybrid undersides. If our outward agitation is disturbing on the screen of printed sheets, how much more shocking it is on the stage, where materiality seems to rise up in a gratuitous obstruction. Yes, the Book or the monograph it becomes, about a type (the closely packed pages like a coffin, defending, against the brutalities of space, a refolded infinite delicacy constituting intimacy for the being to itself), suffices along with many new processes analogous in rarefaction to the subtlest aspects of life. Through a mental operation and no other, as a reader I abstract the character's physiognomy, without the displeasure of an exact face leaning out over the footlights over my source or soul. All his features reduced to words, a stance giving way

†Henri Meilhac (1837–1897), who did much of his work in collaboration with others, co-signed many operettas of Offenbach and many adaptations of novels (for example, *Manon Lescaut*). [—*Trans.*]

to the identical disposition of the sentence, this whole pure result obtained for my noble delectation, objects to any actor that one can go and see as his public somewhere. Unless, like me, you enjoy reopening, each winter, one of the exquisite and poignant works of Messieurs de Goncourt; for you'll learn—although the cadence of my sentences slows down and moves farther away and defers what I'm going to say about one of the princes of contemporary letters—that all this dilatory artifice of respect is aimed at the interesting, clever, and quasi-original adaptation that he himself made of his masterpiece. To the lack of taste, it's easy to whisper truths that the written work trumpets better, but I bring an attenuation: I call, not from a theatrical point of view, but for the integrity of the literary work, because of the even more coarse context it is now in, for a scenic restitution of what was, beforehand, extracted from the novel by some delicious, subtle strategy of analysis.

And . . . and—I'm speaking here of a perception of an atmosphere transposed from poetry to the world—answer if there remains a satisfactory relation, here, between the actors' way of appearing and speaking, and the ungraspable character of life's subtlety. Conventions! You will be able to show, in the theater, a paradise more believable than a salon.

Monsieur Daudet, I think, has pondered without preconception the birth of the novel on the stage, and his gifts, to further that end, follow no law but an impeccable tact. He produces an art that disturbs and seduces as if some truth lay behind the ambiguity between the written and the played, neither of these two. There pours from the stage, almost omitting the volume, a charm unknown to the theater. If the perfidious and cherished present intrudes in the form of an advertisement—a path toward the thought of someone else, toward a writing—it flashes the talisman of the page; but here one is captivated, on the other hand, by the ancient enchantment of a gilded hall, the show implying something direct and as if coming from everyone, like a liberated vision. The actor avoids scanning his steps by dramatic habit, but he steps over a silent carpet on a sonorous trampoline between stepping and leaping. There is an infinite—up to delight—subdivision of what would have to be called, to modify a famous formula, *a scene not to attempt,* at least at the present time, when people can think of only one thing: to eradicate every code from the past. "Never to do or say anything that can be exactly copied in the theater." The soul-shock, without the possibility of abandoning oneself to it as in a poem, occurs briefly now and then: a shout, a start, with a lightness of touch and the insight of a man who keeps his eye focused, exceptionally, on our world.

New, concise, luminous features, even if the Book loses thereby, urge us toward a limited theater.

The intention, come to think of it, lying in the folds of French tragedy was not to reanimate the ashes of antiquity but to produce, in almost no real context, some of the grand human poses or something like our moral raw material.

To find a sculptor making statues equal, for example, to the internal operation of Descartes: if the signifying stage of those days didn't benefit from it, with their unity of character, joining theater and philosophy, we have to blame the notorious taste that era had for erudition, refraining from inventing, though ready to; failing to breathe life into the abstract type, though analytical and neutral. One page of those Greek and Latin fanatics might have helped the transfer. The figure of an ideal leap didn't eliminate or satisfy the modes or scholarly obsessions of that century.

Only something instinctual, something that gave a beautiful musculature to phantoms, survived.

If I detail the contrary or perhaps similar idea of that man with such a simple viewpoint, Monsieur Zola, accepting modernity as the definitive era (above which flies away the heroic Louis XIV cameo), he aims to establish there, as on a general and stable ground, the drama of oneself underpinned by no fable, except what has been in the headlines. The poets, our ancestors, used as a means of sublimation an old charming vice, too much ease in identifying the rhythmic elegance of a synthesis, coming near the sought-after formula, differing today only by an analytic hinge, multiplying the lifelikenesses and the bruises of chance.

When one of life's storms comes to an end, people of our time, let's remember the care we take to counter every sudden gesture or outcry disturbing our sobriety and sit down to a conversation. Thus, and during that sober talk, the orchestra begins its surge from underneath, catching up the spectator; that's when his Phèdre, *Renée*, subjugates me . . . Each emotional attitude, barely hinted at, is firmly resolved by even familiar characters. What is specific about the attitude of our time, or even the supreme human one, is never to speak before deciding, which is quite different from the earlier habit of letting the emotions of indecision furnish our beloved raw material; thus, we carry within us the impersonality of grand occasions.

This law, which excludes traditional art, no! dictated classical theater to an uninterrupted debate; thus, it's through that relation, and not through analogies between now and, say, the seventeenth century, that I maintain that the recent comedy of manners resembles the former!

See for yourself: you always knowingly, either before or after, treat the situation; a contemporary tries to elucidate it by a pure appeal to one's judgment, as if it always concerned someone else, and without considering the judge at stake. The triple combat between Saccard and the father of the heroine, then with Renée, resolving into a trade the sinister forebodings, illustrates this, to the point where no dramatic overture seems to me more modern, because of everyone's anticipated self-mastery.

This voluntary effacement of anything external, however, cannot be extended without outbursts, and the succinct bolt of lightning that will serve as the trigger against so much constraint, and so many useless precautions against the magnificent act of living, brands with violence the poor wretch, as if caught red-handed, who suffers such an interdiction against appearing as he is.

There you can see a present-day tragic theory, or, better, the last one: drama, which is latent, appears only through a gash in the surface spectacle, affirming the irreducibility of our instincts.

When a novelist adapts one of his novels for the theater, it seems, to someone who has become blasé, like just another so-called genre play, except for the splendor, at every turn, of qualities magnified until they merit a point of view: refining into an intuition the whetted curiosity which suggests that there exists between that and the things played daily, a difference—
An absolute difference . . .

The conventional veil of tone, concept, etc., that hovers in each hall, hanging from the crystal chandeliers—perspicacious themselves—its fabric of falsity, and presenting the stage as banal, has seemed to catch fire on the gas jets! And innocent, morbid, surly, brutal, with classic nudity, step forward each of the characters.

Meanwhile, not far away, the thorough washing of the Temple, accomplished to my astonishment by the orchestra, pouring out its floods of glory or sadness—don't you hear it?—of which the restored but still invisible Dancer, finishing her preparatory ceremonies, seems the topmost moving foam.

There was once a theater, the only one I willingly went to, the Eden, significant of today's state, with its godlike Italian resurrection of dances offered for our vulgar pleasure, while around back waited the monotonous promenade. The glow of false electric skies bathed the modern crowd, in jackets, holding satchels; then, through the sounds' exaltation of an imbecilic gold and laughter, there descended on the glitter of sequins or skin the irremissible lassitude, mute with all that isn't first illuminated by the spirit. Sometimes, I thought, when the conductor lifted his baton, it was the tap of an old-time fairy's magic wand, transforming a multicolor crowd gradually into a glittering, garrulous sorcerer, a rare and charming effect; but of all this and of the light shed on the masses' movements according to their subtle leaders, the watchword remained for the collection plates of the finales, glumly mourning the beyond, followed by the polyglot idiocy of amazement before the exhibition of the means of beauty, in a hurry to spread the enlightenment around, toward some simplifying rendering of accounts: for prostitution in this place—and that was an aesthetic sign—in front of the satiety of frills and nudity, swore off even the puerile extravagance of plumes, trains, or makeup, and only triumphed in the underhanded and brutal fact of its presence among uncomprehended wonders. Yes, I returned again and again to that place and to its flagrant case which occupied so much of my reverie, but in vain, without such music as we know equals silence or the gushing of voices, or the claims of the ones who occupy an ideal function—La Zucchi, La Cornalba, La Laus—setting aside with a kick of the leg the banal conflict, new, enthusiastic, and designated by a supreme foot above the venalities of the surrounding atmosphere, higher even than the stars painted on the ceiling.

Time to bid that very instructive exploitation adieu.

In the absence of a ballet expiring in luxurious tiredness, this singular local spot, for two years already, has enthroned the purified symphony via the Sunday vesper bells, not by enlarging the cherished French melodrama until there is harmony between the verse and the instrumental tumult (which is the aim of dance and sometimes of the poet), but by creating a whole art, the most comprehensive art of our time, such that through the omnipotence of a still-archaic total genius it landed and planted itself among us, validating the origins of a rival race: it was *Lohengrin*, by Richard Wagner.

O the pleasure of hearing, with a reverence found at the altar of any poetic sense, what is, until now, the truth; then to be able, through an expression even foreign to our own hopes, to emit, meanwhile and without misunderstanding, words.

Never has the elite, concerned to worship properly something splendid, received a worse slap in the face than that given by the mob demanding, with or without the government, that such a masterpiece, panicked itself by itself, be suppressed: this type of possible shame had not been envisaged by me; I've seen worse, and can only greet this with indifference, but now some tempest in a sewer strikes out against superiority and spits on it.

A certain carelessness about the initial productions, not to say a certain inattention, perhaps, to their solemnity, where a pronounced presence amid all the striking scenery, demands, instead of these notes scribbled hastily or transcribing the ringing of the aftermath still in my ears, my full attention, facing ahead, orthodox, on pleasures that I only feel half-heartedly: other diffuse reasons were added, even in an exceptional case, to make me neglect the means and the being of raising the French curtain on Wagner. I felt unwell; the rest is known; it's in fleeing the homeland that, from now on, we can satisfy our soul's appetite for the beautiful.

What folly, especially in the political sense that invades everything—even I'm talking about it!—to have lost an elementary occasion, fallen from the sky, and that we should have embraced, to show to a hostile nation the courtesy that can undo the sniping news item; all we had to do was salute a Genius in his blinding glory.

Everyone, again we are faced with the road to the cult of art at the present time (although, in my opinion, Germany's art reveals new and pompous bastardy), obliged to take the road abroad, not without feeling the displeasure the simple instinct of the artist feels, upon leaving home: but he must leave as soon as he can drink his fill from something necessitated by his thirst.

Stages and Pages

THE OCCASION presented itself not long ago to study both a new dramatic work and certain dispositions of the Parisian public that were secret even to itself: along with the proclamation of superior sentiments, nothing captivates me as much as reading their reflection in the undecipherable numerous face of an audience.

I go back to the recent literary gala given by Monsieur Edouard Dujardin to produce *La Fin d'Antonia* [The End of Antonia].

The author presents one of today's interesting figures. That of the man of letters, burning with a continuous and pure flame—novelist with *Les Hantises* [The Obsessions], *Les Lauriers sont coupés* [The Laurels Have Been Felled], poet with *La Gloire d'Antonia* [In Praise of Antonia], *Pour la Vierge du roc ardent* [For the Virgin of the Burning Rock], and *La Réponse de la bergère au berger* [The Shepherdess's Answer to the Shepherd]; but not a professional; a man of the world, sportsman, editor (founder of the Journals called *Indépendante* and *Wagnérienne*); tomorrow he could unfurl the sail, made from something other than vellum, of some remarkable yacht. I'd like to see him for an hour, wearing evening clothes, a shower of orchids on the inside of his suit, three-quarters in shadow because the footlights are out, with a pretty inclination to the whole mysterious attitude, examining carefully, through his monocle, his prologue: Whistleresque. For three

consecutive summers he invited Paris to see the three parts—
each one a modern tragedy—of *La Légende d'Antonia* [The
Legend of Antonia]. This time, specially, for the conclusion,
he did it up big. He rented the elegant, fashionable hall of
Vaudeville, exceptionally, and rows of plants, decorated for
the occasion, stretched into the street, to the point of tying
up traffic. . . . In my view, a mistake! although I don't impute
it to any personal ostentatiousness on the part of the impresario (he strikes me as uninterested in any facile fame, or gull-
ible about the value of the work, frankly): for the impact and
confirmation of the latter, he gathered together, around a
primitive vision, distant and naked, in addition to regular
theatergoers, the boulevard.

The adventure might have turned out differently from the
smattering of laughs that were exalted to the point of uneasiness, interrupting the respectful attentiveness of the magnificent hall, with its forthright applause. In fact, if, in place of
the supreme or intact aristocracies of literature and the arts,
one begins to feign a need, almost a cult—one turns away,
aesthetically, from the intermediary games proposed to the
bulk of the public, toward the exception or the minor indication, everyone wanting to show that he is capable of understanding something rare. I perceive in this the worst of all
things, and the best way to smother the delicate idea for the
future (there won't remain anything withheld); and finally, I
lament hypocritically, there is a danger for this artificial elite.
Stupefaction, more intense than boredom, which twists mouths
that have stifled a yawn, for one feels that it's out of place and
that the play is delightful, only for someone else, very far
away. Relaxation from this new torture would come with the
possibility of laughing, abundantly, with a whole room, if an
incident helps it along—for example, if an actress trips on her
train, or says a word with an unintended double meaning. I
have been able, along with the quick intelligence of the majority, to perceive the beginnings, on several faces, of this cruel

contemporary phenomenon: *to be where you want to be and feel foreign there.* I'm just pointing it out to psychology.

Armed in advance with an argument or program in hand, as is the custom at concerts, isn't the spectator going to recognize here a musical celebration of life, confining the mystery to language alone or to the development of mimicry?

Let me here transcribe the program notes:

"In the first part of the legend, the female lover meets the male lover; the male lover dies. In the second part, 'Le Chevalier du passé' [The Knight of the Past], the female lover has become a courtesan; but in the midst of her triumph, the past reappears and teaches her the vanity of her glory; she leaves.

"Now she is a beggar. She has given up her former desires, and wants nothing but the silence and solitude of withdrawal; a spiritual life outside the world and above nature (as religious life used to be) was the goal she thought possible. Thus, her ascetic's pride has accepted being the beggar who holds out her hand for her daily bread."

I would not know how to characterize the dramatis personae better than this, except to say that with respect to each other and unbeknownst to them, they execute a kind of dance, the measure of the progress of the work. Very melodically, with utter smoothness; moved by the inner orchestra of their diction. Modernity fits well with these somewhat abstract traps and turns, really unexpected if one didn't already know to what extent the general and the neutral predominate, or see how apt our clothing is to express style, even a topcoat, as we saw in the two performances before this; the third did not require this reflection. Here the relation, according to the setting and the costumes, which have become pastoral, establishes it-

self effortlessly between a naïve art and broad emotions and
truths, ample, grave, primordial.

This parenthesis—

I don't reject, by taste, any simplification, and even hope
for one, equal to parallel complexities: but theater institutes
prominent characters who act and are seen so as to block
metaphysics, just as the actor makes one not see the presence of the *lustre*. They will not turn toward anything outside themselves except through the elemental and obscure cry
of passion. Without this rule, one would succeed too easily,
through scholastic or analytical illuminations, in naming the
absolute: the invocation addressed to it by the woodsmen
seems to me to proceed too directly. The summit of a holy
mountain in the background, itself intersected by a patch of
sky, undeniably suggesting a beyond, sufficed, remaining invisible; and, reinforced by the purity of souls, dawn could
break, as an unconscious hymn on the day of liberation . . .
What good is a setting, if it doesn't maintain that image:
the human translator has, poetically, only to let himself be
haunted by and render this obsession.

The main attraction Monsieur Dujardin's experiment exerts
on me comes undoubtedly from his verse forms. I want to
keep, for some extraordinary use of speech, which, to an inexpert ear, sometimes dilutes itself into prose, the name of
verse. In what, exactly, does verse inhere? not always in the
artifice of blanks or the arrangement on the page in books; every piece of cut-up text by itself doesn't make one; and it's
only through the repetition of its multiple game that I perceive the metrical pattern at all. This transformable fabric
around everything undulates until, at a certain point, it bursts
with the luxury essential to versification, spaces itself out, dis-
seminates itself, and preciously fits the verbal action on stage:

is this a happiness? more! I've almost reached an instinct! Here are some rhymes shooting out from a short stem, gathering together, spreading out, spinning wildly, calling attention to a certain emotional theme, which becomes a major crux. The well-known traditional prosodic devices cluster here, there, fading away by layers, in order to reappear, suddenly, in a burst, of extreme altitude. This is readily called recourse to the Wagnerian stamp: it indicates, rather, how everything French tends to limit itself. In the intermission that French poetry is going through right now, given that now is the time to give it this leisure, it seems to me obvious that the old and perfect effects, taken apart piece by piece by Monsieur Dujardin or any other, deconstructed and lined up in order, should be, in his work, spontaneously remolded according to their originary sympathies, in order to improvise some entirely new state. I'm happy to stay with this explanation, especially since it designates a memorable rhythmic case.

Everything—the magnificent instrumental polyphony, the lively gestures of dance or the voices of men or gods, the excess attention paid to the material sumptuousness of the decoration—we consider, with Wagner, blinded by such cohesion or a whole artform, in the triumph of genius, what poetry has become today. Does this mean that the traditional writer of verse, he who works with the humble and sacred artifices of language alone, will try, crowned somehow by those very constraints, to compete? Yes, like an opera without orchestra or song, just spoken; at present now the book will try to suffice to open up the inner stage and whisper echoes into it. A versified collection summons one to an ideal representation: motifs of exaltation or dream are linked together or detach themselves, according to the design or their individuality. One portion sways in a rhythm or movement of thought, another opposes it: both of them swirl around, where there intervenes, emerging like a mermaid whose tail is taken for foliage or the curlicues of an arabesque, a figure, which the idea remains.

Anyone who has really looked at nature contains inside himself a theater inherent to the mind, a summary of types and correspondences; just as any volume confronts them, opening up its parallel pages. The haphazard collection, and there are indeed such, the present volume not excepted, where chance, and the author's obsessions should be understood here, should never be anything but simulated. There is a certain symmetry, like that which reigns in every edifice, even the most vaporous, of vision and dream. The pleasure vainly sought by the late Dreamer-King of Bavaria in solitary attendance at the unfolding of scenery, is found, in retreat from the baroque crowd rather than in its absence from the bleachers, achieved by restoring the text, in its nakedness, to the spectacle. With two pages and their lines of verse, and the accompaniment of my whole self, I supply the world! Or at least I perceive, discreetly, its drama.

The modern tendency to remove the work or poem from all representational contingency, whether coarse or exquisite, has dominated very strict intellects, especially that of Monsieur de Regnier, as a look at his *Poems* will suggest. To install one's work in the convergence of fragments that harmonize with a center, which then becomes the source of the latent drama that ebbs and flows throughout the poem, designates the resulting manner, and I admire no less the direction of Monsieur Ferdinand Herold, giving us openly and without reticence the action of the play; the actors noticed for their bearing and their pronunciation, or for the site, or for the songs, a whole multiple score with integral speeches.

Quite different is the art of Monsieur Maeterlinck, who also inserts theater into the book!

He doesn't do it symphonically as we have just described, but with a purposeful succession of scenes, à la Shakespeare; it is fitting to pronounce the name, even though there are no apparent similarities with that god, except the necessary ones. Monsieur Octave Mirbeau, who safeguards the honor of the press by making sure each exceptional work gets talked about, at least once, by him—but with what fire!—was right, to awaken every eye, to invoke Shakespeare, as an enormous, peremptory literary sign; he then nuanced his descriptions with delicate senses.

Lear, Hamlet himself, and Cordelia, Ophelia, I cite only those who go deep into the legend and their special distance, influence every life, tangible, intense: when read, they leap off the page and are suddenly corporeal. I envisaged *La Princesse Maleine* differently when I read the play one afternoon; she remained the innocent and strange character I knew, where abandon dominated, with reason, a context where nothing simply human would go. The walls, massively blocking off all reality, shadows, basalt, the emptiness of a hall—the walls, of a certain width but far from the hangings, and weathered with the local weather—before becoming holes, their faded inhabitants stretched, one tragic time, a member that was normally stiff, and smiling, stuttered or mumbled, alone, the word of their destiny. And all this time the vulgar swear that no one existed and nothing happened on those slabs. Bruges, Gand, land of primitives, decay . . . we are far away, with these phantoms, from Shakespeare.

Pelléas et Mélisande exhales on stage the delight of pages. What do I mean? These brief tableaux are supreme: anything preparatory or mechanical has been rejected so that the essential, which for the spectator comes out of the performance, can appear. It seems that the piece is a superior variation of the admirable old melodrama. Almost silently and abstractly, to the point where in this art, where everything becomes music in the strict sense of the word, even the part of a pensive instrument like the violin is disturbing, as unnecessary. Maybe such a tacit atmosphere leads to the anguish the author feels that makes him say things twice, to be sure they are said, or to assure them, for lack of anything else, a consciousness modeled on the echo. A frequent charm, otherwise inexplicable, among hundreds; which could be wrongly called devices.

The Poet—to return to my obsession—outside of prodigious occasions like a Wagner, awakens, in writing, the Master of Ceremonies of everyone's private feast day; or, if he convokes the public, he shows it the authenticity of his intimate munificence, which blazes forth with charm.

Solemnity

BUT WHENCE comes my affliction, exhibited with such dandyism, that gives me my incompetence about anything other than the absolute? It's the doubt that makes one at first abominate the intruder, with wares different from the ecstasy and the feasts the priest knows, who vainly puts on a vacuity of insignia, in order to, nevertheless, officiate.

With the impudence of a trompe-l'oeil news brief, to fill a theater and exclude Poetry, playing sublimities (keeping the spectator's hope alive), does not seem to me worse than to seem to show it and throw it into the spectator's yawn as something special; or to instate the deity in some doltish and vulgar—but perhaps meritorious—design is about the same as omitting it.

The quibble, the only quarrel I have with a false temple, even if called the Odéon, is not that it favors one side over the other—its side is composed of pseudo-attributions and depends on architecture—but, as the façade of an artificial cult, caring for a vestal virgin in order to feed with a pharmaceutical flame *the great art nevertheless!* that it resorts meticulously and accurately to the same mixture as that used by great art, to preserve the ho-hum inscription *Ponsard* as if it were something fundamental and true. A denial of justice for the year gone by or the one to come affirms itself here, as an observation, where I see with some displeasure a national stamp put on the realization that the present is not fertile for such products, and one prefers to fill up the void with what pretends to exist so that no one will notice the lack of what is not. On the contrary, and first of all in my notes, we are in the half-light, and you, priestess of an empty crypt, have not had to put your hand on any of the well-labeled vials which decorate themselves at birth, through thrift and once and for all, with the dust of their eternity. Ponsard wouldn't get my back up more than anyone else, if it weren't for the fact that, and I almost applaud him for this—his fame derives from it—he had the unheard-of effrontery, risked, extravagant, of persuading a clique that he represented, in the lack of all splendor, Poetry in the theater, whenever the god appeared. I admire him for this, having kept Hugo in mind, of whom he was certainly well aware, to the point where, of humble, unwell, and impoverished birth, he played the part of one duty-bound to surge into the spotlight, for lack of anyone else; he constrained himself, after all, to efforts with a vigorous stamp. Mischievousness a bit broad, but funny! which many of us recall; but its commemoration is not a reason to suddenly summon a new generation. How ardently, in my heart of hearts and from the bottom of my naïve, just soul, I harbor a predilection for nourishing, without wanting to revive them to the detriment of any contemporary, as authentic substitutes for the Poet, who bring out our smile, or theirs perhaps if they feign one, with the sole purpose of modestly denying, in the space of the total extinction of lyricism—and the Luce de Lancivals or Campistrons that haunt it—that harmful vacancy: they have, around what was once their soul, pulled tight as clothing a rag worn thin to expose their procedures and techniques rather than to admit the Goddess's veil gone in a rent or a loss to mourn. These larvae remain touching, and I pity their descendents, too, like people who maintain the honor of an altar whose fists are curled with sleep. All are instructive before becoming grotesque, imitators or forerunners, they receive a sacred deposit from one century and transmit to the next what precisely is not, or, if it were, it would be better not to know! a residue of art, axioms, formulas, nothing.

One evening empty of magnificence or fun, I opened, in quest of compensation, the radiant poem "Le Forgeron" [The Blacksmith]† in order to learn from it some solitary truths.

Any poem composed for a reason other than to obey the ancient genius of verse, is not a poem . . . You might—before the invitation of the rhyme, here extraordinary because it is one with the alexandrine, which, in its poses and the multiplicity of its play, seems devoured by its rhyme as if that sparkling cause of delight triumphed from the very first syllable; before the sudden wing beat that carries you off—you might once, and that's even every day's occupation, have had an idea of the concept to treat, but undeniably in order to forget it in its ordinary sense, and to give yourself wholly to the dialectic of Verse. As a jealous rival, to whom the dreamer yields mastery, it resuscitates, to the degree that it, glorious and philosophical and imaginative, revives a celestial vision of humanity! without it, there is just beautiful discourse out of some mouth. In this new—sublime—state, there is a fresh beginning of the conditions and materials of thought, laid down naturally for a prose study: the vocables, by themselves, after this difference and the experience of the beyond, find their virtue.

No one, ostensibly, ever since the explosion of the poetic phenomenon, has summed up with more daring and candor than perhaps that unmediated and original spirit, Théodore de Banville, and the years' purification of his individuality in verse designates him a special being, superior, and drinking from an occult and eternal source; for, made younger in the admirable sense that a child is closer to nothingness and transparency, it is something other than enthusiasm or lyric delir-

---

†"Le Forgeron" was collected in the poetic volume *Les Villages illusoires* (Illusory Villages) by the Belgian poet and friend of Mallarmé, Emile Verhaeren (1855–1916). [—*Trans.*]

ium that lifts him to continual poetic heights: outside of any breath, perceived as gross, virtually in the juxtaposition of words alone, according to an absolute meter which requires a speaker, the poet dissimulated or the reader, whose voice is modified toward mellowness or loudness, in order to sing.

Thus emerges from itself the principle that is nothing other than—Verse! It attracts as well as sheds for its unfolding (the time it takes for it to shine and then die like a rapid flower, on something transparent like the ether) the thousands of elements of beauty crowding together and ordering themselves according to their real, essential value. A Sign! in the central abyss of a spiritual impossibility that says that nothing can belong exclusively to everything, the divine denominator of our apotheosis, some supreme mold for something that doesn't exist in the same sense as other objects: from which it borrows, in order to revivify a seal, many scattered veins of ore, unknown and floating like unclaimed riches, and forges them together.

This—I slide into an observation—is why, in our language, lines of verse go by twos or more, by reason of their terminal accord, that is, the mysterious law of Rhyme, which reveals itself with the function of guardian, and prevents any one of them from dominating, or peremptorily staying: in what thought was *this* made! Who cares? given that as soon as its material is debated, it becomes debatable, gratuitous; momentary and double like flight, the identity of the two halves being stamped by their parity in sound.†
Every page of the program announces and tosses up, like vibratory gold traits, those sacred rules of the first and last of

†This is the superiority of modern verse over ancient verse, which forms a whole but doesn't rhyme; it fills up, once and for all, the metal used to make it, instead of taking it, rejecting it, becoming it, proceeding musically: taking a stand, making a Diptych. [—*Author*]

the Arts. It's an intellectual spectacle that impassions me: the other, drawn from storytelling or pretexts, is comparable to it.

Venus, from the blood of Love begat, is immediately desired by the Olympians and especially Jupiter: upon whose orders Venus, a virgin refusing every suitor, in order to reduce their depredations, subjects herself to the chains of Hymen with Vulcan, the latent maker of masterpieces, whom woman or human beauty, blending them all, compensates by her choice (this has to be explained in the fewest words possible, given that language is the substance of the artwork itself).

What a show! the whole world is in it; a book in our hand, if it pronounces some august idea, takes the place of all theaters, not through the oblivion it causes but by imperiously recalling them, on the contrary. The metaphoric sky that spreads around the lightning bolt of verse, the artifice par excellence to the point of simulating little by little and then incarnating the heroes (just enough not to be disturbed by their presence, one trait); this spiritually and magnificently illuminated backdrop of ecstasy is what is purest in ourselves, ready to surge up when the occasion arises, which in existence or outside art is always lacking. Music, too, is necessary, but the instrumentation of an orchestra tends to reproduce or fake it. One has to admire, in its all-powerful simplicity, or faith in the vulgar and superior technique, elocution, then the metrics that hone it to its ultimate expression, like a spirit, hiding among the pages, defying a whole civilization that neglects to build for his dream, so that they will take place, the prodigious Hall and the Stage. The mime absent and the preludes and finales, too, by the woodwinds, the brasses, and the strings, that spirit, placed above circumstances, expects the obligatory accompaniment of all the arts, or does without it, indifferently. The only one to arrive on time, because the time is ceaselessly or never, he appears like a messenger, bringing the book with a gesture or his lips, before effacing himself; and whoever retains the general bedazzlement multiplies it to everyone, from the fact of communication.

The marvel of a real Poem, as here, seems to me to be that—arising from conditions that authorize its visible unfolding and its interpretation—it first lends itself, and then little by little, ingenuously if need be, it only replaces all for lack of all. I imagine that the cause of going out together and assembling, in view of festivals inscribed in the human program, will not be the theater, limited or incapable of responding all by itself to subtle instincts, nor music, which in any case is too fleeting not to disappoint the crowd: but founding in oneself something vague and brutal that these two isolate—an Ode, dramatized or cut up knowingly; these heroic scenes making an ode in several voices.

Yes, the cult that was promised to ceremonials, imagine what it could be, think! It's simply the mystery, old or of all time, that the wave, for example, of recent symphonic concerts tried to put in the shadows, instead of freeing it, badly installed on stage, and making it reign.

Even in Wagner's work—which a poet, the most superbly French poet, consoles one for not invoking everywhere here—I perceive not theater, in the strict sense (without contest one would find more, from a dramatic point of view, in the Greeks or in Shakespeare), but the legendary vision which suffices under the veil of sonorities and blends in there; what's more, neither are his orchestral scores, when compared with those of Beethoven or Bach, simply music. Something special and complex results, situated in the convergences with other arts, issued from and governed by Fiction or Poetry.

A work like that given to us, in full wisdom and vigor, by Théodore de Banville, is literary in its essence, but doesn't fold back entirely into the mental instrument par excellence—

the book! The fact that the actor, squeezed into the obviousness of prose, and inserted in the rests of the orchestral sumptuousness which translate the rare lines of prose before the
precious stones and fabrics of the next scene, spread out better
than it would be before the amazed gaze, each scene having a
stage-set or a site that is certainly ideal, all this in order to
divinize the character's approach, already summoned only to
show through the majesty and amplitude of Place! I assert
that, as a proud and enlightened subject of the modern era—
aesthetic and industrial—the culmination of that spring that
began to flow in the Renaissance, but was limited to inventing
technical refinements; this grandiose and persuasive development of the actor's recitation—for one must have recourse to
this term when speaking of verse—charm and instruct; despite the gods' classical origins, but stormy for their type (are
we very far away, now, from mythic invention?), above all
will impress the People; in any case, nothing so well presents a
character of textuality, for the celebration of official festivities
in traditional and contemporary taste: like the Opening of a
Jubilee, notably in the figurative sense of concluding a cycle
of History; which seems to me to require the ministry of the
Poet.

Music

and

Letters

How DIFFICULT it becomes for a Frenchman, even perplexing in his case, to judge things in other countries! Such confusion, to say nothing of the fog, is what I bring back from England. Invited to "lecture" at Oxford and Cambridge, and, politeness obliging me to accept the tour of local marvels, presented by two very different visits—one impressive, perhaps, and the other intimate—I'd like now to draw some generalizations.

The well-known path comes to an end at penetrating, enveloping, definitive London. Its monumental fog can no more be separated from the city in one's mind than the light and wind lifting layers of material up above the buildings, in order to drop them again, suffocatingly, immensely, superbly. The mists, reliquefied, seem to flow nearby with the Thames.

It took the trains an hour and a quarter to reach the learned cities: I had my reasons.

Ask anyone in this amiable communion—that of study—and they will tell you that among these colleges in every style, nothing clashes: medieval, Tudor, interspersed with airy fields of cows and deer, with flowing springs, perfect for training exercises. Great Britain places great store in giving its generations an athletic upbringing. The University links these convents or clubs, the princely heritage, liberalities.

Everything—that the youth of England are able to shelter their growth in the architecture of pensive buildings—would be simple, including even congregating with a presence of men, their elders, unique across Europe and the world, who, in my opinion, are more important than the storied stone, and I was thoroughly amazed by them. Today, if asked how to perfect an impression of beauty, truly the flower and result I would choose would be these same *Fellows*.

Each collegial residence for centuries has secluded a group of these lovers of learning, who succeed each other by electing each other. A vacancy comes up; "So-and-so [they agree], in London or anywhere, could be one of us." They vote, and then call him. There is only one condition: the chosen individual must be a university graduate. From then on, for his entire life, he simply draws on his stipend. Invariably. If he prefers some British landscape to constantly meditating by the same window, or wants to compose, in his designated chair, one of the tomes that line the walls, or to haunt the refectory—big as a cathedral, built over a considerable wine cellar—he can do so, or even find his stipend, if he's a traveler, waiting in some bank of Italy or of the whole world. Most of them stay put, and respect the clause that forbids marriage within these monasteries of science. Experiments and discoveries are made in this setting more easily than elsewhere; here I met the most accomplished prose writer of our time. There's no need to bargain for anything, even tacitly; they live freely, unconstrained. That's the most important feature. A voluntary renunciation of the present goes along with the post: after one has been named a Somebody, the only rule is that one should persist, and all the means are provided except adversity. It's a luxury to be able to praise others for their esteem of precious fellow men, and isn't completely useless.

We would cry scandal.

In order for this exception, whose charm stays with me, to work—ordinary, elegant, prestigious—one needs an untroubled traditional ground: one where the populous provinces of iron and dust eagerly pant to support the twin flowering, in marble, of cities built for thought.

Our own structure seems organized so that nothing comparable to these privileged retreats can cast a doctoral shadow, like a robe, around the steps of a few delightful gentlemen.

A single motive suffices for one to deprive oneself in this way: mistrust, in which an instinct for absolute justice can be discerned. The English conception testifies to a different social generosity.

The Académie, here, is not comparable, with its plans and rules.

So near the end of the term and the summer vacation, I like to fix in my mind these retreats that I should forget (granted, they're not to our taste), and to avoid, without some equivalence for my friends and me, a mental farewell.

From the past, I saw immediately, there is a perpetual new beginning, along with the season, of sunsets to come: like the concept of Cloisters. There is a certain distaste for it in a democracy: in our case, we abolish, deny, disparage. I insist on the phrase "from the past"—it helps us to disengage, with a sigh, from a lesson, majestic as a choir, which will not be silenced; and neither will the droning of some Fellow, who continues to speak, not without insight, on a French topic, refined, literary—provided that some still exist—undeniably, on this spring day a hundred years or more from now. I even wonder whether such institutions, neutral to any violence that might tear down their walls, *remain*, in a sense, because they are *in advance*. Certainly, it seems—to an impartial observer—as if the perpendicular Gothic thrust of the "Jesus" basilica and the vigilant tower of "Magdalen" College surge up out of the past, and go, very deliberately, straight into the future.

I myself contradict what I've said about things at home; imbued with a sort of hostility toward states of rarity sanctioned from outside, or which are not purely the act of writing, I retract those aspirations toward a necessary solitude when it seems to be only a matter of *appearing* to dream. We need that flight—into ourselves; recently we could still do it.

But the Self—isn't it already becoming distant, in order to withdraw?

Here is a longstanding idea I had for us before this trip, but revived through the foreign contact: it might well appear banal, perhaps, and for that reason I've said it aloud often, without thinking much about it; its import is just too applicable. I confess that I give practical or direct ideas the same kind of inattention given to everything, in the street, by passing women. The pleasure I got from this one, mentioned in conversation, results from the startled response of friends highly placed in the administration or the State, and consequently embattled, who acquiesced immediately as if to a self-evident truth, about which, by chance, no one has done anything yet. It would interest me to see, or the fact would be instructive, whether, spoken in public, the idea would have the same effect.

Very few words suffice: it's now or never.

Every nation known for its brilliant writing (for lack of pious cement foundations, which I also admire) possesses a sum that can't be called anything but its literary "fund"; this indeed applies to us French. In modern times and in hard currency, to supplement the State, so long as it takes an interest, meddling or solicitude, in Letters.

The rumble of poetic glory for any people through the ages isn't confined to pure splendor; it stocks, in the course of generations, out of the limelight, a cash register—since great authors succeed through their books, which sell.

It adds up to quite a treasure, compared to the effusion of intelligence, which, in fact, according to my calculations, is, in itself, moderate—and I don't hide my satisfaction in that— but absolute: the money suffices, taken out of the principal, for a delicate and legitimate use.

Let me point out that there is no risk the classics won't be reprinted, to keep up with demand. The expected benefits of this enterprise should apply to the material conditions of life, luxury or cheapness, according to the interest: while to erect a monument is to divulge. Newly invented styles of type, of layout, of illustrations, or paper, are an offering to the master-piece from the era, and constitute a suitable—that is, bene-ficial—gift. But there is, and here I intervene with confidence, something, little—*some little nothing,* let's say explicitly—*which exists,* for example, *equal to the text;* where the profit doesn't merely belong to the fans of Rabelais, Molière, Mon-tesquieu, or Chateaubriand. It is reserved, like a loan, and, in all honesty, a small amount escapes them. I would like to have the Revenue Ministry's perceptiveness, as a guardian, and call this fund "dues": reduced to centimes, or, if coins exist else-where than in consciences, to a "scruple."

Light thus shed on a strangeness in commerce, where the time to dream freely in the course of their careers was not without making an impression on the gallant young man in-habiting the honorable editors; that reasonable being, I think, was happy to see clearly spelled out the effects of the difficult circumstances that stood in his way. All of them, I guarantee, had, of their own accord, lots of doubts about the nation's generosity toward their persons—granted that it works for sublime, dead writers, whose sales are certain; but acquiring the habits and undergoing the prolonged distraction of manip-ulating vast business affairs!

The public domain, where, after a lapse of fifty years, the ownership of works of the spirit changes hands, unlike other forms of inheritance, cannot have been created for the partic-ular benefit of even the most honorable of speculators . . . The present affords the right, taken away from the family, to be the sons of genius. As if the writer, before he came into his own, or rather *our* own, had derived a benefit, our custom, sin-gular and beautiful, provided he adds to it; then after a short time, the usual transmission is cut short. With this idea in mind: that the inheritance, after a while, goes from natural filiation to the line of the mind. Or that those people, young ones, in their time and at their peril, who are researching a trace of supernatural ancestors, if there was money, would know it was there: by reason of the significance of this patrimony, the only one appropriate for them.

Various signs of encouragement, prizes, which might affect the revenue, in the absence of needs, can underwrite diverse literary celebrations; using the regular mechanism (personally, I know it), figuring in the modestness of a tax on all publications, even scholarly ones: a job, if the point is admitted, divided between the Press and Parliament.

An objection—that books would become more expensive, and that the masters would lose in popularity—is false (the small tax would be taken off the merchant's gains).

Have I laid out a project? Veritably. I stop there, because working out the details is so far beyond my competence; without regrets, since the idea of gold gleaming next to the hand is appealing and provocative, like the gold edges of pages, compressed and closed on the sides of slumbering volumes. There is, as they say, a lot to do: a campaign, starting with this indisputable observation.

Every trip happens after it's over, in the mind; its value, through research and comparison, is known only when one is back home. The memory of the two English towns is fading, with their reliquaries of learning becoming merely steeples: leaving me off, some would say, down to earth. Never mind, if the land is our own, and if I discover in it this noble treasure.

1894

(Several paragraphs of this brief essay became, as it were, juridically developed by me in the *Figaro* of August 17 [1894] into the following article.)

To go suddenly from reverie to facts requires a few decisive words, as they are presented in the newspapers: it is important, for the achievement of success, that the notion come from the Press to Parliament. It would be a small modification, to clarify the meaning, of the law which for the moment governs our public Domain.

Everyone knows, and I remind you without details, that a provision in the legislation, unique in our system, limits to fifty years, after the death of a writer, the revenue of his works.

But the law stops halfway in its plan, which remains hidden from it.

If the law suspends heredity, under the circumstances, or withdraws it from the ordinary heirs, is it in order to suppress it altogether? I maintain that that isn't what happens. The publisher that gives us today the works of Racine becomes, in a sense, the poet's heir when he benefits from the favor accorded to those noble verses. The proof of this lies in the fact that, if ingenuity is deployed in the making of the book, the gain is less if the reprint is of Pradon.[†] I hope no one will recriminate: "To choose between the two Phèdres precisely—that is bound to make money. What acumen!"

The result is that the publisher inherits, or gains from, besides his personal merit, the intrinsic and public value of the text: for, as much as by its sublimity, the works of a great name are magnified by the accumulated admiration of readers.

Thus, the law does not suppress heredity, for the reason that it cannot, but the revenue channels itself toward a third party, or several, who have no claim to it: the law merely proposes to interrupt it.

To effect a transfer.

For whose benefit, certainly, that will take place, without any intrusion. You can see here the ideal inheritors, substituted for direct filiation by blood. In addition, in the case of literature, there is the particularity that the famous author did not always enjoy, while he was alive, or while his heirs were alive, the financial benefits of his works. The gain, withheld

---

[†]Jacques Pradon (1632–1698), a competitor of Racine's, wrote *Phèdre et Hippolyte* in 1677. [—*Trans.*]

from him, goes to those distant children who continue his thought.

There's no other explanation for this leap in the transmission of a property whose valuation is about the same as that of any other property.

I bow before the intention, which I recognize to be just.

Whoever has looked closely at the mirage of Immortality knows that, besides the uncaring opinions of the future crowd, it consists in hero worship, renewed by new generations of young people, at the beginnings of life. This elite group, which breaks away, by zeal, from the expected career paths, often encounters suffering and hesitation. From whom would its members accept aid, better or more proudly, than from their own spiritual ancestors, from whom they get their vocation?

The State should not be entirely indifferent to a source, a very pure source, of national pride, and it is not in a position to use public moneys. Here, therefore, is a link.

What will the means of acquisition and distribution of this patrimony, which sounds rather old-fashioned, soon to be called the "Literary Fund," look like? There is no reason to hurry to give details. Above all, I wanted to put forward the principle; but I know that, in many cases, people are convinced by knowing how it might work. Vagueness about practicalities would get in the way. The mechanism in fact already exists; I'll show how it would work, at least enough to satisfy those who are curious.

The small tax taken on reprints, even scholarly ones, implies the compatibility of an office, if necessary, next to the Registry of Books, which is part of the Ministry of the Interior. Wouldn't you prefer that it be located, decoratively or to enhance the thing's significance, in the very Palace of the Book, the Bibliothèque Nationale?

The revenue should go to beginners, by way of their literary elders, an impartial representation of the past. Either in the form of prizes for outstanding works, or as help in publishing works still in manuscript. The procedure isn't so unfamiliar to the Académie, in the first case, that its tasks couldn't be extended to the second, as well. The mechanism is in place, or the Académie could be replaced by a committee, recruited for this purpose.

The only resentment opposing this idea would come from heirs whose rights are violated, and there aren't any. I don't think I'm here presuming on the well-known delicacy of publishers, when I say that none of them will rise up against a tax, in any case minor. Will they be grateful? Perhaps indeed yes, given that the privileges of an incomplete law are susceptible to abuse. The nation will have the opportunity to install, for a moderate price, a system totally worthy of praise. I ask the newspaper which lends support to this project by announcing it to go even further, and, in its *interviews,* to solicit the opinions of a corporation for which both the editor and I wish the best.

In a peremptory argument, something lingers—it may be, in an article almost entirely about business, the displaced introduction of an image. You should see this, rather, as an administrative problem. The public Domain we spoke about earlier perfectly represents the public square, or some public building. The place belongs to the mass of citizens; it doesn't belong to any one. One doesn't do business there for one's own sake without executing oneself. The speculator who convokes people to the public square to testify to his hard work ceases to be a part of all, and divests himself of a right.

Music and Letters

In Oxford on March 1st, and on the 2nd in Cambridge, I had the opportunity to give this talk, differently.

The *Taylorian Association* was inaugurating a series of foreign lecturers, whose job was to communicate to its members the state of literary affairs in our country. Unforgettable. . . .

What an honor, leavened with good grace, my friend of three days and of eternity did me, the historian York Powel, of *Christ Church*. The evening before the lecture, he offered to read, in my place, because of my terror at speaking a foreign language, his admirable translation, which had flowed out in one continuous stream during several sleepless hours. The charm and certainty of the enterprise were contagious from that moment on. In hindsight, I also attribute to respect for this master the interest that greeted the activity I was to perform myself the following day. I was able to imagine the hour—the end of a wintry day—and the huge windows; but not the boredom that showed on the faces of that carefully selected crowd.

As for *Pembroke College*—Poe was supposed to have lectured there, in front of Whistler. It was evening. The heavy drapery of the bow window behind the speaker, who stood against a chair and at a table that held two silver candelabra, which were lit. The mystery: worry that maybe you'd knock them over; and the elite making, in the dark, to mark their attention, the sound of muffled respiration, as if breathing behind a veil. Finally Mr. Charles Whibley was found by his brother, the *Don*, and we could all go on to the game of transmitting reveries between one man and others.

DEAR SIRS AND MADAMS

Until now and for a long time, two nations, England and France, the only ones, have evinced a parallel superstition of Literature. One passing the torch with magnanimity to the other, or taking it back and shedding light on their mutual influence; but—and this is the object of my talk—not so much this alternative (which somewhat explains my presence before you, even speaking my language), than, first of all, the special aims of a certain continuity in masterpieces. In no way can genius not be exceptional, with the height of an anomalous crown sticking up above the angle; yet it only projects, as elsewhere, vague or abandoned spaces in order to entertain, on the contrary, an order and almost an admirable ability to gather together lesser structures—chapels, colonnades, fountains, statues—and produce, all together, some uninterrupted palace, open to the royalty of everyone, out of which arises a taste for homelands: which, in this double case, hesitates, in its delight, before a rivalry of comparable and sublime architectures.

Your having asked me to tell you about the state of our literature does not come at an inopportune time.

I do indeed bring news. The most surprising kind. Such a thing has not been seen before.

Verse has been tampered with.

Governments change, but prosody always remains intact: either because, during revolutions, it goes unnoticed, or because, whatever violence the government sustains, it is never accompanied by the thought that the latter dogma could vary.

It is fitting to speak of it already, just as an invited traveler immediately unburdens himself of gasping words that testify to an accident he witnessed and is pursued by: the truth is, verse is everything, as soon as one writes. Style, versification, if there is cadence, and that is why any page by a sumptuous writer, using language withdrawn from its habitual haphazardness, ornamental, works like a broken line of poetry, playing with its sounds and its hidden rhymes, like a more complex thyrsus. It is really the culmination of what used to be called the *prose poem*.

Very strict, numerical, and direct, with the play of its two parts, the former meter subsists, alongside experimentation.

That's where we are now: the separation.

In place of the way the powerful Romantic ear, at the beginning of the century, combined the doubleness of their undulating alexandrines with their stressed caesuras and enjambments; fusion undid itself toward integrity. A lucky discovery which seems to bring to a close yesterday's experiments is *free verse*—an individual modulation (as I say frequently), because every soul is a rhythmic tangle.

Then the squabbles started. A few experimenters—it was inevitable—went far, thinking they were done with the official canon (I call it that for its guarantee). Official verse forms will remain, nevertheless, for official functions. There was something audacious in this disaffection. Back to the drawing boards . . .

Those who take a dim view of this consider it all a waste of time.

By no means.

Because some real masterpieces have come out of it, independently of any debate over form; and even if one doesn't think so, the quality of silence that would replace them, around an overused instrument, is precious. Verse, on grand occasions, thunders forth, a rarity (although I said a moment ago that everything, measured, becomes verse): just as Literature, despite the need, proper to you and to us, to perpetuate it in every age, represents something singular. French meter, especially, which is delicate, would be used intermittently; now, thanks to its period of stammering rest, the eternal verse can rise again, with perfect intonation, fluid, restored, with perhaps supreme complements.

Everything was stormy but bright, and, in the upheavals, all to the credit of the recent generation, the act of writing was scrutinized down to its origins. Very far, at least, when it comes to the point, which I formulate thus: that is, whether writing itself is out of place. Monuments, the sea, the human face, in their natural fullness, conserve a property differently attractive than the veiling any description can offer—say, evocation, or, I know, *allusion* or *suggestion*. This somewhat haphazard terminology bespeaks a tendency, perhaps the most decisive tendency that literary art has undergone; it limits it, but also exempts it. The literary charm, if it's not to liberate, outside of a fistful of dust or reality without enclosing it, in the

book, even as a text, the volatile dispersal of the spirit, which
has to do with nothing but the musicality of everything.

Thus, with respect to the devastation of the recent period, its rapid crises or its noble hesitations; you already know as much as anyone.

Should I stop there? Or why do I get the feeling I've come here about a vaster subject, perhaps unknown even to me, than such a renovation of rituals and rhymes—to rise to it, if not to treat it? With such benevolence as an invitation to speak about what I love; and also the considerable apprehension of a foreign audience, brings back an old wish, many times denied by solitude, to account deeply and completely for the ideal crisis, which, as much as the other, social, roils many: or, right away, despite what might be abrupt about such a question in front of an audience dedicated to scriptural elegance, ask: Does something like Letters exist? Something other than the refinement (which was a convention in the classical age) toward their most polished form of expression, of all notions, in all domains. The observation that an architect, a jurist, or a doctor raises his structure or discovery up to language in order to achieve final form; in short, everything that comes from the mind is reintegrated into the mind, generally, whatever the subject.

Very few have stood face to face with the enigma, which casts a dark cloud, as I am, rather late in the game, suddenly seized by a doubt concerning what I wish to speak about with liveliness. This type of investigation has perhaps been eluded in peace as dangerous by the very people who, summoned from a university faculty, come running at its call; afraid of diminishing the faculty's value in light of the response. Every pattern endures: on which one imposes the notion that it is what it is, in one's opinion, by its faith or facilities. Admire the shepherd, whose voice, reverberating against treacherous rocks, never comes back to him, in turmoil, as a sneer. So much the better for him; on the other hand, there is ease and maturity to call for some light, even fading light, on the causes of a vocation.

Now, at this extraordinary putting-on-notice we mentioned a moment ago, revoking the titles of a well-known function, when we were supposed to be stringing garlands on its altar; at this sudden invasion, like some undefinable defiance (and not of my strength), I reply with an exaggeration, indubitably, and warning you against it: Yes, Literature exists and, if you will, alone, in exception to everything. It's an accomplishment, at least, that couldn't be better named.

A man can seem entirely oblivious—it's best to be ignorant only intentionally—of the contemporary intellectual burden; in order to find out, according to something simple and primitive, for instance the symphonic equation proper to the seasons, a habit of ray and cloud; two remarks or three analogous to those ardors, those storms that suggest that our passions derive from several types of sky: if he has saved from the disaster a kind of reverence for the twenty-four letters as they have fixed themselves, through the miracle of infinity, in some existing language, his, then a sense for their symmetries, their actions, their reflections, all the way up to a transfiguration into the surreal endpoint, which is verse; he possesses, our civilized inhabitant of Eden, above everything else, the element of felicity, a doctrine as well as a country. Whenever by his initiative, or whenever the virtual force of the divine characters teaches him, he begins to put them to work.

With the ingenuity of our foundations, our legacy from antique magic books—spelling—Literature spontaneously isolates itself, a way of taking note. A means; nay—more!—a principle. The turn of a certain phrase or the weave of a diptych, copied upon our confirmation, aids the hatching, inside us, of observations and correspondences.

Strictly, I envisage, putting aside your scholarly notebooks, rubrics, parchments, reading as a desperate practice. Thus, industry has failed to make happiness, which may not lie within our reach: I've known moments where anything one tries, in the name of a secret disposition, cannot satisfy.

Something else . . . It seems as if the scattered quivering of a page only wants either to defer or to hasten the possibility of that something else.

We know, held captive by an absolute formula that, doubtless, only what is, is. But to wave aside, incontinently, under any pretext, the attraction of the lure, would testify to our illogic, denying the pleasure we want from it: for the *beyond* is its agent—and its motor, I would add, if I were not reluctant to take apart impiously, in public, the fiction, and consequently the literary mechanism itself, in order to lay out the principal part or nothing. But I admire how, by means of a trick, we project, to a great, forbidden, thunderous height, our conscious lack of what, up there, gleams.

What is this good for—

For a game.

In light of a superior attraction like a void, we have the right to be lured on by nothingness; it is drawn out of us by the boredom of things if they are established as solid and preponderant—we frantically detach them and fill ourselves up with them, and also endow them with splendor, through vacant space, for as many solitary festivals as we wish.

As for me, I ask no less of writing, and I'm going to prove it.

Nature has taken place; it can't be added to, except for cities or railroads or other inventions where we change the form, but not the fact, of material.

The one available act, forever and alone, is to understand the relations, in the meantime, few or many: according to some interior state that one wishes to extend, in order to simplify the world.

Equal to creating: except that the notion of object, escaping, is lacking.

Some such occupation suffices, to compare aspects and count

their number as it touches our intelligence, so often brushed aside: arousing, like a décor, the ambiguity of a few beautiful figures, at the intersections. The total arabesque, which ties them together, has dizzying leaps into known fears, and anxious chords; warning rather than disconcerting by moving aside, or so similar to itself that it is subtracted by being confounded. It is a stilled, melodic encipherment, of the combination of the motifs that compose a logic, with our very fibers. Whatever agony, also, the Chimera suffers, pouring out of its golden wounds, obvious for every like creature, no untwisted curve has falsified or transgressed the omnipresent Line spaced out from any point to any other in order to instate the idea; if not beneath the mysterious human face, then to the extent that a Harmony is pure.

To surprise this habitually, and mark it, strikes me as a fitting obligation for one who has unleashed the Infinite; to which rhythm, among the keys of the verbal keyboard, lends itself, as if under the interrogation of fingering, by the usage of apt, quotidian words.

Truly, what are Letters but this mental quest, carried out as discourse, so as to define or to evince, with respect to oneself, proof that the spectacle corresponds to an imaginative comprehension, true, in the hope of mirroring oneself in it.

I know that Music—or what we have commonly agreed to call by that name, limiting it to orchestral performances involving the support of strings, brass, and winds, with permission to be joined by words—hides the same ambition, although this is never spoken of, because music seldom confides. On the other hand, to the trace we mentioned a minute ago of the sinuous and mobile variations of the Idea, which writing claims to stabilize, has there been, perhaps among some of you, occasion to compare certain phrases with a memory of the orchestra? where the return to shadow is succeeded, after an anxious period of turmoil, by a sudden burst of clarity, like the bright radiation of the breaking of day: it is all vain, unless language, dipping and soaring on the purifying wings of song, gives it meaning.

Consider well (our investigation is almost over): an exchange might, nay, must occur, with the triumphal return of the magnificent supplement, the word, which, whatever happens, accepts instrumentation for a brief moment, so that the forces of life won't remain totally blind to their own splendor, even though it is latent or goes nowhere. I call for the restitution, to impartial silence, in order to help the mind repatriate, of the whole—shocks, glidings, known and unlimited trajectories, an opulent state suddenly turned evasive, a delicious inability to finish, this shortcut, that feature—apparatus; minus the tumult of sonorities, still transfusible into dream.

The great, magic writers all bring convincing proof of this generalization.

Then we justly possess the reciprocal means of Mystery. Let us forget the old distinctions between Music and Letters, which only divide them, voluntarily, for their subsequent fusion: the one evocative of prestige situated at the highest point of hearing, or almost abstract vision, being well versed,† which, spaciously, grants the printed page an equal range.

I pose, at my own risk aesthetically, the following conclusion (if, by some grace usually absent from a public talk, I have managed to get you to ratify it, that would be the honor I sought this evening): that Music and Letters are two sides of the same coin; here extending into obscurity; there dazzling with clarity; alternative sides to the one and only phenomenon I have called the Idea.

One of the modes inclining to the other, disappearing there,

---

†"L'entendement." [—*Trans.*]

reemerges with borrowings: twice, disturbing the finishing touches with its oscillation, it transforms a whole genre. Theatrically, the audience, unconsciously and obliviously, hears its own grandeur: or the individual asks for lucidity in an explicative and familiar book.

Now that I can breathe free of anxiety, less out of remorse about introducing this subject to you than, at the start of a lecture, from the fear that the subject I wish to speak to you about implies no authenticity on my part, which is necessary to be convincing; and that you granted that fundamental requirement through the sympathy of your solemnity, while, with predestined speed, almost impersonal, the divulgings came rapidly, new to me, or lasting if one acquiesces to them; it seems to me that almost without daring to hope for it, I perceive you with more intimacy, as the vagueness dissipates. Then, having a chat among friends, for whom the charm is just to get together, seduces me; pardon me if I have been slow to fall in line; I blame the serious shadows that descend on your city, where everything falls into decline except thinking, which moves toward this sonorous room particularly comfortable to Dream. Have I, when I should have chatted, pronounced a dissertation? Added to your morning's courses? In short, taught a class? The grandiose title of Head of a School that the press and the rumor mill have given to one who always works alone, and by that fact attracts the attention of juveniles, must have preceded your lecturer and sounded hollow. None of that, of course, is true. Nevertheless, however reclusive I might be in my laboratory of thought, as a mystagogue, I'm in favor of one who plays his part in several meditations yet to be determined; the procedure capable of pulling him out, a loyalty, almost a duty, to communicate to adolescents a fervor that they look for in their elders. I approve of that habit: no gap in literary succession should ever be allowed to exist in your country or in mine, even in discord.

And that is why I find myself quite at home before this group
of masters and elite youngsters.

What can we knowingly take to laugh about, if not misunderstandings?

The worst, without leaving this room—and this one is indeed annoying, I'll mention it in order to reject it—would
be that there hovers over all we say here a disappointment
coming from you, dear Ladies. Maybe you wanted a brilliant
commentary to whisper to your piano; or maybe you found
me incompetent on your vacation reading of novels and other
volumes. Why should I talk about them, when we can see the
act of writing at its source? I was thinking, on the train, about
all the unpublished masterpieces, the nightly correspondence,
inside those sacks of mail, like a load of prizes behind a loco-
motive. You are the privileged authors, and to make you
dreamy or eloquent or good in terms of the pen, or evoke
with intensity a form of beauty turned inside, you don't need
abstruse theoretical considerations, you just tear off a blank
white page and, according to your mood, start writing.

The situation of the poet, I dreamed of saying, does not
fail to present difficulties, or comedy.

A lamentable lord exiling his ghost from ruins slow to swal-
low him up, in legend and melodrama: this is how the press
pictures the poet. They also, this time rightly, derive from him
the presentation, as explosive as a bomb, of a concept too virginal for Society.

Newspaper clippings sort of whisper my part, oh! hardly
modest enough, in the scandal propagated by explicitly using a name intended to furrow the brows of important people everywhere to designate a volume making the rounds
these days. Frequently used terms like "idiot" and "madman,"
rarely tempered into "stupid" or "fool," are so many stones
thrown at the haughty importunity of a feudality of minds

that apparently threatens Europe—not in every point displeasing, given that there's an excess of goodwill (I don't dare knock it) among people who become ecstatic at empty symptoms, so eager is everything to be built. The bad thing, in this case, is that science meddles with it, or that people drag it in. *Degeneration* is the title. *Entartung*, the title that comes from Germany, is the name of a work, let's be explicit, by Max Nordau. I forbade myself, so as to maintain a level of generality for these remarks, to name anyone, and don't find, at present, that I have broken my rule. That vulgarizer did make one observation: Nature doesn't make a genius fully formed: he corresponds to a type of man and not to any individual. But practically, the occult touch of an immune thumb almost abolishes a faculty in someone who gets large doses of the opposite; those are pious or maternal perpetrations designed to thwart the critic's or judge's clairvoyance, not exempt from tenderness. Focus! What happens? Drawing strength from his privation, the handicapped chosen one grows toward plenary intentions, and leaves in his wake, of course, innumerable waste products, such as his brothers, cases labeled for medicine, or used ballots when a vote is over. The mistake of the pamphleteer in question was to treat everything as waste. Thus, we should make sure that the subtle arcana of psychology and destiny don't fall into the hands, too large to manipulate them, of some excellent foreman or some honest laborer. Who would stop halfway and look! for some divination beyond that, he would have understood, on one point at least, the poor and sacred natural procedures, and would not have published his book.

The opposite insult stutters forth from the newspapers, for lack of audacity; this leaves a barely articulated suspicion: Why the reticence? The devices, whose explosion lights up parliament with a summary illumination, but pitifully disfigures the curious bystanders, would interest me, because of the light—without the brevity of its instruction, which allows the legislator to claim eternal incomprehension; but I'm against adding bullets and nails to the bombs. Like an opinion; and to blame all damage only on the fact that there are writers, a little out of the spotlight, who believe, or not, in free verse, captivates me, especially by its ingenuity. Nearby, they keep to themselves; at a distance, as though for a grand occasion, they offend the miscellany of daily facts. What are they hiding? What discredit are they casting, not as much as a bomb, on what best, indisputably and expensively, furnishes investment capital as a current list of apotheoses: on condition that it decree neither the first word nor the last, relative to certain illuminations, also, that speech can draw out of itself. I would hope that one would push an opinion until the following insinuation slips out: proclaiming, as healthy, the chaste retreat of a select few. It is important that in any contest of multitudes for interest, amusement, or commodity, certain rare enthusiasts, respectful of the common motive insofar as they show indifference to it, institute, by following a different drummer, a minority: given that, however deep the furious conflict among citizens, under the sovereign eye, it adds up to unanimity—agreement, at least, that what they are devouring each other for matters. In any case, given the need for an exception, like salt!—a veritable one which, indefectibly, functions—there are in our time on earth a few minds, I'm not sure, to their credit, how to call them: gratuitous, foreign, maybe vain—or literary.

There is no one—did you notice my attempt to lift the tone, rather somber, which my lecture had taken, with its point of dogmatism, by joking about the incoherence that the street assails anyone with, taking the profit and saving up the rest—who doesn't ruin it. Is it general miasma, or, when certain subjects are mentioned, is it that their grave vibrations persist? In any case, it seems that my fireworks, lit by a concession unnecessary here, have fizzled.

Preferably.

No kidding, now I'm free to finish anytime, with impenitence; keeping my surprise that certain poets have been considered at all, but only through the double meanings that oppose to them a double unintelligence.

While the intuitive understanding is pleased to discern the kind of justice, in the contradictions the fight is based on, to be mastered and the glories in the distance—the interpreter, through a wager, and not even as a virtuoso, but charitably, allies together as materials in order to render the illusion, the words, the perfect words, belonging to some school, dwelling, or market. Verse will emote through some sort of balancing, fierce and mellow, like an orchestra, on outstretched wings; but with flowerbeds rooted in you. Over there, wherever it is, denying the ineffable, which lies.

A humble man, my double, whose word occupies his lips, according to this mediocre—not!—means, if he agrees to join in, as an accompaniment, as a never-heard echo, will communicate, in the appropriate vocabulary, all pomp and all illumination; because, for each, it is appropriate that the truth reveal itself as it is—namely, magnificent. As a docile taxpayer henceforth, it's through his assent that he pays the tax that allows his children to have a homeland.

Because, peremptorily—I infer it from this celebration of poetry we've spoken of, not to speak of the hour I spent talking about it, combining the attributes of Music and Letters: let's just call it Mystery, or it isn't the evolutionary context of the Idea—I said *because* . . .

Great damage has been caused to terrestrial togetherness, for centuries, by conflating it with the brutal mirage, the city, its governments, or the civil code. Otherwise than as emblems or, vis-à-vis our estate, what necropolises are to the heavens they make evaporate: an earth surface, almost not bad-looking.

Tollbooths and elections are not here below, though they seem to sum up democracy, what makes a popular cult, even when such formalities are followed augustly, as representatives—of the Law, seated in all transparency, naked and marvelous.

Mine those substructures, when obscurity invades your perspective; no!—string up some lanterns, in order to see: the point is to get your thoughts to demand, from the ground, a simulacrum.

If, in the future, in France, religion comes back, it will be the amplification of the sky-instinct in each of us, rather than a reduction of our instincts to the level of politics. To vote, even for oneself, does not satisfy, as the expansion of a hymn with trumpets sounding the joy of choosing no name; nor can a riot be sufficiently tumultuous to make a character into the steaming, confounding, struggling-again-into-life hero.

Well, I'll end here, in order not to expand, for once, too much upon this subject on which everything depends—literary art—and being incapable of making you laugh, and wanting to avoid, at least, the ridiculousness, to you as well as to me (if you'll allow me to say so) of droning on and on.

The transparency of thought blends together, between public and speaker, like a mirror melting, when the voice is silent: you will pardon me if I collect, for clarity, some leftovers here, or omissions, or consequences, or unexpressed thoughts. That's what will be found in these Notes.

Page 182, §2
As elsewhere, vague or abandoned spaces.

Discontinuity in Italy; Spain, at least for an outside eye, dazzled by a Dante, a Cervantes: even Germany accepts that there are intervals between its moments of greatness.

I stand by what I said.

Page 183, §6

. . . The separation.

Verse sketches itself out by throwing out two darts, less successively than simultaneously for the Idea, reducing duration to a spiritual division proper to the subject: it differs from the sentence or other temporal development, which prose plays with, in concealment, in its twistings and turnings.

The one has its regulation by the pious capital letter or the alliterative key of rhyme: the other, from a precipitated leap to a sensitive settling down, takes its place thanks to punctuation, which, arranged on blank paper, already signifies.

Along with free verse (on which I won't repeat myself) and prose with calculated linebreaks, I don't know any other use of language that even remotely resembles these two: except the poster or advertisement, which has taken over the newspapers—it has often made me fantasize as if before a new language and the originality of the Press.

The articles known as First Nights, admirable in the only contemporary form possible, because they belong to all eternity, are really poems, simply more or less good poems: rich, void, enameled, or glued together.

People have made the critical mistake, in my opinion, in editorial rooms, of seeing them as a separate genre.

Page 184, §4

. . . Around an overused instrument, is precious.

Suddenly the history of the alexandrine is closed by internal freedom, caesuras and hemistichs wherever one wants; Parnassian poetry, so vilified, stopped there: it instated poetry that pronounced itself on its own without the help of some preexisting breath in the reader, or moved by the placement or size of the words. Its lag behind a fairly definitive mechanism was its failure to spell out its operation or poetics. That this mechanism should have gone on evolving since, on empty, according to the immediacy of wheel or rein, is not the worst thing; but what *is*, in my opinion, is the pretense of enclosing within expression the material of objects. Time has perfected the work; and who among us speaks of a schism? To the impersonal and pure verse form, an instinct for picking out song from the world will adapt, in order to make visible fundamental rhymes, and reject, as vain, the remainder.

Page 184, §4
. . . French meter is used intermittently.

I neither blame nor disdain the periods where art is eclipsed; it is instructive insofar as the wear shows what pious manias have gone into its weave.

Page 187, §5
. . . In light of a superior attraction. . . .

This point of view is no less pyrotechnical than metaphysical, but a fireworks show, at the level and by the example of thought, bursts out with ideal pleasure.

Page 190, §1
. . . Asks for lucidity in an explicative and familiar book.

The Truth, if one wants to work out the routes, orders that industry end up in Finance, as Music does in Letters, to circumscribe a domain of Fiction, the perfect comprehensive term.

Music without Letters seems like a subtle cloud; Letters, like an everyday coin.

It was appropriate not to separate them further. The title, proposed before the Oxonian messenger once at the end of a chat, was *Music and Letters*, half of the subject, intact: its social counterpart omitted. At the heart of the harangue, here I am serving up this piece whole to my listeners, on a background of speculative staging or dramatization: from cursive preliminaries to dissipation in gossip, brought back to clarity precisely to try to bridge the lack of nonfinancial interest.—Everything is summed up between Aesthetics and Political Economy.

In treating the motif whole (rather than cutting it up into pieces), I would still have avoided Hellenizing with the name of Plato; having, myself, no intentions other than those of a modern man directly expressing an unchallenging enigma, just as he wears, in public, a black suit.

Page 194, §4

. . . A humble man, my double . . .

Eternal myth: communion, through the book. Everyone gets the whole.

Page 195, §1

. . . Demand from the ground a simulacrum.

A government, in order to have value, will mirror that of the universe. Which is it? Monarchical? Anarchical? . . . All conjectures are welcome.

The City, if I'm not wrong in my citizen's sense, reconstructs an abstract, superior place, situated nowhere, as the right place for man.—A simple sketch of this grandiose watercolor, this one doesn't wash down, marginally, to a footnote.

What a taste for demonstrating (no one, irresistibly, has so much to say!), I succumbed, one last time, to the mortarboard, with the English universities, and a past that was fated to be professorial. Also, this somewhat crude language . . . I expressed myself, in our language, not here.

The Speech, or lecture, or, better still, Discourse, seems to me to belong to a genre to be used outside our borders. You here, at our place, speak; if it's required of us to pay homage, we agree to do so.

Literature, like hunger, consists of suppressing the person writing. What do his loved ones think he does every day?

Sleepiness that makes one put down the spoon on the saucer, having read an article in some journal to the end, glancing at the distended shadows of the slippers at the foot of the bed ready for the morning or for midnight. This is my opinion as a member of the public; and as an explorer from no sandy wastes, not curious looking, if I sought to parade around in my milieu, I should grab, en route, from a furrier, a jaguar or lion rug, to begin by strangling it, and present myself to familiars or to the world only in the midst of this vigorous action.

Crisis

of

Verse

A MINUTE ago, dropping my hand, with the lassitude that is caused by one afternoon after another of bad weather, I let fall—without curiosity, though it felt as though I had read everything twenty years ago—the string of multicolored pearls left by the rain, reflected in the glass of a case full of books. Many a work, under the beaded curtain, will align its own illumination: I enjoy following their light, as under a saturated cloud, against the window, one follows storm lights across the sky.

Our recent phase, if not achieving closure, takes a break or perhaps takes stock: close attention uncovers the creative and relatively confident intention.

Even the press, whose information is usually twenty years old, is writing about the subject, suddenly, when it happens.

Literature is here undergoing an exquisite and fundamental crisis.

Whoever grants this function a place, or even the primary place, will recognize in this the current event: we are witnessing, in this fin-de-siècle, not—as it was during the last one—a revolution, but, far from the public square: a trembling of the veil in the temple, with significant folds, and, a little, its rending.

A French reader, his habits interrupted by the death of Victor Hugo, cannot fail to be disconcerted. Hugo, in his mysterious task, brought all prose—philosophy, eloquence, history—down to verse, and, since he was verse personified, he confiscated, from whoever tried to think, or discourse, or narrate, almost the right to speak. A monument in the desert, surrounded by silence; in a crypt, the divinity of a majestic unconscious idea—that is, that the form we call verse is simply itself literature; that there is verse as soon as diction calls attention to itself, rhyme as soon as there is style. Verse, I think, respectfully waited until the giant who identified it with his tenacious and firm blacksmith's hand came to be missing, in order to, itself, break. All of language, measured by meter, recovering therein its vitality, escapes, broken down into thousands of simple elements; and, I add, not without similarity to the multiplicity of notes in an orchestral score, but this one remains verbal.

The change dates from that, although Verlaine's underground and untimely experiments prepared the way, so fluid, going back to primitive names.

As a witness to this adventure, where others want to see me as more effective than it would be suitable for anyone to be, I at least directed my fervent attention to it; and it is time to speak about it, preferably from a distance and, as it were, anonymously.

Grant that French poetry, because of the primacy accorded to rhyme, in its evolution up to us, is intermittent: it shines a while, exhausts its inspiration, and waits. Extinction, or rather a refusal to expose worn-down threads, repetition. The need to poetize, as opposed to many accidental circumstances, leads, now, after one of those periodic orgies that lasted almost a century, comparable only to the Renaissance, when shadow and chill should have followed, not at all! the brilliance changes, continues: the rethinking, ordinarily hidden, fills the public eye, through recourse to delicious approximations.

I think I can break down, in its triple aspect, the treatment that the hieratic canon of verse has undergone, in sequence.

This prosody, with its brief rules, is nevertheless uncompromising. With its hemistich, an act of prudence, a statue to the smallest effort needed to simulate versification, rather like those codes that tell us that refraining from stealing is proof of honesty. Just what I didn't need to know; not having guessed it myself establishes the uselessness of constraining myself to it subsequently.

Those who remain faithful to the alexandrine, our hexameter, loosen internally the rigid and childish mechanism of its meter; the ear, freed from a gratuitous inner counter, feels pleasure in discerning all the possible combinations and permutations of twelve beats.

Consider that taste very modern.

One intermediate case, in no way the least curious, follows:
The poet with acute tact who considers the alexandrine the definitive jewel, but not to bring out, sword, flower, very often and according to some premeditated end, touches it shyly or plays around it—he gives us neighboring chords before releasing it, superb and naked: letting his fingers drag against the eleventh syllable or go on to a thirteenth, many times. Monsieur Henri de Regnier excels at this kind of play, of his own invention, discreet and proud like the genius he has instated, and revealing of the transitory trouble poets have with the hereditary instrument. Another thing, or simply the opposite, can be detected in a voluntary mutiny against the old

tired mold, as when Jules Laforgue, in the beginning, initiated us into the certain charms of lines that were slightly off.

Up to now, or in the two cases we've just cited, there has been nothing but reserve and abandon, because of lassitude at the frequent use of the national cadence, whose appearance, like that of the flag, should remain exceptional. With this proviso, however: that voluntary infractions or knowing dissonances call only on our sensitivity, whereas, barely fifteen years ago, the pedant we have remained used to rail against departures from the rules as against some ignorant sacrilege! I would say that the recollection of strict verses haunts these approximations, and that they benefit from it.

What is new about free verse, not as the expression was understood in the seventeenth century when people spoke of fables or operas (which was only an arrangement of known meters), but let's call it "polymorphous": and let's imagine the dissolution of the official verse form, the form now becoming whatever one wants, so long as a pleasure repeats in it. Sometimes it's a euphony broken up with the assent of the intuitive reader, ingenuously and preciously right—that was once the work of Monsieur Moréas; or else a gesture languid with dreaminess, suddenly jumping awake, through passion, which provides meter—that's Monsieur Vielé-Griffin; before that, Monsieur Kahn invented a very learned notation of the tonal value of words. I'm giving only these names, and there are other typical cases, as proof of what I say: Messieurs Charles Morice, Verhaeren, Dujardin, Mockel, and all of them: I send my reader to their publications.

What is remarkable is that, for the first time in the literary history of any people, concurrently with the grand general and historic organs, where, according to a latent scale, orthodoxy exults, anyone with his individual game and ear can compose an instrument, as soon as he breathes, touches, or

taps scientifically; he can play it on the side and also dedicate it
to the Language.

This is quite a bit of liberty to count on, the newest: but I
don't see—and this remains my intense opinion—an erasure
of anything that was beautiful in the past. I remain convinced
that on grand occasions, poets will obey solemn tradition, of
which the preponderance comes from the classic genius: it's
just that, when there's no reason, because of a sentimental
breeze or for a story, to disturb those venerable echoes, a poet
will think carefully before doing so. Each soul is a melody that
needs to be renewed; and for that, each becomes his own flute
or viola.

According to me, there arises quite late a true condition or
the possibility not just of expressing oneself, but of modulat-
ing oneself, as one likes.

Languages imperfect insofar as they are many; the absolute
one is lacking: thought considered as writing without accessories, not even whispers, still *stills* immortal speech; the diver-
sity, on earth, of idioms prevents anyone from proffering
words that would otherwise be, when made uniquely, the material truth. This prohibition is explicitly devastating, in Nature (one bumps up against it with a smile), where nothing
leads one to take oneself for God; but, at times, turned toward
aesthetics, my own sense regrets that discourse fails to express
objects by touches corresponding to them in shading or bearing, since they do exist among the many languages, and sometimes in one. Beside *ombre* [shade], which is opaque, *ténèbres*
[shadows] is not very dark; what a disappointment, in front of
the perversity that makes *jour* [day] and *nuit* [night], contradictorily, sound dark in the former and light in the latter.
Hope for a resplendent word glowing, or being snuffed out,
inversely, so far as simple light-dark alternatives are concerned.—*Only,* be aware that *verse would not exist:* it, philo-

sophically, makes up for language's deficiencies, as a superior supplement.

What a strange mystery: and, from no lesser intentions, metrics appeared, during incubatory times.

What caused a medium extent of words, under the gaze's comprehension, to take on definitive traits, surrounded by silence?

If, in the case of French, no private invention can surpass the prosodic heritage, displeasure would nevertheless break out if a singer couldn't—to the side and as he liked, not in the infinite, wherever his voice encountered a rule—gather blossoms nevertheless. . . . The experiment, a while ago, took place, and, aside from erudite research into accentuation etc., ongoing or forecast, I know that a seductive game is being played with recognizable fragments of classic verse, to be eluded or to be discovered, rather than involving a sudden discovery, totally new. It will take time to loosen the constraints and relax the zeal that got official schools into trouble. All very preciously: but from this liberation, to hope for something else, or to believe, seriously, that every individual possesses a new prosody in his very breath—and also, of course, some new spelling—is a joke, or inspires the platforms of many prefaces. It's not arbitrary that there should be similarities between poetry and ancient proportions; some kind of regularity will last because the poetic act consists of seeing that an idea can be broken up into a certain number of motifs that are equal in some way, and of grouping them; they rhyme; as an external seal, the final words are proof of their common measure.

It is in what has happened to verse, so interesting, during this period of rest and interregnum, less than in some virginal mental circumstance, that the crisis lies.

To hear the indisputable ray—as particular features gild and tear a wandering melody; or Music joins Verse to form, since Wagner, Poetry.

It's not that one or the other can't still, in its integrity, separate triumphantly from the other (Music without articulation gives a mute concert, and Poetry alone can only enounce): from their combination and mutual influence, instrumentation is illuminated until it becomes obvious beneath the veil, just as elocution descends into *the* twilight of sonorities. The modern meteor, the symphony, according to the intention or unbeknownst to the musician, approaches thought; which no longer claims descent only from common speech.

Some explosion of Mystery to the skies in its impersonal magnificence occurs, where the orchestra couldn't *not* influence the ancient effort that long claimed to translate it uniquely through the voice of the ancestor.

Consequently, a double indication—
Decadent, Mystic, the Schools naming themselves, or being labeled in haste by the press, have adopted, as what they have in common, the viewpoint of an Idealism that (as in fugues or sonatas) rejects natural materials as too crude, even when thought organizes them; to retain from them only a suggestion. To institute an exact relation between images, and let detach there a third, blendable, clear aspect, presented for divination. . . . Abolished is the claim, aesthetically an error, even though it produced some real masterpieces, of including in the subtle paper of a volume something other than, for example, the horror of deep woods, or the scattered mute thunder of foliage: not the intrinsic and dense wood of the trees. A few spurts of intimate pride truly trumpeted evoke the architecture of a palace, the only one habitable: outside of any stone, on which the pages couldn't close.

208

Crisis of Verse

"Monuments, the sea, the human face, in their natural fullness, conserve a property differently attractive than the veiling
any description can offer; say evocation, or, I know, *allusion*
or *suggestion:* this somewhat haphazard terminology testifies
to a tendency, perhaps the most decisive tendency that literary
art has undergone; it limits it, but also exempts it. The literary
charm, if it's not to liberate, outside of a fistful of dust or reality without enclosing it, in the book, even as a text, the volatile dispersal of the spirit, which has to do with nothing but
the musicality of everything."†

Speaking has to do with the reality of things only commer-
cially: in literature, one contents oneself with alluding to it or
disturbing it slightly, so that it yields up the idea it incorporates.

Under those conditions arises song, which is joy made even
less heavy.

This aim, I call Transposition; Structure, another.
The pure work implies the disappearance of the poet speaking, who yields the initiative to words, through the clash of
their ordered inequalities; they light each other up through reciprocal reflections like a virtual swooping of fire across precious stones, replacing the primacy of the perceptible rhythm
of respiration or the classic lyric breath, or the personal feeling driving the sentences.

An order innate to the book of verse exists inherently or
everywhere, eliminating chance; it's also necessary, to eliminate the author: now, any subject is fated to imply, among the
fragments brought together, a strange certainty about its appropriate place in the volume. It is susceptible to this because
any cry possesses an echo—motifs of the same type balance

†Extract from "Music and Letters." [—*Author*]

each other, stabilizing each other at a distance, and neither the
sublime incoherence of a romantic page, nor that artificial
unity that adds up to a block-book, can provide it. Everything
is suspended, an arrangement of fragments with alternations
and confrontations, adding up to a total rhythm, which would
be the poem stilled, in the blanks; only translated, in a way, by
each pendant. I find traces of such an instinct in many publications and, given the type, it doesn't long remain without companions; young people, for once, when poetry seems to be
thundering and harmonious with plenitude, have stuttered out
the magic concept of the Work. A certain symmetry, in parallel fashion, which, to the place of the verse in the piece links
the authenticity of the piece in the volume, steals, in addition
to the volume, written by diverse hands, inscribed on spiritual
space, the amplified signature of genius, anonymous and perfect, giving art existence and being.

It may be only a chimera, but merely to have thought of it
attests, reflecting off its scales, how much the present cycle, or
the final quarter-century, has been struck by some absolute illumination—of which the unceasing stream of water against
the panes of my windows washes away the streaming trouble,
until it lights up this thought—that, more or less, all books
contain the fusion of a few repeated sayings, few enough to
count, or even only one—in the world, its law—bible as the
nations simulate it. The difference between one book and another constitutes its entry into an immense contest, offering its
proposed reading of the one true text, sought in vain by all
civilized—or literate—ages.

Certainly, I never sit on the terrace of a concert without
perceiving, within its obscure sublimity, an outline of one of
the poems immanent to humanity, all the more comprehensi-
ble for being stilled, in its original form, and that, if asked to
trace the line of its vast progeny, the composer felt this facility
of suspending even the temptation to explain himself. I imag-

ine, following an unextractable and no doubt writerly prejudice, that nothing will remain without being proffered, that we are stuck at precisely the point of searching, faced with the breaking up of classic literary rhythms (I've spoken about this above) and their dispersion into articulated shivers close to instrumentation, for an art of achieving the transposition into the Book of the symphony, or merely to take back what is ours: for it is not through the elementary sounds of brasses, strings, or woods, but undeniably through the intellectual word at its height that there should result, with plenitude and obviousness, as the totality of relations existing in everything, the system otherwise known as Music.

An undeniable desire of my time is to distinguish two kinds of language according to their different attributes: taking the double state of speech—brute and immediate here, there essential.

To tell, to teach, and even to describe have their place, and suffice, perhaps, in order to exchange human thought, to take or to put into someone else's hand in silence a coin, this elementary use of discourse serving the universal *reporting* in which, except for literature, all genres of contemporary writing participate.

What good is the marvel of transposing a fact of nature into its vibratory near-disappearance according to the play of language, however: if it is not, in the absence of the cumbersomeness of a near or concrete reminder, the pure notion.

I say: a flower! And, out of the oblivion where my voice casts every contour, insofar as it is something other than the known bloom, there arises, musically, the very idea in its mellowness; in other words, what is absent from every bouquet.

As opposed to a denominative and representative function, as the crowd first treats it, speech, which is primarily dream and song, recovers, in the Poet's hands, of necessity in an art devoted to fictions, its virtuality.

Verse, which, out of several vocables, makes a total word, entirely new, foreign to the language, and almost incantatory, achieves that isolation of speech; negating, with a sovereign blow, despite their repeated reformulations between sound and sense, the arbitrariness that remains in the terms, and gives you the surprise of never having heard that fragment of ordinary eloquence before, while the object named is bathed in a brand new atmosphere.

About

the

Book

Several times the same Comrade, this other, came to me and confided his need to act: what did he have in mind?—especially since his coming to me announced on his part, in his youthfulness, also the occupation of creating or succeeding with words, which would seem to dominate. I say again, what did he have in mind, exactly?

To unclench one's fists, to break out of a sedentary dream, for violent fisticuffs with the idea, like a need for exercise: but the younger generation seems hardly restless, besides being politically disinterested, to stretch or test the body. Except in the monotony of unrolling, between one's ankles, on a track, according to today's most fashionable instrument, the fiction of a dazzling, continuous rail.

To act, otherwise, and for someone who doesn't begin the exercise by smoking, meant, visitor, I understand you, philosophically, to produce on many a movement that gives you the impression that *you* originated it, and therefore exist: something no one is sure of. This praxis can be understood in two ways: either, by will, unbeknownst to others, to spend a whole life toward a multiple outburst—which would be *thinking:* or else, using the means available now—journals and their whirlwind—to send a force in some direction, *any* direction, which, when countered, gives you immunity from having any result.

At will, according to one's disposition, plenitude, or haste.

Your act is always applied to paper; for meditating without a trace is evanescent, nor is the exalting of an instinct in some vehement, lost gesture what you were seeking.

To write—

The inkwell, crystalline like consciousness, with its drop, at bottom, of shadows relative to letting something be: then, take the lamp away.

As you noted, one doesn't write, luminously, on a dark field; the alphabet of stars alone does that, sketched or interrupted; man writes black upon white.

This fold of dark lace, which holds the infinite, woven by thousands, each according to his own thread or extension, not knowing the secret, assembles distant spacings in which riches yet to be inventoried sleep: vampire, knot, foliage; and our job is to present them.

With the indispensable touch of mystery that always remains, somewhat expressed, nevertheless.

I don't know whether the Guest perspicaciously circumscribes his domain of effort: I would be happy to mark it, along with certain conditions. The right to accomplish anything exceptional, or beyond reach of the vulgar, is paid for by the omission of the doer, and of his death as so-and-so. He will commit exploits only in dreams, so as not to bother anyone, but still, the program is posted for those who don't care.

The writer, with his pains, dragons he has cherished, or with his light-heartedness, must establish himself, in the text, as a spiritual *histrio*.

Stageboards, *lustre*, obnubilation of fabrics and liquefaction of mirrors, in the real, all the way up to excessive leaps of our gauzy form around a still center, on one foot, of virile stature, a Place presents itself, on the stage, the enlargement in front of everyone of the spectacle of the Self; there, because of the intermediaries of light, flesh, and laughter, the sacrifice the inspirer makes relative to his personality, completes itself; or it's the end, in an uncanny resurrection, of so-and-so: his word henceforth vain and echoing through the exhalations of the orchestral chimera.

In a hall, he celebrates himself, anonymous, in the hero.

Everything functions like a festival: a people testifies to its transformation into Truth.

Honor.

Seek, anywhere, something similar—

Will one recognize it in one of those suspect houses that detach themselves, overburdened by the banal, from the common alignment, claiming to synthesize the diverse goings-on of a quarter; or, if some façade, according to the French taste for divination, isolates, in a square, its ghost, I salute. Indifferent to what, here and there, is whispered, as along a gas line the tongues of flame are turned down.

Thus, Action, in the mode we agreed upon—literary action—does not go beyond the Theater; is limited to that, to representation—an immediate disappearance of writing. If it ends up in the street or elsewhere, the mask falls away; we don't have to do with a poet: abjure your poetry—anyway, it doesn't have much power out there—you would prefer to add to the pile of acts committed by individuals. What good would it do to spell out, which you very well know, like me, who kept it through a quality or lack of childhood in exclusivity, this point, that everything, vehicle or placement, which is currently offered to the ideal, is contrary to it—almost a speculation on your lack of externalization, your silence—or defective, not direct and legitimate, in the sense that a moment ago we called for a surge, now tainted. Since a malaise never suffices, I'll clarify, assuredly, with the right number of digressions coming next, this reciprocal contamination of work and means: but first, doesn't it make sense to express oneself spatially? like a cigar tracing circonvolutory patterns, whose vagueness, at the very least, is outlined against the harsh electric light?

A certain delicacy has, I hope, suffered—

Externally, like a cry of distance, the traveler hears the wail of a whistle. "No doubt," he says to himself, "we're going through a tunnel—*our time*—that runs for a long way beneath the city before getting to the all-powerful station of the virginal central palace, which crowns it all." The underground will last as long, O impatient one, as your concentration in preparing to build the crystal palace swiped by a wing of Justice.

Suicide or abstention, why would you choose to do nothing?—This is your only time on earth, and because of an event I'll explain, there's no such thing as a Present, no—a present doesn't exist . . . For lack of the Crowd's declaring itself, for lack of—everything. Uninformed is he who would proclaim himself his own contemporary, deserting or usurping with equal imprudence, when the past seems to cease and the future to stall, in view of masking the gap. Outside of those All-Paris occasions whose job is to propagate faith in the quotidian nothingness, and inexpert if the plague measures its period to a fragment, important or not, of a century.

Therefore, keep yourself, and be there.

Poetry is sacred; some people attempt hidden chaste crises in isolation, while the other gestation takes place.

Publish.

The Book, where the spirit lives satisfied, in cases of misunderstanding, one feels an obligation toward some sort of purity of delight to shake off the dregs of the moment. Impersonified, the volume, to the extent that one separates from it as author, does not demand a reader, either. As such, please note, among human accessories, it takes place all by itself: finished, it exists. Its buried meaning moves and arranges, into a chorus, the pages.

Afar, it dares to forbid, even at celebrations, the present: one notes that chance denies to certain dreams the materials of confrontation; or a special attitude helps them.

You, Friend, whom it's unnecessary to frustrate for years just because there's a parallel with voiceless general labor, will find the case strange: I ask you, without judgment, without sudden factors, to treat my advice as, I admit, a rare kind of folly. Nevertheless, it is tempered by this wisdom, or discernment: that it might be better (than to bet on, at the very least, an incomplete context around you) to risk certain conclusions of extreme art that might burst out, glittering like a cut diamond, now or forever, within the integrity of the Book—to play them, even through a triumphal reversal, with the tacit injunction that nothing, palpitating in the unconscious flank of the hour, shown clear and evident to the pages, will find the hour ready; while nevertheless it may be in another time that it will cast illumination.

Displays

THUS not even; it wasn't; I began naively to feel comfortable. A semester had passed into oblivion, and the summer brought out the abundance, blooming, and spreading of our literary production, as usual.

With the autumn wind, a rumor spread through the market and lodged in the leafless trees: I don't know whether it makes you laugh retrospectively, as it does me; there was talk of a disaster in the publishing business; the word "krach" [crash] was bandied about. Unsold volumes littered the ground; because, people said, of the public's disinclination to read, probably in order to contemplate things themselves, without intermediary; sunsets, for example, which in that season are magnificent. Triumph, despair, at the level of the sky, is matched by the trade in Letters; so much so that I suspect there is an advertisement joined to the trepidation, otherwise it wouldn't make sense that the novel, which everyone agrees is contemporary, attracts attention to itself precisely because it is hit with this calamity.

During this time, no one alluded to verse.

Nothing was left out of this farce (importance, consultation, gestures) to signify that we were thus, thanks to the ideal, being assimilated to disappointed bankers: to have a position, subject to declines and to reversals in the stock exchange: to have a footing there, almost by taking a step.

No: it seems that even to complain about this calamity was bragging; back to the drawing boards.

Mental nourishment—like the other, indispensable kind—keeps its currency, and I come back from spending the morning outside, in springtime, charmed like any city-dweller by the small amount of headiness in the street; having never, during my excursion, felt, except in front of a modern grocery store or shoe store for books, a worry, but acute then, about the architecture demanded by these displays, their construction of piles or colonnades along with their merchandise.

The annual launching or distribution of reading matter, formerly held during the winter, now advanced to the threshold of summer: the windowpane which cast a chill over the acquisition has disappeared; and the open-air editions burst their wrappers toward the hand setting off for the gloved distance, the purchaser in a hurry to choose something to place between her eyes and the sea.

Observe this interception—

It is what a fan is for the Far East, Spain, and delicious illiterates, with the difference that this other paper wing is more lively: infinitely and summarily it unfolds and hides the site, in order to bring against the lips a mute painted flower like the intact and meaningless word of fantasy approached by its flutter.

Thus, as a poet, I believe, to my detriment, that writing even a diptych there would be too much.

It functions as an isolator, with the virtue of mobility constantly renewing the unconsciousness of a delirium without a cause.

The volume—and here I mean the volume of narratives or of genre—goes the other way: it avoids the lassitude given by direct encounters with others, but also takes care that one not come too close to oneself; attentive to the double danger. Expressly, it neither detaches nor conflates us, and, through an adroit oscillation between promiscuity and emptiness, provides our likeness. Thus, each novel is an artifice showing that each circumstance into which fictive contemporaries rush, however extreme, presents nothing foreign to the reader, but is part of a uniform life. Or, there are only people like us in the world, even among those it is possible, while reading, to imagine. With the initial characters of the alphabet, of which each touch corresponds to some attitude of Mystery, the clever practice will evoke, of course, people, always: without the compensation that by making them such, or borrowing them from the meditative means of the spirit, they do not intrude. These bores (the door to whose home sweet home we will not open), through the fact of loosened pages, penetrate everywhere, come out, insinuate themselves; *and we understand that they're us.*

That's precisely what a modern person requires: to be reflected even in his averageness—served by his obsequious phantom woven out of everyday language.

Whereas there was, when language reigned, a first attunement to the origin, in order for an august sense to be produced: in Verse, the dispenser and organizer of pages, master of the book. Visibly, whether it appears in its integrality among the margins and blanks, or dissimulates itself, call it Prose, but it's still there if there's any secret pursuit of music within the storehouse of Discourse.

At any rate, I won't interrupt a plan to discern, in the volume, whose consumption is de rigueur for the public, the results of its use. Which are (without the concern to see literature as working toward this effect, but rather the opposite) that it is incontinent to reduce the horizon and the spectacle to a medium-sized breath of banality, scriptural and essential: made to fit the human yawn, incapable, by itself, of discerning its principle, in order to emit it. Instead of banning the vague or the common or the unpolished—which would be quite a job!—they should be applied to oneself as a state: then worry if the very simple thing called a soul doesn't agree faithfully to scan its flight according to some innate rhythm or according to the recitation of a few well-known verses, new and yet always the same.

A type of business, that of numbers, the summary of enormous and elementary interests, employs the printing press for the propagation of opinions, the narration of miscellaneous news stories; and this all becomes plausible in the Press, restricted to publicity, it seems, leaving out an art. I disapprove only of the return of some triviality into the original book, which agreed to share with the journal the monopoly on intellectual equipment, perhaps to unburden itself. Rather, among us at least, the Press wanted its place among writings—traditionally grounded in the *feuilleton* [serial novel], which sustained the whole format: just as, along the avenues, above the fragile dazzling stores, their windows glistening with jewels or brushed with fabrics, securely rests a building with numerous stories. Furthermore, fiction in the literal sense or imaginative narratives parade around through well-stocked "dailies" up to the top, dislodging the background article about current events, which appears secondary. It contains a suggestion or even a lesson of some beauty: that today isn't just the replacement for yesterday, presaging tomorrow, but gets outside of time, as general, with a clean, new integrity. The vulgar sandwich-board open wide at intersections thus reflects a sky over the dust, a distant echo of the political text. Such an adventure leaves some indifferent, because, they imagine, with a little greater or lesser rarity or sublimity in the pleasure people feel, that there is no change in the situation of what, alone, is most immeasurably precious and highest, known by the name of

Poetry: it will always remain excluded, and the quiver of its wings elsewhere than on the page is parodied, not more, by the breadth, in our hands, of the hasty and vast pages of the newspaper. To gauge today's extraordinary overproduction, in which the Press cedes its means intelligently, the notion nevertheless prevails that something very decisive is being elaborated: as if, before a new era, there is a competition for the founding of the modern popular Poem, or at least some innumerable *Thousand and One Nights;* at which a suddenly invented reading majority would marvel. Come participate in whatever happens in this thunderous accomplishment, as in a festival, all you contemporaries! Otherwise, the intensity of the fire heating it up is much greater than that needed in daily consummation.

Quite simply, our walk ends with this objectless divagation: in order to provoke a tenuous but precise sentiment in some of those present, to whom, moreover, I have cautiously referred. Their discomfort—and it's a lot!—their stumbling block, would make them, these people of letters, more the newspaper hawkers, speed up or avert their eyes before a vulgarization of the sacred format, the volume, under our gaslights; it seems like language stripped naked and flung out to the street corner.

Stores only increase the hesitation to use, with the same contentment as before, privileges, nevertheless theirs, to publish.

Nothing follows; how little any of this matters!

The person one is concerned about (at least one wishes him to be somewhere, out of immediate hearing range) is guessed at: he does not seek ordinary or handy facilities; his name swirls around or rises with its own force, which is never attuned to mercantile considerations.

An era, as a matter of course, knows the existence of the
Poet.

In order as to keep the number of guests small, he shows
the manuscript only to a few friends, but he's immediately famous! Whether with leaves of Antique Holland or Japan, an
ornament of consoles, in the shadows; or anything, decidedly
if the book takes off extraordinarily without any advertisement, the fact just takes place. There isn't a young friend in
the heart of the provinces that doesn't, silently, inform himself. Just as it is about to be refuted, the network of communication, having omitted some journalistic facts, activates its
wires, and produces this result.

Listen! or to come back to where I started, pushing an
idea as far as it will go, even if it bursts in the manner of a
paradox.

The discredit that falls on the bookstores has to do less with
a diminution of its operations (I don't find any), than with its
notorious impotence before the exceptional.

For the author, hitting it big or glowing with a mediocre
monetary return would amount to the same. Indeed, there is
no colossal gain to expect from any literary production. Met-
allurgy is better in this respect. Beside an engineer, I would always become secondary: and preferably would have another
job. What good is it to traffic in what, perhaps, shouldn't be
sold, especially when it doesn't sell?

As the Poet has his revelation, so he lives: outside and unknown to advertisements, to counters sinking under unsold
books, or to exasperated vendors: according to an anterior
pact with Beauty, which his only duty is to note with his comprehensive and necessary gaze, and of which he knows all the
transformations.

A PROPOSITION said to emanate from me, cited in my praise or dispraise—but I claim it here, along with others that will gather around—says, briefly, that everything in the world exists to end up as a book.

The qualities required for such a work, assuredly genius—which scares me, since I'm one of the ones who lack it—don't stop there, given that the volume entails no signatory, so what is it like? Hymn, harmony, and joy, a pure cluster grouped together in some shining circumstance, tying together the relations among everything. The man charged with divine sight, because of the willed limpidity of the links, has only, before his gaze, the parallelism of pages as model.

When I see a new publication lying on a garden bench, I love it when the breeze flips through the pages, and animates some of the exterior aspects of the book. No one, perhaps, since there has been reading, has remarked on this. This might be an occasion to do so, when, freed, the newspaper dominates, mine, which I put aside, it blows over to a rose hedge, where it struggles to cover the blossoms' ardent and proud confabulation, unfolds in the flower bed; and I'll leave it there, along with the flower-words in their muteness, and, technically, I propose to note down how this discard differs from the book, which is supreme. A newspaper remains the starting point; literature unburdens itself there as much as it wishes.

Folding is, with respect to the page printed whole, a quasi-religious indication; the large sheets are less striking than the thick stacks of pages, which offer a tiny tomb for the soul.

Everything the printer created is summed up, in the name of the Press, in the newspaper: the open page, receiving the imprint, unpolished, the first layer of a text. This employment, immediate or anterior to closed production, certainly contains conveniences for the writer, panels joined end to end, proofs, which render improvisation. Thus, a "daily," before the vision—but whose?—presents a meaning, or even a charm, like that of a popular fantasy or fairy tale. Follow—the summit or Premiere, the height of detachment, despite thousands of obstacles, precipitates or represses, as if by electric light, after the articles that follow in their wake, the original servitude, the notice, on the fourth page, among an incoherence of unarticulated cries. It is certainly a moral spectacle—what does it lack, along with the exploit, in the paper, of erasing the book; although, visibly, down below, or rather, at the bottom of the page, it is attached by pagination, like a serial novel, heading the generality of the columns. Nothing, or almost nothing—if the book is slow in coming, as it is, an indifferent outlet where the other is emptied . . . Including the idle format; and vainly competes, gathered like a flight, but ready to take wing again, this extraordinary intervention of folding or rhythm; initial cause that an uncut book contains a secret, and silence haunts it, precious, succeeding evocative signs, for the spirit literally abolished from everything.

Yes, without the folding back of the paper and the undersides it installs, which spreads around the black letters in shadow, the book would not present any reason to propagate itself like a fragment of mystery, in the surface opened up by a finger lifted to part the pages.

A newspaper, the open sheet, full, borrows from the printer this undue result, this simple maculation: there is no doubt that the spectacular vulgar advantage is, in everyone's eyes, the multiplication of copies, and lies in the print run. A miracle lies in this benefit, in the elevated sense that words, originally, come down to the use, endowed with the infinite, up to the consecration of a language, of some twenty letters—their becoming, as everything hides there to later burst forth, the principle—making typographic composition approach a rite.

The book, total expansion of the letter, should derive from it directly a spacious mobility, and by correspondences institute a play of elements that confirms the fiction.

There is nothing fortuitous there, where chance seems to capture the idea, the apparatus is equal to it: don't judge, in consequence, these words as too industrial or having too much to do with materiality: the fabrication of the book, in the whole thing that unfolds, begins at the first sentence. Immemorially, the poet has known where each verse belongs, in the sound that is inscribed for the spirit or on pure space. In turn, I mistrust the volume and the marvels announced by its structure, if I can't, knowingly, imagine a certain motif in a certain place, page and height, casting its own light on the work. Along with the back-and-forth movement of the eye, finishing one line, starting another: there is no parallel practice to represent the delight, having, immortally, broken off, one hour, with everything, of translating one's chimera. Otherwise, or in the absence of any execution, like pieces on a keyboard, active, measured by pages—why not just close one's eyes and dream? Neither the presumption nor the enslavement is tedious: but the initiative, whose lightning can strike anyone, ties up the fragmentary notations.

Through the act of reading, a solitary tacit concert is performed for the spirit, which regains, with a lesser sonority, signification: none of the mental ways to exalt a symphony will be left out—just rarefied from the fact of thought, that's all. Poetry, close to the idea, is Music par excellence—doesn't admit inferiority.

Here, in the case at hand, is what I do: when it comes to booklets to read, according to common usage, I brandish my knife, like a poultry butcher.

The virgin folds of a new book, still, lend themselves to a sacrifice whose blood stained the edges of ancient volumes red: they await the introduction of a weapon, or paper cutter, in order for possession to take place. Without this barbaric simulacrum, the more advanced conscience is more personal: when it takes up a book from here or there, with its varied melodies or figured out like an enigma, it is almost rewritten by the one who reads. The folds will perpetuate a mark, intact, inviting one to open or close the page, according to the leader. However blind and haphazard, the strike is used up in the destruction of a frail inviolability. Sympathy would go to journalism, sheltered from this treatment: its influence is nevertheless unfortunate, imposing on the organism, complex, required by literature, the divine book, a certain monotony— it's always that same intolerable column that is distributed, made to the dimensions of the page, hundreds and hundreds of times.

But . . .

—I understand, *can it stop being this way;* and I'll try, in an aside, since the work—all alone or preferably—needs an example, to satisfy curiosity in detail. Why couldn't a line—a spurt of grandeur, a considerable thought or emotion, a sentence in bold type that continues for pages, one line per page in graduated placement—keep the reader breathless, calling upon his powers of enthusiasm, for the length of the book;

along with little groups of secondary importance, explanatory or derivative—a sowing of frills.

It's an affectation to surprise the gaping crowd with a statement: an acquiescence if several people I'm cultivating, remark, without noticing, in the instinct coming from elsewhere that makes them arrange their writings in an unusual manner, decoratively, somewhere between sentences and verses, certain traits like those; if one wants the same thing in isolation, so be it, to uphold the fame and claim to clairvoyance of an epoch where everything appears. One person divulges his intuition, theoretically, or maybe even, on empty, on a certain date: he knows that such suggestions, which reach the art of literature, should be delivered firmly. Nevertheless, I understand the hesitation to uncover, brusquely, what does not yet exist. That hesitation weaves, modestly, with the general surprise, a veil.

Let's ascribe to dreams, before reading, in the pit, the attention drawn by some white butterfly, who flits everywhere, nowhere, and disappears; not without mimicking the sweet nothing, sharp and guileless, down to which I reduced the subject, passing and repassing a minute ago, insistently, before the crowd's amazement.

P<small>URE</small> prerogatives would be, this time, at the mercy of low jokers.

Every piece of writing, outside of its treasure, must, toward those from whom it borrows, after all, for a different object, language, present, with words, a sense even indifferent: one gains by not attracting the idler, charmed that nothing concerns him, at first sight.

Each side gets exactly what it wants—

If, nevertheless, anxiety is stirred by I don't know what shadowy reflection, hardly separable from the surface available to the retina—it attracts suspicion: the pundits among the public, averring that this has to be stopped, opine, with due gravitas, that, truly, the tenor is unintelligible.

Ridiculously cursed is he who is caught up in this, enveloped by an immense and mediocre joke: it was ever thus—but perhaps not with the intensity with which the plague now extends its ravages.

There must be something occult deep inside everyone, decidedly I believe in something opaque, a signification sealed and hidden, that inhabits common man: for as soon as the masses throw themselves toward some trace that has its reality, for example, on a piece of paper, it's in the writing—not in oneself—that there is something obscure: they stir crazily like a hurricane, jealous to attribute darkness to anything else, profusely, flagrantly.

Their credulity, fostered by those who reassure it and market it, is suddenly startled: and the agent of Darkness, singled out by them, can't say a single word thenceforth, without, a shrug indicating that it's just that enigma again, being cut off, with a flourish of skirts: "Don't understand!"—the poor author announcing, perhaps, that he needed to blow his nose.

At the same time, following the same instinct for rhythm that chose him, the poet doesn't forbid himself from seeing a lack of proportion between the means unleashed and the result.

In his opinion, individuals are wrong, in their supposedly species-specific design—because they draw from an inkwell with no Night the vain layer of intelligibility that he, too, observes, but not only—they act indelicately to foment the Crowd (which contains the Geniuses) to let loose waves of vast human incomprehension.

About something that doesn't matter.

—Playing the hand, for free or for minor interest: exhibiting our Lady and Patron to show her dehiscence or her lack, with regard to certain dreams, as the measure of all things.

I know, in fact, that they crowd the stage and expose themselves, actually, in a humiliating posture; since to argue that something is obscure—or, no one will get it if they don't, and they don't—implies a prior suspension of judgment.

Although it is representative, scandal breaks out, beyond all proportion—

To an enterprise that does not count literarily—

Theirs—

To exhibit things in the imperturbable foreground, spread out like street vendors' wares, under the pressure of the instant, all right—why write, in that case, unduly, except to display the banality; rather than to spread a fog, a precious cloud floating over the intimate abyss of each thought, given that to discern the immediate character of things, no more, is vulgar. If in place of the labyrinth lighted up with flowers, where leisure invites us, these stabilizers, in spite of the fact that I avoid evoking an image that puts them personally "up against the wall," are imitating, along a head-racking path, a plaster reproduction, erect, of the interminable blindness, with neither a spring nor green underbrush, finding only bottle pieces and shards.

Even advertisements hesitate to follow that concept of writing.

—You talk as though clarity could just pour forth, uninterrupted: or that it doesn't take from momentary interruptions the brief character of deliverance.

Music, in its time, came to sweep this all away—

In the course of the piece, through feigned veils (the ones around us remain), a subject arises from their successive layers amassed and dissolved with art—

That's the usual disposition.

One can, of course, begin with a triumphal blast, too sudden to last; inviting the shreds of surprise to group themselves after the fact, freed by the echo.

Or the opposite: in a return to closed folds, dark with anxiety to attest to the present mental state on a point, trampled and thickened with doubts, then a definitive simple splendor breaks out.

This twin intellectual procedure, notable in symphonies, which found it in the repertoire of nature and sky.

I know, people want to limit the Mystery in Music; when writing aspires to it.

Supreme instrumental tears, a consequence of transitory winding, burst out more truly than any possible argumentation; one asks oneself, by what terms of vocabulary, if not in the idea, they should be translated, given this incomparable virtue. A direct adaptation with I don't know what, and, during the contact, the feeling slipped in that a word would clash here, would be an intrusion.

Writing, tacit flight of abstraction, takes back its rights faced with the fall of mere sound: both it and Music presume a prior disjunction, that of speech, for fear of adding to the idle chatter.

Both have the same, but contradictory, adventure, where one descends while the other escapes: but not without trailing some of its original webs behind it.

All, apart, under my breath, or to concentrate. I started out from intentions, as one wants a style—neutral, one imagines—and neither too dark by plunging deep nor too blinding by getting out of the water, glistening and dripping: opposing the alternative that is the law.

What pivot, in these contrasts, am I assuming for intelligibility? We need a guarantee.—

Not its spontaneous leaps, included among the facilities of conversation; although this artifice excels in being convincing. A language, French, retains its elegance by sometimes appearing in its négligé, and the past testifies to this fundamental exquisite quality as a racial gift. But our literature goes beyond the "genres" of correspondence and memoirs. The abrupt high, beating wings will be reflected too! whoever guides them perceives an extraordinary appropriation of structure, limpid, the primitive rumbles of logic. The sentence sounds like a distant stammering, repressed by the multiple use of incidents, but is composed and elevated up to some superior equilibrium, with the planned balancing of inversions.

If anyone, surprised by its wingspan, looks for something to blame . . . it's just Language, playing.

—Words, all by themselves, light each other up on the sides that are known as the rarest or meaningful only for the spirit, the center of vibratory suspense; whoever perceives them independent of the usual context, projected onto cave walls so long as their mobility or principle lasts, being what is not said in speech: all eager, before they are extinguished, to exchange a reciprocity of flames, or presented obliquely as a contingency.

The debate—which the average evidence necessary deflects into a detail—remains one for grammarians. Or even an unfortunate who is wrong on every occasion differs from the popular gimmicky discourse of the day only because, perhaps, in him is born the need to differentiate himself from denouncers. He refuses the insult of obscurity—why not incoherence, sloppiness, plagiarism, not to speak of some special and preventable sin—or another one, platitude: used by those who, in telling the crowd it doesn't have to understand, are the first to simulate embarrassment.

I prefer, faced with aggression, to retort that contemporaries don't know how to read—

Anything but a newspaper; which has, of course, the advantage of not interrupting the chorus of preoccupations.

To read—

That practice—

To lean, according to the page, on the blank, whose innocence inaugurates it, forgetting even the title that would speak too loud: and when, in a hinge, the most minor and disseminated, chance is conquered word by word, unfailingly the blank returns, gratuitous earlier but certain now, concluding that there is nothing beyond it and authenticating the silence—

It is a virginity which solitarily, before the transparency of an adequate look, divides all by itself into fragments of candor, nuptial proofs of the Idea.

The melody beneath the text, conducting divination from here to there, applies its invisible floral or lamp-bottomed ornament to mark the end.

Services

THE PITCH, now that it is time for a return to the capital, is sounded by the opening of a new season of concerts.

It's the same spectacle every season: an audience—and the back of a man who gains, I think, he seems to, prestige from its invisibility.

A breeze, or fear of missing out on something that requires a return, blows, from the horizon to the city, just when the curtain is about to rise on the deserted magnificence of the autumn. The close glory of luminous fingering, not seen in the foliage, is mirrored in the vigilant orchestra pit.

The conductor's baton awaits a signal.

Never would the sovereign wand fall, beating out the first measure, if it were required that at this special time of the year, the *lustre*, in the hall, represent, in its multiple facets, the public's lucidity about what it is doing there. It's an elite crowd: the usual artists, the worldly intellectuals, and so many little positions. The music buff, although at home, disappears. It's not about aesthetics but about religiosity.

My temptation would be to understand why something that seemed like a forerunner of art, has acquired, since, an altogether different power. It is understood that, apart from official celebrations, Music seems like the last plenary human religion.

I went there out of curiosity, trying to sniff out the occasion in advance. I might have recognized the melody, which
today influences every work, even painting, even fresh-air im-
pressionism, and the rising of life in the grain of a block of
marble. Or even the audible whispers of reason or a speech in
Parliament. Everything is worth only a tune sustained for a
long time, and in a pleasant key. The poet, a verbal artist,
defies this rule, he persists, in a pretty prejudice, not a narrow-
ness, but his supremacy in the name of the means, the humblest and therefore the most essential: speech. No matter how
high strings or brasses go in their exultation, verse, from the
fact that it can most immediately approach the soul, can attain
the same thing. I went, then, with many other people, and
suddenly—a familiar intruder—was assailed by a doubt, only
one, but it was, I must admit, extraordinary.

This multitude satisfied by the petty play of existence, enlarged up to politics, as the press designates it every day; how
is it that—is it true that—does it depend on some instinct
that, scaling the literary distances, it suddenly needs to find itself face to face with the Unspeakable and the Pure, poetry
without the words!

A question—where, better than in the volume, whose level
and threshold are at eye-level and definite, directly . . .

What relation exists between a contained, sober crowd and
a shower of sparks, like orgies, from time immemorial or from
evenings or fame? or other infinite breezes; otherwise one is
setting oneself up, because of the disproportion between oneself and such fireworks, for a mystification—

The idea is haunting, in the same way that an enormous
and superior report is: see to what extent, on Sundays, the au-

dience is actually experiencing the pleasure it has elected—
yes, whether the service, the concert, takes place, for someone—whether it isn't, for example, a vomiting of inanity into
absence.

You see before you a lost pair of eyes, lost in ecstasy,
beyond their curiosity! Not that reflecting an innate sua-
vity doesn't suffice: inside is imprinted a bit of the feeling,
even if not at all understood, to which one's features are ad-
justed. To maintain one's honorable bearing is to take part, according to the conventional pretext, in the figuration of the
divine.

Seriously.

The crowd which begins to surprise us so much as a virgin
element, or ourselves, fulfills for sounds the function of guardian of mystery! Its own! It compares its rich muteness to the
orchestra, wherein lies collective greatness. At the cost of
the individual's unwittingly accepting to appear mediocre at
present.
Ah! The art of speaking well: at least French is utilitarian
and social, rather than dilettantish. That's what has been made
of the symphony.

A surreptitious initiation is illuminating, like the Sunday
laundering of banality.

Coiffed—if the crowd is female, look, a thousand heads! A
partial consciousness of the dazzling spectacle runs through
the crowd, depending on the city clothes chosen for afternoon
concerts: stops, like the sound of cymbals finishing, in the
golden filigree of little hoods, or is reflected in the jet orna-
ments; many a plume shines prophetically. The imperious velvet will bisect the shadow with a fold, which will take on the

coloration of a nearby instrument. Over the shoulders is a mantle of lace, the intervals of the melody.

The presence of the orchestra conductor details and contains the chimera, within the parameters of his gesture. His hand is about to redescend.

Following the external silence, it seems presumptuous to say that many a vibration of certainty and shadows combined into a meditative unison has ceased—

Thus—

Simply in people's inability to perceive their nothingness otherwise than as hunger, a profane misery, outside the accompaniment of the absolute thunderclap of organ music, which is Death.

A race, our own, which has the honor of lending guts to the fear of itself felt by the metaphysical and monastic eternity, appeared, then bayed out the abyss throughout the ages, and would be, no, I laugh, despite this celestial treatment, as if none of this had happened, ordinary, immune, vague; since there remains no trace, to a minute of posterity—when not even reconquered, native life flourished.

At the very least, such effacement, without the will of the beginning, after long periods, calling, intimately as it strikes a solitude, to the spirit to sum up again the somber marvel—

But the spirit, disdaining syntheses, prefers to lead research astray—empty in any case if it doesn't agree that the astonished, the banal, and the vast public masses are also capable of answering the call to salvation. The most direct, perhaps, having visited unconsciousness; the most elementary, summarily of course, Divinity, which is never anything but Oneself, to which prayers have risen, in ignorance of their precious secret, in order to measure how far they have traveled, prayers leaping upward and being knocked down—to our level, and taken up again, as a starting point, humble foundations of the city; faith in everyone. This trajectory from layers of earth to sidewalk level is illuminated, every night, within reach, by the circle of an ordinary streetlight.

Unrecognized religion and common virtues presented by a nation: above all, let the packed-earth platform we stand on take place, one harangues, according to mutual piety—from there, the soul is free to exile itself higher and higher. The rest surges up, drawing subtle materials from deep in the individual, materials no less important than stone for the steeple or lace for the design.

With her contrary precaution, the Mother who thinks and conceives us, always, even if these exaltations abort as buried treasure—which it will later be opportune to deny—wants us to begin with arduous zeal and sublimity.

We will not fail to obey her order, in this case.

The Middle Ages will remain forever the incubation period, as well as the beginning of the world, the modern world: at the threshold of a bountiful era, I want, from earthly well-being to entire ease—everything, for fear that the projection of sainthood will not suffice, will clearly fail, to gather in the darkest part of us in order to file out veritably if possible, with joy, or something like the time of times, oh! if only that could be!

A current pretension, which claims to be of the "laity" without that word's having a definite meaning, linked to the refusal to get any inspiration from above, imitates, habitually, the dogmas and philosophy that, intellectually, are omitted by the discipline of science.

The only interest that grabs us is the question of dreams . . .

Even if one of the Chimeras is allowed to survive, religion, or in this preliminary trial, Justice—

Will a rite exteriorize itself from this daily practice as pomp and seal: or are we finished with this grandiose genre of distraction.

A question closely bound up with what might unfold, not so much with our subject: one needs some evening reading like the one I'm coming from—the exceptional book by Huysmans—to suggest, with the hope of defending oneself from his superb influence, my adaptation or the transports of such madness—

The intrusion into future celebrations.

What must they be: derived, first of all, from Sunday leisure—

No one, unless he hangs, as his vision, the heavy *lustre*, evoker of multiple motifs, will cast light here; but one can nevertheless deduce the means and necessities involved.

The multitude bifurcates into some amphitheater, like the wings of human infinity, terrified before the sudden abyss opened up by the god, man—or Type.

The performance offers representation with a concert.

The miracle of music is this penetration, in reciprocity, of the myth and the house, topped by the sparkling of arabesques and golds, which trace the blockage of the pit, the vacant space, facing the stage, the absence of anyone, where the audience parts and which characters can't cross.

The orchestra floats and fills in, and the action in progress does not seem isolated or foreign to the spectator, who is no longer just a witness: but, from each seat, through tortures or gleams, one is each by turns, circularly, the hero—who is pained at not being able to reach himself without storms of sounds or of emotions displaced onto his body or onto our invisible surges. He is no one, according to the rustling, diaphanous curtain of symbols and rhythms he opens over his statue, for everyone.

It is a mystery, something other than representative, and, I dare say, Greek. Theatrical play, church service. You feel how much more "objective," detached, illusory, are, in classical plays, even Prometheus or Orestes, where the point is to wrap up the stairway of legend, whose shiver remains, of course, in the spectator's robes, but without the terror of such a grandiloquent vicissitude's affecting whoever contemplates it, thus becoming, unwittingly, a protagonist. Here we recognize, henceforth, in drama, the Passion, to enlarge the canonical view, or, as was the case with the celebratory aesthetics of the Church, accompanied by the turning fire of hymns, a human assimilation to the tetralogy of the Year.

Its haunting, of the theater that the spirit carries within it, will grow larger, expanding to the majesty of a temple.

Our communion, or part of one in all and all in one, thus, withdrawn from the barbarous food that designates the sacrament—in the consecration of the host, however, the prototype of ceremonials, is affirmed, despite its differences from a tradition of art, the Mass. The enthusiast that one is, with regard to something, either would no longer know how to attend as a passer-by to tragedy, even if it included an allegorical return to the Self; and, at the very least, requires a fact—

or at least belief in a fact—in the name of results. "Real presence": or—the god had better be there—diffuse, whole, mimed from afar by the effaced actor, known by us trembling, because of all the glory, if latent then undue, which he assumes then gives back, struck by the words' authenticity and luminescence, triumphant with Homeland, or Honor, or Peace.

Without thought, to light up the glass of the dome to mark the elevation and transparency of what is rumored to be called the social edifice, a few steps ahead would matter little; except in order to enter, inaugurate, and thus greet a subtle resemblance to gravities of the past, darkly packed away in the memories of the instating crowd.

I don't believe, at all, that I'm dreaming—

A certain parity with liturgical reminiscences, exclusively our own avowedly original reminiscences, inscribed at the threshold of certain profane apparatuses, imposes itself: but don't go and make the same mistake some preachers do, and lighten, through I don't know what dilution into the color of electricity and of the people, the archaic elsewhere of skies. Everything effective in history is interrupted, there's little transfusion; or the relation consists in the fact that the two states existed, separately, to be brought together by the spirit. The Eternal, or what appeared to be the Eternal, doesn't get younger, crawl into caves, and hibernate: nor will anything new henceforth be born, unless it comes from the source.

Let us forget—

Some day a magnificence will unfold, seeming like nothing, analogous to the Shadow of long ago.

Then people will notice, or, at least, will retain some sympathy, which upsets me: but maybe not; all I've wanted to do here, seeing that the time isn't ripe, is to push Dream against the altar found next to the tomb—its feet are pious with respect to ashes. The fog around it was purposeful: it would be a mistake to be too precise. To do more would be to intone the ritual and to substitute a false glow for a dazzling sunrise covered by an officiating priest's vestments, while the server should fill the altar with incense, to mask a nakedness of place.

The Same

A MAGNIFICENT contemporary pleasure, due to the many charms of Poetry, can have merit only if mixed with the functioning of the capital, and results as if it were an apotheosis. The State, because of unexplained (and therefore demanding faith) sacrifices required of the individual, needs a system: it's improbable, in fact, that we should be, with respect to the absolute, the same little men we ordinarily appear to be. A certain royalty surrounded with military prestige, formerly sufficient publicly, has ceased; and the orthodoxy of our secret aspirations, which still endure, put back in the hands of the priests, has weakened. Nevertheless, let's go into the church along with art: and if—one never knows!—the sparkling of old songs consumed the shadow and lit up a divination long veiled, there might suddenly be lucidity about the joy to be instated.

It always happens that, in this place, what proffers itself is a mystery: to what degree does one remain a spectator, or to what degree does one presume to have a role? I ignore any simplification whispered by the doctrine, and stick to liturgical solutions: not that I listen as a music lover, except to admire how, in the sequence of the anthems, prose works, or motets, the voice, of both boy and man, divided, joined, alone, or without accompaniment other than a touch on a keyboard to give the pitch, evokes, for the soul, the existence of multiple and unified personalities, mysterious and totally pure. There is something like Genius, an echo of the Self, in there, without beginning or decline, but simultaneous with the delirium of a person's superior intuition: he makes use of the players, by quartet, duet, etc., just as if they were the chords of a single instrument, playing virtuality—the opposite of opera, where everything exists to interrupt the celestial freedom of the melody, the only condition to counteract if one hopes for some verisimilitude in depicting regular human development.

A conflation obsesses me, in the midst of pleasure, concerning certain extraordinary effects rediscovered here, contributing to our future festivals, attributable perhaps to theater, just as, in the sanctuary, there was the rare dramatic representation: a performance that never took place elsewhere, and was constituted for the object.

Follow me here: three elements are necessary.

The nave full of people, I'm talking not about servers but of the elect: anyone who, however humble his roots, can span with his voice, from the origin to the uppermost arch, the responses in an incomprehensible Latin, exultant if not understood, who participates in an exchange of sublimity between everyone and himself, folding back toward the chorus: for that is the miracle of singing, one projects oneself as high as one can shout. Tell me if this communion is an artifice, better and more widely prepared, egalitarian, at first aesthetic, changing everyone into the hero of the divine Drama. Even though the priest in this does not have the quality of an actor, but officiates—designates and distances the mythic presence with which we just conflated ourselves, far from obstructing us with the same intermediary as the actor, who arrests thought at his encumbering character. I'll end with the organ, relegated to the doors, expressing the outside, a huge murmuring of shadows, or their exclusion from the shelter, just before the surges of ecstasy break out, a deepening of the entire universe pacified and a cause of pride and security among the hosts. Such, divided into the authenticity of distinct fragments, is the staging of a state religion, as yet unsurpassed by any frame-

work, and which, divided into a triple work, proffers a direct
invitation to the essence of a type (here, Christ), then proffers
his invisibility, and then by vibrations outlines the enlargement of place to the infinite, strangely satisfying to a modern
hope of philosophy and art. Plus, I forgot to mention the very
hospitable free admission.

The first hall owned by the Crowd, at the Trocadéro Palace, is premature, but interesting, with its setting reduced
to the size of the stage (the platform in front of the chorus),
its considerable bank of organs, and the crowd jubilant to
be there, in an edifice made for festivals, implying a vision of
the future; please note the unconscious borrowings from the
church. The performance, or service, is lacking: the cere-
monial pomp will hesitate between two terms, deliberately
spaced. When the old religious vice, so glorious, which was to
divert toward the incomprehensible sentiments that were natural, in order to give them a solemn grandeur, is diluted in the
waves of the obvious and the plain-to-see, it will nevertheless
remain true, that devotion to one's country, for example, if it
is to find its backing elsewhere than on the battlefield, needs a
religion, is of the order of piety. Let us also consider that
nothing, despite the insipid tendency of our day, partakes exclusively of the laity, since this word doesn't quite have a
meaning.

Full of surprises as solitary as they are general even for the
Poet, this meditation, restricted by chance to several pillars of
the local parish, loses its strangeness after a moment; its conclusion, nevertheless, holds: indeed, it was impossible for the
race not to bury in religion, even if since abandoned, its intimate, unknowable secret. The hour has come, with the necessary detachment, to start digging, in order to exhume ancient
and magnificent intentions.

Important Miscellaneous News Briefs

THE HIGHLY vain universal deity with neither exterior nor pomp—

This refusal to betray any brightness must perhaps cease, in despair and if light shines from without: then, sumptuousness like a ship that founders, will not give up, and celebrates sky and sea as it burns.

Not, when the time comes for show—

At the crash of a Bank, vague, mediocre, gray.

Currency, that terrible precision instrument, clean to the conscience, loses any meaning.

By the light of phantasmagorical sunsets when clouds alone are sinking, with whatever man surrenders to them of dreams, a liquefaction of treasures runs, gleams on the horizon: I thereby gain a notion of what sums can be, by the hundreds and beyond, equal to those whose enumeration, in the closing arguments during a trial involving high finance, leaves one, as far as their existence goes, cold. The inability of figures, however grandiloquent, to translate, here arises out of a case; one searches, with this hint that, if a number increases and backs up toward the improbable, it inscribes more and more zeros: signifying that its total is spiritually equal to nothing, almost.

Mere smoke and mirrors, those billions, outside the moment to grab some: or the lack of resplendence, even of interest, shows that electing a god is not for the purpose of sheltering him in the shadows of iron safes and pockets.

No complaint from my curiosity disappointed by the effacement of gold under theatrical circumstances in which to appear blinding, bright, cynical: to myself thinking that, no doubt, because of money's incapacity to shine abstractly, the gift occurs, in the writer, of amassing radiant clarity with the words he proffers, such as Truth and Beauty.

Accusation

THE INSULT is barely articulated in the press, for lack of
daring: a suspicion ripe and ready to fall; why the reticence?
Devices whose explosion lights up the houses of Parliament
with a summary glow, but pitifully disfigures the passers-by, I
would be interested in this because of the light—without the
brevity of its ability to teach, which permits the legislator to
allege a definitive incomprehension; I refuse to stock up on
bullets and nails. This, according to one opinion, helps cast
blame on writers who keep to themselves, and are, or are
not, in favor of promoting free verse, captivated by ingenuity.
Up close, they are reserved; from afar, as if for some occasion, they offend the miscellaneous news item: whatever they
hide, they cast discredit, less than a bomb, upon the best a capital provides, at great expense, like an up-to-the-minute tran-
script of its apotheoses: on condition that it not decree the last
word, or the first, about certain illuminations, also, which
thought can draw out of itself. I would hope that one could
push this opinion so hard that it wouldn't rely on mere insinuation; proclaiming healthy the chaste retreat of a few. It
is important that, in any contest involving the multitudes for
interest, amusement, or ease, there will be rare enthusiasts,
respectful of the common motive as a way of showing indifference, who instate, through their different tune, a minority; given the fact that, however divergent the sides in the furious conflict of citizens, they all, to a sovereign eye, agree
on one thing: that what they are eating each other up for

matters. Once you've granted the need for an exception—like salt!—the real one that, indefectibly, functions rests in this sojourn of several spirits, I don't know how, to their credit, to designate them: gratuitous, foreign, maybe vain—or literary.

Cloisters

How DIFFICULT it becomes for a Frenchman, even perplexing in his case, to judge things in other countries! Such
confusion, to say nothing of the fog, is what I bring back from
England. Invited to "lecture" at Oxford and Cambridge, and,
politeness obliging me to accept the tour of local marvels, presented by two very different visits—one impressive, perhaps,
and the other intimate—I'd like now to draw some generalizations.

The well-known path comes to an end at penetrating, enveloping, definitive London. Its monumental fog can no more
be separated from the city in one's mind than the light and
wind lifting layers of material up above the buildings, in order
to drop them again, suffocatingly, immensely, superbly. The
mists, reliquefied, seem to flow nearby with the Thames.

It took the trains an hour and a quarter to reach the learned
cities: I had my reasons.

Ask anyone in this amiable communion—that of study—
and they will tell you that among these colleges in every style,
nothing clashes: medieval, Tudor, interspersed with airy fields
of cows and deer, with flowing springs, perfect for training
exercises. Great Britain places great store in giving its generations an athletic upbringing. The University links these convents or clubs, the princely heritage, liberalities.

Everything—that the youth of England are able to shelter their growth in the architecture of pensive buildings—would be simple, including even congregating with a presence of men, their elders, unique across Europe and the world, who, in my opinion, are more important than the storied stone, and I was thoroughly amazed by them. Today, if asked how to perfect an impression of beauty, truly the flower and result I would choose would be these same *Fellows*.

Each collegial residence for centuries has secluded a group of these lovers of learning, who succeed each other by electing each other. A vacancy comes up; "So-and-so [they agree], in London or anywhere, could be one of us." They vote, and then call him. There is only one condition: the chosen individual must be a university graduate. From then on, for his entire life, he simply draws on his stipend. Invariably. If he prefers some British landscape to constantly meditating by the same window, or wants to compose, in his designated chair, one of the tomes that line the walls, or to haunt the refectory—big as a cathedral, built over a considerable wine cellar—he can do so, or even find his stipend, if he's a traveler, waiting in some bank of Italy or of the whole world. Most of them stay put, and respect the clause that forbids marriage within these monasteries of science. Experiments and discoveries are made in this setting more easily than elsewhere; here I met the most accomplished prose writer of our time.

There's no need to bargain for anything, even tacitly; they live freely, unconstrained.

That's the most important feature.

A voluntary renunciation of the present goes along with the post: after one has been named a Somebody, the only rule is that one should persist, and all the means are provided except adversity. It's a luxury to be able to praise others for their esteem of precious fellow men, and isn't completely useless.

We would cry scandal.

In order for this exception, whose charm stays with me, to work—ordinary, elegant, prestigious—one needs an untroubled traditional ground: one where the populous provinces of iron and dust eagerly pant to support the twin flowering, in marble, of cities built for thought.

Our own structure seems organized so that nothing comparable to these privileged retreats can cast a doctoral shadow, like a robe, around the steps of a few delightful gentlemen.

A single motive suffices for one to deprive oneself in this way: mistrust, in which an instinct for absolute justice can be discerned. The English conception testifies to a different social generosity.

The Académie, here, is not comparable, with its plans and rules.

So near the end of the term and the summer vacation, I like to fix in my mind these retreats that I should forget (granted, they're not to our taste), and to avoid, without some equivalence for my friends and me, a mental farewell.

From the past, I saw immediately, there is a perpetual new beginning, along with the season, of sunsets to come: like the concept of Cloisters. There is a certain distaste for it in a democracy: in our case, we abolish, deny, disparage. I insist on the phrase "from the past"—it helps us to disengage, with a sigh, from a lesson, majestic as a choir, which will not be silenced; and neither will the droning of some Fellow, who continues to speak, not without insight, on a French topic, re-fined, literary—provided that some still exist—undeniably, on this spring day a hundred years or more from now. I even wonder whether such institutions, neutral to any violence that might tear down their walls, *remain*, in a sense, because they are *in advance*. Certainly, it seems—to an impartial ob-server—as if the perpendicular Gothic thrust of the "Jesus" basilica and the vigilant tower of "Magdalen" College surge up out of the past, and go, very deliberately, straight into the future.

I myself contradict what I've said about things at home; imbued with a sort of hostility toward states of rarity sanc-tioned from outside, or which are not purely the act of writ-ing, I retract those aspirations toward a necessary solitude when it seems to be only a matter of *appearing* to dream. We need that flight—into ourselves; recently we could still do it. But the Self—isn't it already becoming distant, in order to withdraw?

Huysmans, in a work that does something infinitely different from providing documents, however extraordinary (a comparison between fifteenth-century souls magnificently given over to evil, and us), denounced the bizarre lingering, in contemporary Paris, of demonism. The Middle Ages were an incubator; everything since then has blended with classicism to compose this vain, perplexing, just-out-of-reach modernity—beyond the petrified Roman laws stagnates a religion, that of the cathedrals, similarly. Even with closed eyes, one cannot not see, watching over the city as in times gone by, about to take flight, the hovering shadow of Notre Dame.

The witches' Sabbath, underneath, conducted by a restored frieze of gargoyles and other disgusting creature, refuses to come down.

A segment of the public, uncounted by the census, retains a taste for practices whose maintenance at the papal court, tasked with confounding them, is labeled vivacious. Stupor whipped up with blasphemy, this worldly Black Mass spreads, naturally, to literature, where it is an object of study or criticism.

A certain deference, or more, toward the extinguished laboratories of the Great Work, would consist of taking up again, without a forge, the manipulations and poisons cooled into something other than precious stones, in order to continue by intelligence alone. Since there are only two ways open to mental research, where our need bifurcates—aesthetics, on the one hand, and political economy, on the other: it is of the latter, principally, that alchemy was the glorious, hasty, and unclear precursor. Everything at eye-level, pure, as if lacking meaning, before the apparition of the crowd, must be restored to the social domain. The nondescript stone, dreaming of gold, the philosophers' stone: it presages, in finance, the future credit, preceding capital or reducing it to the humility of coins! How disorderly the search going on around us is, and how little understood! It almost bothers me to proffer these truths, implying prodigious, neat transfers of dream, rapidly and at a loss.

A new, almost involuntary piety toward science doesn't omit anything that haunted its grandiose and childish origins: this chimera-apparatus, signifying for the literary being something isolated and innate, has value as a museum: but to bring his soul back to the virginity of a blank piece of paper is not the way to produce any blazon there. I claim that, between the old procedures and the magic spell that poetry will always be, a secret parity exists; I proclaim it here and perhaps personally have marked it a bit too emphatically, in various essays, to an extent that exceeded the penchant for enjoying it attributed to me by my contemporaries. To evoke, with intentional vagueness, the mute object, using allusive words, never direct, reducing everything to an equivalent of silence, is an endeavor very close to creating: it is realistic within the limits of the idea uniquely put in play by the literary sorcerer, until an illusion equal to a look shines out. Verse is an incantation! And one cannot deny the similarity between the circle perpetually opening and closing with rhymes and the circles in the grass left by a fairy or magician. Our job is to learn the subtle dosages, deleterious or revitalizing, of the essences we call feelings. Nothing that once emanated, for illiterates, from this human artifice, summed up in the book or floating imprudently

outside it at the risk of volatizing anything similar, wants to
disappear today, at all: but will regain the pages, which are,
par excellence, suggestive, and full of charm.

Guilty is he who, on this art, blindly operates a doubling: or
separates out, to realize them in a substitute magic, these delicious, modest—but expressible—metaphors.

THE RATHER easygoing fellow that some have the habit of greeting by my name—while I, a spirit, up there, am reflecting off of space—demands respect during the hearing of grievances. What a strange case he would draw up, wouldn't he, if one consented to listen—like this case, touching upon a question, singularly, of staying here, where the venereal spring has introduced something of twilight to the window-panes. I will transcribe his speech, which bringing before the public might ruin; the utterer, as soon as the haunting presence appears, through frequenting me, begins.

Some aspiring writer goes to the fields, June exhales, to dictate, in a moderate tone, an *O rus quando te* for our day.[†]

Let the reasoner be silent—
He proffers, to mark his complaints, not without deprecation—

It has to be said that the artist and man of letters, who goes by the unique name of poet, has nothing to do with a space reserved for the crowd or for accident; he's a servant, in advance, of rhythms—

But perhaps it was necessary for him to be held there and even to hold fast; in order to return, instructed and, anywhere,

---

[†]Horace, *Satires*, 2,6: "O rus, quando ego te aspiciam?" (O rural home, when shall I see you again?) [*—Trans.*]

burying as expendable his precious tribute, which he's sure to
have no use for.

But smiling to himself, judging the adventure profitable,
contradictorily: for the simple reason that, for such subjects,
an agglomeration of vagueness should determine a repulsive
illumination, furious with intelligence.

Which consists in speaking ill of the City—

Of the City properly understood—or else I would stop
talking—in its current state, full of expectations, yet giving
the false impression of functioning, because of the torrent of
life it launches, even though it lacks a social basis and is not
crowned by art.

Long suburbs prolonged by endless rails leading to a central nothing extraordinary, divine, or sprung completely from
the fictive ground in exchange for miles of asphalt, to trample,
in order to run away.

Always without excuses that I'm on stage, intellectually and
from memory I testify like destiny, which some confuse with
their reverie; this has always made me feel cherished. The
double stimulant added to Letters, exteriority and means, has,
in my case, in absolute order, graduated its influence.

Nature—

Music—

Terms to be taken in their common definitions of foliage
and sounds.

Let's dig around again, simply, in destiny.

The first in terms of date—nature, the Idea that is tangible, so as to intimate to the uncultivated senses some reality, and direct—imparted to my youth a fervor I call passion, while its funeral pyre transforms the days that have evaporated into majestic suspense; it was lighted with the virginal hope of being able to defend its interpretation to the reader of horizons. Any clairvoyance that, in this suicide, sees that its secret is not incompatible with man clears away the vapors of desuetude, existence, the street. Thus, while being led by a well-known instinct, one evening of agedness, toward music, irresistibly into the subtle origin of all, I recognized, without doubt, the backgrounded but reviving flame, where woods and skies are sacrificed in public; there, fanned by the lack of dream it consumes, it spreads shadows around like the roof of a temple.

Aesthetically, the succession of two sacred states thus invited me—the one, primitive or fundamental, still with the density of materials (it's no scandal that industry either shapes it or purifies it): the other, more volatile, a reduction into corresponding features, now nearing pure thought, along with a textual abolition if the image is forbidden. The marvel, chronologically, is to have layered their concordance; and that if it was oneself, So-and-so, pursued to the woods, scattered, all the way to a water source, another concert, this one instrumental, doesn't exclude the notion: this phantom, right away, with echoing clarities, the same, in the course of his transformation from natural to musical, is identified.

What good is it to loiter in palaces? That which, today when we have no history, they have at their disposal is an orchestra; I, for my personal use, have measured its delight against its chimera. To think of it or invincibly to sing, to follow a joyous inner surge, albeit quietly, in verse: one notices that most walls reverberate the echo by means of inscriptions that have nothing to do with it, advertising instead utensils or clothes, with their prices.

The place is therefore not here.

Paris, like London, advances its season into the summer, because each accessory, whether carriage or clothing, sparkles and froths luxuriously outdoors; a dust dissipated everything at the beaches.

The sea—which one would do better to keep silent about than to inscribe in parentheses, if the firmament doesn't enter along with it—becomes disjoined, properly speaking, from nature. A certain exceptional drama works its ravages between them, and this has its rationale in no one.

My theater, at spectator-level; and I, the only actor, march out—why not?—inspired by the scenery, represent myself by fragments, to see how it feels, out of everyone's view and taking leave of all.

A certain security known as the tranquillity of the fields, when it encounters those dissipations or that verbiage, gathers up enough silence for the grandeur of what one cannot say to show through.

Waste time, several voices advise—without remorse, or, worse, become conscious of disgust as soon as you find yourself face to face with leisure, as in your apartment: that is where the spatial illusion intervenes. The summer resident's gaze is satisfied halfway up the tree trunks, and spends many days sunk in a pool, looking for buried treasure.

It suffices to go an hour and a half away, although the noise is continued by the train; a little further and urban obsessiveness ceases; and rushing toward you, with a certain thickness, or the parity of ulterior plantings, is a wood. The fields of grain, happy to define that environment, stretch out as far as the eye can see, and celebrate by their luminous self-confidence the population center, in which the old city keeps vigil. Any further flight comes back as a waterway.

A well-known rural page accompanies the vacationer, however idle, and is never out of place—this habitual spot, under the reflection of a classic cloud and a commonplace: has it succeeded, writing, later rarefied by the symphony, in confining itself to a few mental abbreviations, all the more so if it rises toward the irreducible or the impossibility of a beyond—on the ground where I place my foot, its ordinary mirage remains. Nothing transgresses the figures of the valley, the meadow, the tree.

Never ask, at the height of the season, Will we retrace our steps?—but, when Autumn ought to flaunt worldly success, if we shouldn't allow it to retain, once and for all, decidedly, rather than looking for fellow men, incompetents, a solitary prerogative.

The experiment stops short with this stupor—

Veritably, it's amazing how much a capital city, where the present nearly dies of exasperation, contains, outside, the range of this miasma . . . it barely extends fifteen leagues, over the leaves and the grasses . . . no interest will recall now—to what extent the fortress was constructed by people expressly against their magnificence, as nature disperses them, except for a recourse to music, whose high transmutatory furnace sits idle for these months—I say, to what extent, up on the ramparts, beats, nearby, the drumming of actuality: let the noise cease at a short distance for anyone who, in imagination, whittles a flute on which he can bind together his joy according to various motifs, especially at perceiving himself, simply, infinitely on earth.

Solitude

Does literary existence, apart from one, the real one, which is spent in awakening the inner presence of harmonies and significations, take place, in the world, otherwise than as an inconvenience—

Certainly I have in mind the Poet who, possessing no interests, anywhere, works with the gratuitousness of his product or his commercial disdain: doubtless both, knotted together quite simply. The guaranteed miracle of his material existence or a bitter compromise, since everything should flow from an assent and certify, while it lasts, the contemporary mental luxury: this bursts forth only through missing destiny—at least, social destiny; even if one were, finally, to draw a subsidy from a fluke of fortune.

Such a personage doesn't even have a taste for the instituted honors reserved for letters.

Familiarity with one's close friends leads one to assert that there is—no one, in the situation of genius, among them any more than anywhere else and with better reason, who fails to believe himself its model. A fundamental ridicule; also, latent evidence. Even to hear others, having finished with the worldly pleasantries, reduce art summarily to talents that fill up essays, along with things that are mainly technicalities, is worthwhile, if only for the sudden urge to insinuate that there is only oneself, and to enjoy the polite withdrawals and the denials veiling their stupid despair. This alternating concern remains the pretext for society and the exchange of opinion: for I'm not implying, either, that one takes undue pleasure in this; or that chattering about how many failures it took to produce one success suffices to arm, erect, our enigma, or to explicate or broadcast the means, aiming at a lesser glory, which Mystery will forever remain.

Such a bizarre initiative visits itself upon a writer only in one case—when, in his extreme distraction, and letting his composition be put aside, he improvidently and peremptorily allows himself be recognized under the name of Master, and emerges from his dreams thinking he hears it murmured gravely in front of him, and, however laughable this farce may be, perhaps, for once, here—it touches a scrupulous and punctilious man, obliged by inner proprieties, instead of disavowing it, to respond by pronouncing, precisely, a few general remarks, proper to disciples. As if any young person, faced with a predecessor, didn't retain the flower of his independence: any approach contains homage; and the certainty of haunting the same region comes from evasive words exchanged during a walk, as steps are taken in tandem, between different ages. Whether one be on the verge of old age or an adolescent, one gains, in reserve, or respects the inverse leap between one era and the next, as time marches on. Teaching constrains the one who gives and the one who receives, except if a work is produced: always an intimate act. Ah! A festival, for example: nothing celebrates it, outdoors, but this intoxication, the fusion of recent illuminations with older lights—no duty but to produce a book favorable to this honeymoon of the spirit, or comradely handshake between thinking people. If immortality presents survival but in thousands, the Poet, who enjoys singing or raising his voice, in purity, over the conversations about a particular subject: does he listen for the future echo, or does he hear again the crisis undergone, for awhile, at the beginning of the youth of each generation—

when the child about to die suddenly glows with a blinding light and becomes the virgin of either sex. Outside of schools, walls, forms; everything that, completed, will officially serve: in a mental cloister, cradled from one age to another, illuminated by the fleeting light of election. To argue from experience today with those who are already the future, through doctoral pronouncements, is vanity, or even if one has to do it, it reveals disdain for the sovereign rule—that one should never linger, even in eternity, longer than the time it takes to draw something up from its depths; but, to be more precise, to attain one's own style, or as much so as necessary to illustrate one of the aspects and veins of language: one should begin again, differently, as a student if the risk of becoming a pedant looms—thus disconcerting, with a shrug, the genuflection attempted by others, and safeguarding one's multiplicity or impersonality or even anonymity, in front of the gesture of arms raised in stupefaction.

Unless, if one escapes the pitfall of schools, there remains, to amplify any joy, the press, between some crash and some private scandal, intoxicated with curiosity. Who? It can't wait until tomorrow.—What?—Just what you're thinking: a messenger is dispatched to fetch the oracle from here.—Precisely: I don't think anything, ever, and if I give in, this meditation is joined to my smoke, to the point where I follow them, quite satisfied, as they diminish together, before I sit down to a poem, where they will reappear, perhaps, under a veil—and holding out toward the visitor my literary cigar, which makes up for the interview. ". . . What you think of Punctuation." "Sir," very serious, "no subject, certainly, is more imposing. The use or rejection of the conventional marks indicates whether the passage is in prose or in verse, in other words, our whole art: the latter dispenses with them, through the privilege of offering, without this typographic artifice, the vocal rhythm that gauges intensity; in contrast, the former requires it, so much so that I would prefer, on the blank page, a design spacing out the commas and periods along with their secondary combinations, imitating the pure melody—to a text, advantageously suggestive, even sublime, if it were not punctuated." Or some other such blather that becomes so whenever you elaborate it, but is persuasive, dreamy, and true when you mutter it to yourself. Fine, then, he got what he wanted, the close friend terminates the conversation without giving me time to alert him that, when his newspaper wants to discuss this question extensively, I'm ready to do so in ten articles, at a cost of . . . as, moreover, I don't have the faintest desire to do. He has stuck his toe in the cavern; extracted the subtle remains. "A sentence," his presence demands right away, just as he gathers it and brandishes it, "that sums up the point of view." Completely without—he knows what he's doing, the sly one—frills; basic and finished. "Is that really a sentence?" or "Wait a minute," I shout after him, "while I add, out of modesty, at least a little obscurity!"

An interlude to divert the pleasantries far away from the feeling that leads the beginner to cling to those who itch to indoctrinate him. The rare practices marking literary existence or capable of simulating it turn out, there, to possess a fatal reciprocity. The same kind of stagnation is brought from one group to the other, whether it starts with admiration or with advice. People of the ideal should seldom, except during the initial years of surprise, among adherents discovering the same rite, converse: they are then free to make a sudden move . . . except for that of usurping; parallel to all the ordinary tasks given up, as the vocation requires, and the absence, later, of duties, vague, with no relation to preserving any secret tradition. Our bearing is neutral, forgetting the outlets, whatever they are, whether adulterated or noisy, leading to shade trees announcing a forest, or to indifferent asphalt, so long as we carry solitude inside.

Why, then, speciously participate in the interview, if not to utter, as this afternoon's intruder put it, some memorable sentence, as though, in speaking of general things, rhythm has a chance to find its contours and pure lines; why, speaking for myself and, presumptuously, for some of my friends, intone what is charming only if silenced, accompanying any amusement. There's always the threat of dissipating, by playing them crudely or surreptitiously, truths that are true in the state of scales or chords played before a concert begins: better, a silence maintained toward an art, itself made of speech—outside of prestige and inspiration. When a speaker affirms, in one sense rather than the opposite, an aesthetic opinion, generally, besides eloquence, which seduces, he utters some stupidity, because the idea with its contradictory and sinuous flailing is not at all averse to terminating in a fish tail; but it *is* averse to one's unrolling it and displaying it completely in public.

I attribute to consciousness of this case, at a time when two men, despite their pretense to do so, do not speak, for several words, about the same object exactly, the reserve that leads the interlocutors to give away nothing completely and to pay attention; yet they are persuaded—by their common ruse with bravado, the depository of ancient generous and baroque mental combats, or in conformity with the world of which letters are the direct refinement—to withhold as much as reveal their thought, first; second, to seize upon something else—to keep their integrity for themselves, when a cordial need lures them into meeting each other.

Confrontation

In the morning, with summer's lassitude, before the day-light makes everything sparkle, one goes into the fields to shake off insomnia. For everybody, day is beginning, at the haystacks, in the woods, by a stream; one's walking is invariably blocked by work, where sweat takes the place of dew. The same gaze from the same spindly or muscular man, bent over his toil, asking *What are YOU doing here?* With the ill will and scorn felt by a laborer at the approach of someone who apparently does no work. I invite him to reestablish equity, under the sky—veritably embarrassed to stand on an elevation beside the hole he's been digging since dawn.

Quickly to hold up a formula, handy and brief, to this visual interrogation riveted on me, a formula that the worker, in a debate, couldn't deny. "He removes a shovelful of earth, which he dumps not far away, he's productive; and to do the opposite would be a second, paid, job."

Earth, in this pact, has predicated that no force expended, even in response to a counter-order, will be vain.

This man, wherever his ditch opens currently, is reborn from it—

Blessed by the security of effort.

Another, whom I'd like to incarnate, would exist, whose labor cannot be paid by the product, because, perhaps, it admits hesitation. The page, once written, might be torn up, if the boss in me refuses the product—don't envy me, friend—though the client sees nothing wrong with it.

To annul a day of your life or to die a little, consciously, would make you scream in protest: although a parallel divination, in the name of some superiority, interrupts you often in your task, dead drunk.

A vestige of ancient sacrifices; the risk is sufficient for disinterest.

Peremptory, certain, and immediate—shedding light on my case, too: as inspired ones, we spend too much time running after gifts we are slow to master, to know the primitive social roots of a vocation. Suddenly one finds, put off until maturity, the understanding of a man who must be indicated from the outside.

Now gold strikes the race directly; or, as if its dawn had repressed human doubts about a supreme impersonal power, or rather their blind average, it describes its trajectory toward omnipotence—a unique burst, the only one, deferred until some imperturbable noon.

Add to that—he who, immediately overcoming the brutal brightness, declares himself a subject, pays in cash, loyally.

As is de rigueur about another kind of honor, whose shining metal reflects the glow—which is, indeed, the illumination—at least, perhaps an isolated personage who argues, demanding reasons; should flee, to see if the ray will accompany him. The experimenter, at his peril, then, installs authenticity:

what to do on this occasion or if the crowd ceases to intervene, leaving one face to face with one's god; if not to force
him to recognize thinking, the essence, by the residue, coins—
everyone, after that, will operate without shame, under the
law of a private signature.

This function—

To whom—

Unless it is discovered, founded, and usurped by some citizen, in which case the trials are postponed until his eventual
hunger.

The Poet, or pure literary man, regardless of talent, has the
job.

A favorable morning—despite the night spent without disappearance or any harmony with the latent companion who,
inside me, pursues existence, here the half-buried routine shows
it: shall I leave him to the incessant mechanical greeting of the
up-and-down movements of his tool, toward the Sum which
glows on the horizon? My look pressed limpidly on his confirms, for the humble believer in these riches, a certain deference, oh! how a mute handshake makes itself felt—since the
best that happens between two people always escapes them as
interlocutors.

This expression, probably, concerns literature—

Why not write it down, when I get back, as a cursive proof
that, ultimately, on a day of bright sunlight, perhaps, I perceived, in the difference that separates him from the worker,
the exceptional attitude entrusted to the man of letters.

A form of elegance, the last one left, reinforced by the sole
remaining kind of bravura, faced with currency, persists as the

flower of human presentness: which carries with it, anonymously, certain privileges of royalty.

Don't be taken aback and testify loudly to the contrary.

If your misunderstanding limited itself to converting into
everyday procedures an artifice which, drawn out of language, finally, relegates it to everyday speech; then the most
interesting thing, apparently, would be the press—

Whereas I sigh, nothing more, exhaling as if undergoing a
silence cure, far away, my stupor that everything seems to
come down to a transaction; the situation expressly prepared
in order to wager all. Such singularity, of all things, to be mis-
taken there, where—a lesser intuition, certainly, than this triumph of the mind, would dispense one from doing it. Letters
offer no career; the word is used as lyric poets used it, to describe the sun's path to its zenith—which, in a little while, it
will reach—ascension, not advancement. The profession is
lacking, for several reasons, of which one is the rareness of
genius throughout existence, and therefore the obligation to
hide that lack with filler, which compensates, the way a newspaper spaces a paragraph. He who dreams has simple hands
and his compromise is accepted everywhere, here to capture
praise, unsought and precious, there advertising oneself for
definite terms, or aspiring to insignia, which it is pleasant to
make fun of, or angling to become a member of the Légion
d'Honneur, what trivia, or even selling his writings at an
inflated price, unseemly for the hero he has to be, especially
when the case demands some defiance—all these things immediately seem inconsistent and false. Especially if one dedicated
oneself originally to a miracle that began in inspiration and
ended in an elite group of followers—

There can be no selling or trafficking in souls, or else one
just doesn't understand.

The indispensable handful of common metal is profession-
ally useful to him, even before he thinks of living from it, by
performing his trick, the sacred juggler, or by testing the intelligence of gold.

There is, consequently, no sense in cheating or in introducing the push that remains, rather, the creative statue-like caress of the idea.

Wₕₐₜ name, renowned for its famous exploits, can equal
the flourish, among the attractions of splendor, with which its
undulating motifs outline the signature of a grand symphony
orchestra—

The nobility, from now on, will do without a name.

Concurrently, then, with the gleam that comes from dreams,
an impersonal feeling of glory; and, for contemporary kin-
ship, where can it be found, if not in the nonreverberating
hollow of an electoral urn—

With no contribution from fortune.

A lordship announced by wealth, even corresponding, in
someone, to the infatuation with being in charge of the feast
and doling it out to others whose share one possesses, at least
according to oneself, because *they* wouldn't know . . . On the
other hand, to strip away the general means and put it in
doubt indicates, in poverty, a deep racial penchant for solitude.
Any selectiveness, above, can be mirrored below; and the
modern foundation consists in that equivalence, still indicating above and below, parsimoniousness, opulence, all is ambiguous.

The monetary stub is omitted, peremptorily: the attempt at superiority starts by extending, over vulgar distinctions, wiping them out, an equal wing.——

About what——

Essentially, the work of art; it suffices, as opposed to ambitions or interests.

Just so does an essay, this one, turn to facts, hoping, in reporting them, to air out the present for a while, so I won't study a return of nobility, to continue with that word—Ah! really—They say we need one—It appears—Some people are fostering it—The need can be felt—undauntedly, without having faith in that idea, showing the subtle and deep disbelief that such a thing is necessary. If only it were to sweep away, with a word, the ignominious error that obstructs our view of the bestiality of this century——

An outcome, I swear, of the erroneous taste which is the purest and most equitable——

If only such a misunderstanding could really produce itself once and for all! Or if only the flagrant exaggeration of its principle didn't lead to falsification and ruse.

Let's help the hydra dissipate its fog——

It has been said, by vociferation and silence, to the masses: "Everything belongs—in this domain—is placed for your admiration"; and, for lack of anything else, they have been let loose on art. No, whoever traffics; no, whoever digs, how heavily this day weighs on the tribe, it will fall asleep one ear on the bag, where the metal inside serves as dreams: without, moreover, subscribing to every day's immortality, which is lighted up by the evening . . . Or, at least, rest, you in your

simplicity of work assuring daily bread, of which each blast
of clarity echoes as well, magnificently, the perfect opening
salvo.

Oh, who lured a famished crowd here?

Fit for a multitude, there appears a fallacious simulacrum,
made of horsehair plaster and gilding, to block the irrup-
tion of something new, in front of the veil of lies: everyone
is utterly bored: for deep in each person a lantern is going
out, saying that if *this* is the marvel—rather not . . . Worse—
people swore to them, but here they were not completely
fooled—that notably he who claims derivation from the one
and only game, constrained by nature, and strict, feels a fairgrounds satisfaction in pursuing his research, in the public
spectacle, amounting almost to gawking. The yellow bank-
ruptcies with pus on their scales and the candid peddlers bringing to the streets a reform that blows up in their faces, this
repertory—in their absence, the Chambers' running in place
where cold drafts change direction with the current ministerial
crisis—makes up, outside their own drama to which humans
remain blind, the daily spectacle.

Very convenient, for everyone—at hand, like the nearest
open newspaper.

Otherwise, I suspect that the mysterious order pushing the
gratuitous crowd toward false idols is aiming to obstruct the
advance of the Chosen One—whoever wants him, whether
you or me—the only one in whose name social change or revolution occur, so that, once he appears, freely and without im-
pediment, he can live it and know it: testifying to the work of
art, because of a certain dignity, as proof. The attestation
would not defer to the crowd. He foresees, sums up. A temple,
spanning every part of the city, however immense, will not
contain the totality of the people. To a certain law, one, repre-

sentative, the humblest, has to arrive, invited, as if on a pilgrimage, from the depths of an anxious destiny. The last one, morally everyman: on this point, enough—for justice, pleased with itself, to exult, with light shining on the beautiful object that confirms it. I mean—that's where this will is coming from!—that it must come to pass—why him and not this other? Who would be, if it happened, him. Both of them and many others besides, I demand. The Elect isn't chosen by the kind of election you promote, holding the vote on your fingertips, assimilated to factory work. Since you fear, I know, the intervention of mystery or the sky in such a choice.

"Aristocracy," why not say the term aloud—in the face of the much-bruited term "democracy": reciprocity of states indispensable to the national conflict, through which something stands; they clash, penetrate each other, both powerless if one of them isn't there.

The coin, exhumed from coliseum floors, presents, heads, a serene face, and, tails, the brutal universal number.

Only a few conditions will change—and a sacred wind, not to mention history, tosses, plasters, disperses here, and there suspends a precious dust. No one is marked, officially and traditionally, in the composition of an elite, with this character, which, in addition, has no fixity. Thousands of members of the audience, almost alike, begin to move when they hear that beauty is announced somewhere: the masterpiece calls together. Far from claiming a corporate or founding place for the producer: he will appear, showing, fittingly, his anonymity and his back; I'm here comparing him to an orchestra conductor—no interception, before the arising of possible genius—or he returns, as he pleases, to take his seat in the legislative chamber among the rows of those in attendance.

The Court, I would almost say—but who would not dance around the kingly individual if he really were royal, authentically, through spiritual gifts.

A silly person speaks of *snobs*, hijacking foreign slang; a vain epithet, but preferable to its original sense as a joke. The opinion, which is mine, somewhat arbitrary, limits action to the book, for the time at our disposal; but doesn't make me unreceptive to spontaneity and grace, ready to awaken the lover of immediacy. A certain fidelity makes up for what was ordinarily called public.

This initiative seems to me way ahead of a new religion, with which they group—no doubt because of its occultism, prone to inscrutable ecstasies—Music: thus, I have had, all throughout this note, the image, or evocative accompaniment, of the haunting human material seated listening to it.

Bravura and a lot of other qualities in the forepleasure that a presence arouses, a tension in the neck—even though often bent back and disappointed: for the masterpiece is lethal, it plays, after the inviting beginning, somberly to the point of evoking guffaws, so that ridicule will thunder when the chimerical hats get wet as they nod in assent.

A city begins its duty, which, before the temple, or even before the law, rudimentary as the moment, finds, in curiosity if there is only that, or in expectation of the many stories of inhabitants, a fervent reason to meet: above all, the impartial city owes, to the surprise of art, neither more nor less than figuration.

Concerning which, it is seemly—correctly, to lift, in salute—which is your duty, lightly, in favor of anything you like—the very black egalitarian platform fallen upon the bald heads who live there.

THE GREATEST institution, now that the monarchy is finished along with empires, grave, superb, ritual, is not the Chamber of Deputies, direct representative of the country, but another enduring body, whose name it would be disrespectful to postpone uttering: the Académie Française.

What is the meaning of singing its praises, under this dome—

Founded in a very French way, this body is made unique in the world by its collective aim: the bond of Letters transforms into official splendor the efforts of diverse people. As a mark of civilization, what could be better than these portraits of the engineer, the financier, the chemist, the strategist, presented with a scroll, as if the language itself had taken possession of them and given them to the Nation. It's in the same spirit as, in nobler eras, a bas-relief, designed to confer eternal, elegant honors on the country's premier figures. Almost a religion, it stands for a law: that everything stops at writing, comes back to it. Our foundation, in ancient soil, which events put on the eve of a decorative explosion of the proud, practical tastes of the race, was, one might say, conscious, and jealously so: it isolated itself. It is the same logic that flattens everything down to classes in the Institut de France, revealing a political and sacrilegious hand: the decree turns out to be ineffective, even though the art sections, joined with those of industry, do not confuse what is exclusive in their plurality and do not de-

rive a *lustre* from them. Let's go right to the future attack.—
Even when, someday, inscribed in the constitution's programs,
the Institute, completed, modern, including all the relevant
activities, would present itself as a Senate of the opposition, noisily shouting its universal suffrage, forming a majestic
principle taken from the perpetual security of illustrations: if
even with so much grandeur, as I figure it, occupying, like a
sanctuary, the center of the legislative forum, where it only
rarely consents to sit—while this elite body functions by regular votes, the Académie would stand apart or reserve itself for
some special or rare act, one doesn't know what it will be.
Joined with all the intelligences and descending to the real, it
would still organize, for its members, through the strangeness
of their distance, some sort of religion.

The absolute Reign, in itself, of the Spirit—books, which
constitute its mark, are like the paintings and statues that
honor the disused royal apartments: thus is to be understood
the function of the library, in a body impenetrable to palaces;
when a text participates, apotheosis. However big a crowd it
commands, a text undeniably retains a small number of admir-
ers, let's read aloud, let's explain it to the masses; but, even at
its worst, during the silences, the gold of the titles will glisten,
in the learned sepulcher, confronted among themselves, for
light—between this impersonal summary of glory and the
majority knowing it only by hearsay, a secret, honorable communication is established, which suffices for the blessing to occur. No one is in ignorance of, yet no one is stopped by, a
door that looks like a tomb. Be dead, then, less in the ordinary way than through your share of dream, which is diffuse
among other people; or the Volume, enthroned there.

This Room exists, mentally, in everyone's memory, as un-
tapped riches that one suspects.—
To dust off the masterpieces otherwise than by calling them
to mind is a pointless task; their ideal flight should shake it off:

there is no need for a hieratic feather-duster made of ibis plumes, next to crocodiles and mummified ichneumons, which are the usual décor of old books and parchments.

What will the living do here? They are so little alive, if you read the rigorous inscription, which compares them to ghosts.

With some attenuation, they call it a Salon, for its seduction value; there, they ceremoniously converse about beauty, outside of a lady's burst of laughter, touching on subjects whose echo doesn't sound. The muffled murmur of conversation, rather, which marks them as elect, walls them up in their succession—their only branch the naked syntax of a sentence, attentive to the funeral slab of the dictionary, where diverse words lie scattered: or if, as for their metaphor, the double and real death of one of their number—a cause of worry to them—actually occurs, they immediately leap to the platform where the successor is finishing a eulogy understood only by the unquiet ghost, and invites everyone to partake of the empty quiver belonging to someone else, in order to seem invulnerable. The spectacle, in front of an audience, requires some mythic exploit: perhaps the Phoenix arising from its ashes can be dramatized by human beings.

The whole problem can be summed up in this quid pro quo: one wants them to be immortal, instead of their works.

To counteract that doesn't fall to me; and why I'm divagating, and about what, I wonder . . .

With no result, once, I wandered here already; when, to test their indifference to a sure thing, I brought them, with my "Literary Fund," a treasure left by the classics to posterity, so pure that the members of this office are the dispensers and depositors. The haunting unforgettableness emanates from them to whoever, student-like, does not fail to see them in the light of eternity—abstract, general, and vague, outside of any familiarity—I'm content to pronounce my own eulogy, which, following their example, I've lengthened to fit into the conventional folds, and watched out for my reticence and cherished the mystery; I've done it by instinct, as one feels one's way into a game.

One circumstance, concerning this group of dignitaries, can occur, which will heighten its privilege—

Society, an utterly hollow term, inherited from the *philosophes*, has at least something handy and propitious about it: that since nothing exists, in the facts, which resembles in the slightest what is invoked by its august concept, talking about it is the equivalent of talking about nothing at all, or keeping silent out of relaxation. Something lacking braves the violence of contradictions, and in no sense does one risk butting up against an entity. There is a nothingness or an explosion in the void, with fear in the masses that have come to the false shelter, any vulgar arrangement usurping this profitable invocation. The intellectual's cardboard boxes are notorious, open to the gratitude as well as the ridicule of anyone, voting for or against, they're both the same, costumes on the pose of a theater actor, himself vain—it's all very well if he manages to tap his foot in time to his speeches, when it doesn't get stuck in the powder of the stageboards: that's what gives away the artifice.

There it is, with the dots on the *i*'s: we still need the experts to agree—

Imagine a badly educated government confusing itself with allegory, which it comes from; and imagine that, at the same time, a repulsive and delicious Book appeared, concerning Society, beyond the judgments made about it along the lines of "This is beautiful, that is bad"—ordinary, inhuman, foreign—of which the ecstasy or anger at things simply being what they are became more and more absolutely strident: to the point where one often mistook joy and ire for each other, or both, incontestably, for irony. The author is seized, no, sirs, I'm speaking to Academicians, not even his work; he has, closely, joined his work, at least to demand from it, with the assent of the only jurisdiction he knows from the state and from his vocation, the honest bread that is not ratified—oh, don't protest!—either by palms or by prizes. He presents himself loyally, not before the regular tribunal—heads are not going to roll, in effect—but to appear, to defend his thought, in front of his peers. Everyone has recused himself but you. He awaits the judgment that I, for my part, would like to see lampooned—

Meaning that, since the social relation at any particular time, condensed or expanded to allow for government, is a fiction, it belongs in the domain of Letters—because of their mysterious or poetic principle—and thence flows the duty of maintaining the book in general in its integrity.

I add, in your name: so long as the book obeys the rules and is faithful to the complex and numerous arts it uses, of course, O you torn from your jobs, suddenly in the light, who must label an apologue or a periphrasis or stuff explanations into an allusion until it becomes transparent—a kind of leisure which is neither stagnant nor futile, since you must compare established models to the defendant's intuitive use of such devices, and decide, without knowing, amid the unconsciousness of genius, whether the defendant did well or not: which, in advance, is my opinion, provided that the booklet exists.

It is gratuitous to assume that those pages will look the same from the outside—and pardon me for assuming the intervention of the Poet, moreover the vehement sacred rite of the judges did not take place without causing them some discomfort—it was he who took care to evoke you in this inviolable place, the first in the sovereign development of the forces of the nation, as if before high treason or a coup d'état, in this case, spiritual ones: but, preferring the prerogatives of his faith to Christian salvation, he affirms this authenticity, in the case of the condemned work, and orders literary Supremacy to raise, like a sheltering wing, with forty courages making up one hero, your bristling phalanx of fragile swords.

Some of the studies in this first volume of *DIVAGATIONS* have been, with something in mind by the author, displaced from their current publication; others have been added, and others rewritten and reworked, which might disconcert a Reader familiar with them; who, if he exists, has a right to the information that follows—differently beside the point—so that his memory is confirmed.

It would be ungrateful of me not to mention, with respect to these POEMS AND ANECDOTES, the absolute translations they have been given, mainly into English, by George Moore, Stuart Merrill, and Richard Hovey—I had the impression, since I know the language a little, that I was rereading myself—and in Italian, Mr. Pica, dear to everyone here; and several others that have now also appeared, to which I offer a toast, thanking my brothers in all countries. Originally, these little pieces helped to celebrate the opening volumes of the periodicals of friends—from the *Revue des Lettres et des Arts* and the *République des Lettres* to *La Vogue* and many others: except for THE FAIRGROUND DECLARATION and THE WHITE WATERLILY, which appeared in a more worldly journal, *L'Art et la Mode*. GLORY appeared in the course of a biography of the author by Verlaine, and A MAN OF THE CLOTH and CONFLICT were among the "Variations on a Subject" that *La Revue Blanche* gives from time to time. The whole, less the latter, was first grouped with RICHARD WAGNER: THE REVERIE OF A FRENCH

POET and part of SCRIBBLED AT THE THEATER in 1889 to form the volume *PAGES*.

LONG AGO, IN THE MARGINS, or rather on the flyleaf, OF A COPY OF BAUDELAIRE: unpublished—and even unneeded, except for the fact that it accompanies, in the old *Artiste,* a paragraph rescued for the study THÉODORE DE BANVILLE. The emblematic landscape or something like that was new then, and shows the early origins of a hope, pursued since, then merely glimpsed, for a mental transposition.

PIECE: A BRIEF SUMMARY OF *VATHEK:* taken from the note on Beckford that prefaced the French reedition of the famous tale.

VILLIERS DE L'ISLE-ADAM is excerpted from a Lecture, almost a memorial talk, read, in Brussels, a few months after the death of the great man; it occupies with authenticity the threshold of a collection of CAPSULE SKETCHES AND FULL-LENGTH PORTRAITS, in which will be found many, votive, resemblances.

It was impossible not to include the brief, and, I regret, the only words I have said about VERLAINE—on his tomb; they embody, perhaps, enough of a breadth of truth to present, in this particular aspect, that cherished figure, if you take away the circumstantial crepe.

ARTHUR RIMBAUD can be found, in French, in *The Chap Book* of 1896, an exquisite and daring *periodic* out of Chicago.

BECKFORD: printed as the preface to VATHEK, and separately.

TENNYSON VIEWED FROM HERE and THÉODORE DE BANVILLE were published, in French, in the inimitable *National*

Observer, which continued so well the direction of the superb poet Henley. They appeared after the death of the one, and at the dedication of a monument in the Luxembourg Gardens to the other.

EDGAR POE, WHISTLER, and EDOUARD MANET were written for *Portraits du Prochain Siècle.*

BERTHE MORISOT was the preface to the Catalogue published for the Exhibition of the Works of that master—one of the year's great enchantments.

RICHARD WAGNER: THE REVERIE OF A FRENCH POET appeared in *La Revue Wagnérienne.*

SCRIBBLED AT THE THEATER—The remarks below (which appeared in *La Revue Blanche* recently) could not be incorporated into the text *HAMLET* without deforming it: but, in the margins, they complete it. "An impresario, in a province mixed up with my adolescence, once subtitled *Hamlet,* which he was putting on, *Or the Absent-Minded:* that man, with his totally French taste, was trying, I suppose, to prepare the public for the singularity that Hamlet uniquely represents; everyone who approaches him fades, succumbs, disappears. The play, a high point of theater, is, in the works of Shakespeare, a transition between the old multiple action and the Monologue or drama with Oneself, the future. The hero—surrounded by minor versions of himself, walks across the stage, nothing more, reading the book of himself, high and living Sign; negating the others with his glance. He doesn't content himself with the solitude of the thinker among men: he kills indifferently, or, at least, people die. The dark presence of this doubter causes the poison, that everyone dies: without his even always taking the trouble to pierce them, through the tapestry. At this point, in contrast to the one who hesitates, Fortinbras comes in, as a general; with no greater valor, and if death, a vial, a pool of waterlilies and foils, unleashes its varied modes, of which here an exceptional being wears the livery, it matters, as a finale and a last word, as the spectator gathers himself together, that this sumptuous and stagnant exaggeration of murder, of which the idea, and around Whom alone everything happens, remains the play's lesson—the ending seems to go on vulgarly by the passage of an army, emptying the stage with its usual weapons of active destruction, ordinary and within everyone's reach, accompanied by drums and trumpets."

All of the following sections of SCRIBBLED AT THE THEATER except THE FUNDAMENTALS OF BALLET, published in *La Revue Franco-Américaine*, vol. 1, ed. Prince André Poniatowski, the paragraph that starts "The only one would have to be as fluid as the sorcerer," unpublished, and all of STAGES AND PAGES, in *The National Observer*, are part of a dramatic campaign I undertook for *La Revue Indépendante* . . . an unforgettable one, in very particular conditions—I rarely went to the theater: whence perhaps the chimerical exactitude of certain observations, and when I mentioned some failing for the papers, or the reviews, after those, both professional and marvelous, of a Gautier, a Janip, a Saint-Victor, or a Banville, no, not at all, I didn't have in the back of my mind, seriously, that the genre, honored by these great names, would be revived today, and would shine as bright as theirs, despite the clear, supreme, imposing writings of CATULLE MENDES, who is capable of producing something magnificent every day, no matter how mediocre the occasion: I try, faced with such cascades of reason, prestige, loyalty, and charm, which prolong, actually, my lack of interest in the present-day use of the theater, draped in magic and fury, so as to hide the contemporary emptiness that lies behind it.

CRISE DE VERS, a study in *The National Observer*, takes several passages from *Variations*, with the exception of the fragment "Un désir indéniable à mon temps . . . ," which appeared, by itself, in *PAGES*.

ABOUT THE BOOK, a *Variation*, and RESTRICTED ACTION, sent to *The National Observer*, and all that is left of a *Variation*.

A *Variation*, THE BOOK AS SPIRITUAL INSTRUMENT.

At the end of the volume, THE MYSTERY IN LETTERS and SERVICES with CATHOLICISM, a *Variation*—without THE SAME (about hearing the Saint-Gervais Singers) in *The National Observer*, and, in the series IMPORTANT MISCELLANEOUS NEWS BRIEFS, GOLD, SACRED PLEASURE, inserted in journals, MAGIC in *The National Observer*, then the beginning of a page of travel which serves as a Frontispiece to the lecture *MUSIC AND LETTERS* (the "prose writer" is the late illustrious Walter Pater) and ACCUSATION, an appetizer to that lecture—comprise, approximately, the *Variations on a Subject* that were daringly welcomed, despite the initial dismay caused by their typographic disposition, by the kind, ready-for-anything *Revue Blanche*. The reason for the spaces, or blanks—which the long journal article ordinarily stuffs with filler, and indicates inevitably to the reader who samples the text here and there, among the few flakes of interest, why not limit it to those fragments which show a glimpse of the subject, then simply replace with the unwritten-on paper, the obligatory transitions? A fashionable publication, in its table of contents, marks the exact spot between serious journal articles and the mass of other things that flood periodicals. The discontinuities of the text, one will be relieved to know, fit into the text's meaning, and blank space is inscribed only at its points of illumination: a new form, perhaps, comes out of it, timely, permitting what was long called the prose poem, and our research, to become, with a new joining of words, the critical poem. To mobilize, all around an idea, the lights of the mind, at the proper distance, through sentences: or since, really, these molds of syntax, even expanded, can be summed up by a very small number, each phrase, forming a whole paragraph, gains by isolating a rare type more freely and clearly than if it is lost in a current of volubility. Thousands of very singular requirements appear with use, in this treatment of writing, which I gradually perceive: no doubt there's a way, here, for a poet who doesn't habitually practice free verse, to show, in the form of fragments both comprehensive and brief, eventually, with experience, the immediate rhythms of thought that order a prosody.

Valvins, November 1896

IN HIS later years, Mallarmé invented what he called the "critical poem," a genre of theoretical text as stylistically dense and complex as his verse. "Crisis of Verse" (reproduced in this volume) belongs to that genre. In all of Mallarmé's writing, the distinction between "poetry" and "theory" breaks down: every text is a lesson in how language works, weaving and unweaving the poetic act that it is, itself, in the process of not quite accomplishing. The materiality of page, ink, paragraph, and spacing is often just as important as the logic of syntax, figure, and sense.

The crisis of verse about which Mallarmé writes is in one sense peculiarly French. The classical French verse form, codified by François de Malherbe in the early seventeenth century and exemplified by Pierre Corneille, Jean Racine, and Jean-Baptiste Poquelin (Molière), was the *alexandrine*—a line of twelve syllables divided into two halves, or "hemistichs," by a pause called a *caesura*. For almost three centuries, the rules of prosody were strictly observed. The mere displacement of the caesura from its central position in the line caused an uproar when Victor Hugo dared to attempt it in 1830 (in his play *Hernani*). But as of 1886, just after the death of Hugo, the poetic line seemed to Mallarmé to be breaking up altogether. Poets were writing in "free verse." To a French ear, accustomed to counting syllables and evaluating rhyme, this was a revolution. Mallarmé even goes so far as to treat it as a kind of second French Revolution.

Yet in another sense, in Mallarmé's account of the "crisis," this "liberation" of verse is merely a way of rediscovering Language itself and is not, strictly speaking, confined to French: all languages mobilize sound and sense, rhythm and rhyme, deploying words as material, sensual objects with properties that go beyond their meanings, with connotations that create networks of effects, as well as with syntax and rhetoric that provide structure and suggestion. The sounds of words may be related to their meaning, but the very existence of multiple languages indicates that that relation is not one of perfect reflection. Mallarmé notes that unlike God, we do not speak words that are themselves the things they name. While God can say "Let there be light," and there is light, in French the spoken word *jour* ("day") has a dark vowel sound while *nuit* ("night") has a light sound. But our ability to notice this lack of attunement between sound and sense leads us to imagine a virtual language that would be perfectly in tune with itself. One might think that this perfect language would be pure poetry, but Mallarmé does not exactly say so. In fact, he claims that if this language existed, verse itself would not exist, because verse consists of compensating for the failings of language, creating "a total word, entirely new, foreign to the language," suspending the multiple facets of an idea so that its fragments balance in a kind of "musicality of everything."

Mallarmé was not the only symbolist whose highest ambitions for poetry were expressed in terms of music. Paul Verlaine had already asked for "music above all things." And Richard Wagner, the German Romantic composer, had considerable influence on French poetry. That influence sprang less from his music than from his imperfectly understood but enthusiastically endorsed theory of the *Gesamtkunstwerk*, the "total work of art," which would combine music, dance, theater, painting, and poetry. When Mallarmé speaks of Music, he refers simultaneously to two different things: a system of sounds that appeals directly to the senses and emotions, and a system of pure relations and intervals that has no referential but only a structural existence.

French critics and theorists have been not only attentive to, but also influenced by, the writings of Mallarmé. It was largely by learning the lesson of Mallarmé that critics like Roland Barthes came to speak of "the death of the author" in the making of literature. Rather than seeing the text as the emanation of an individual author's intentions, structuralists and deconstructors followed the paths and patterns of the linguistic signifier, paying new attention to syntax, spacing, intertextuality, sound, semantics, etymology, and even individual letters. The theoretical styles of Jacques Derrida, Julia Kristeva, and especially Jacques Lacan also owe a great deal to Mallarmé's "critical poem."

The following essays are a good introduction to Mallarmé, with special attention to the prose, the prose poems ("Le Démon de l'analogie," "La Déclaration foraine," "Le Nénuphar blanc"), and the *Grands faits divers* ("Or").

Johnson, Barbara. "Crise de Prose." In Johnson, *Défigurations du langage poétique: La Seconde Révolution baudelairienne*. Paris Flammarion, 1979. Pp. 161–211.

———— "Allegory's Trip-Tease: 'The White Waterlily'" and "Poetry and Performative Language: Mallarmé and Austin." In Johnson, *The Critical Difference: Essays in the Contemporary Rhetoric of Reading*. Baltimore: Johns Hopkins University Press, 1980. Pp. 13–20, 52–66.

———— "Erasing Panama: Mallarmé and the Text of History," "Les Fleurs du Mal Armé: Some Reflections on Intertextuality," and "Mallarmé as Mother." In Johnson, *A World of Difference*. Baltimore: Johns Hopkins University Press, 1987. Pp. 57–67, 116–133, 137–143.

———— "Discard or Masterpiece? Mallarmé's *Le Livre*." In Rodney G. Dennis with Elizabeth Falsey, eds., *The Marks in the Fields: Essays in the Uses of Manuscripts*. Cambridge, Mass.: Houghton Library, Harvard University, 1992. Pp. 145–150.

See also, for general background:

Leitch, Vincent B., ed. *The Norton Anthology of Theory and Criticism*. New York: Norton, 2001. Material on Mallarmé.

Sieburth, Richard. "The Music of the Future." In Denis Hollier, ed., *A New History of French Literature*. Cambridge, Mass.: Harvard University Press, 1989. Pp. 789–798.